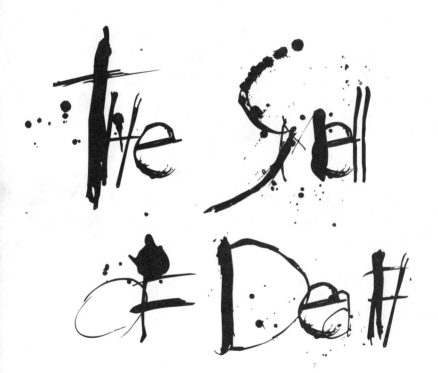

THE SMELL

A BARNACLE BOOK & RARE BIRD BOOKS

OF DEATH

BRUCE DUFF

THIS IS A GENUINE BARNACLE BOOK

A Barnacle Book | Rare Bird Books
453 South Spring Street, Suite 531
Los Angeles, CA 90013
abarnaclebook.com
rarebirdbooks.com

Copyright © 2014 by Bruce Duff

FIRST TRADE PAPERBACK ORIGINAL EDITION

Set in Goudy Old Style
Printed in the United States
Distributed in the U.S. by Publishers Group West

Interior illustrations by A Person

10 9 8 7 6 5 4 3 2 1

Publisher's Cataloging-in-Publication data

Duff, Bruce.
    The Smell of death / Bruce Duff.
    p. cm.
    ISBN 978-1-940207-09-4

1. Duff, Bruce. 2. Rock musicians—Biography. 3. Sound recording ex-
ecutives and producers—Biography. 4. Rock music—California. 5. Rock
music—Biography. 6. Journalists—Biography. I. Title.

ML385 .D84 2014
780/.42—dc23

For Patricia Louise
who encouraged it

Queen Gina
who denied it

Jeff Dahl
who allowed it

Factsheet Three
who survived it

Introduction
by Cheetah Chrome

R EADING THIS BOOK BROUGHT back a lot of memories for me, both of touring myself, with others, and with Bruce Duff himself. Matter of fact, as I type this, things are shaping up for he and I to hit the road again in Spring 2014 for a short jaunt up and down the West Coast. We've done the trip before, as well as one to Spain in 2004, and several recordings and gigs in the eighties in L.A. with Jeff Dahl (one with matching Firebirds!) before the events described in this book. One of those shows was my last time on stage together with Stiv Bators, at the Music Machine in Santa Monica in early 1990.

Two things I can say about Bruce: he knows what he's talking about, and it's always great to see him. Can't say that about everybody, but it comes easy in his case. He's always been a calm force in the most turbulent waters, and a voice of reason in crazy times. And he's funny as hell, too! This book reminds me of that, and makes me wish I'd been along, and that's why I'm glad he wrote it. It also makes me look forward to those gigs in the Spring!

–Nashville, TN
January 2014

Foreword
By Bruce Duff

THIS BOOK WAS WRITTEN by the man formerly known as SL Duff, who had previously been S.L. Duff, which stood for Screamin' Lord Duff. An inappropriate appropriation of one of rock 'n' roll's most unforgettable showmen, I'd nicked it to differentiate the writer from the musician, Bruce Duff. The musician came first, but along the way the musician was asked to become the editor of a start-up local music newspaper being jump-started in the outback of the Inland Empire, here in California. Yours Truly, Bruce, pre-SL, had no experience or knowledge of how such a thing was done but accepted the job. Why not? This was in 1977.

Roll the clock forward a few years and I'd moved to Hollywood to find fame and everything else, and utilized my previous editing and writing experience to sideline into music magazine freelancing. Soon after, I began using the S.L. Duff byline and it stuck. After a time I dropped the periods because SL without them seemed like the way a real writer would do it. SL Duff might one day write a novel about a descent into some kind of hopeless addiction, or maybe a pilgrimage to the third world on an undercover op, or something equally grand.

That didn't happen (and why would it?), because SL Duff was always secondary to Bruce Duff, who maintained real employment within the music industry and was usually the member of at least two or three co-existing performing and recording bands at any given time. Write a book? No. But I would fly to Atlanta on Geffen Record's dime to interview the chainsaw-wielding Jackal because no one else that wrote for that magazine would take the assignment, as they were embarrassed by the very nature of it. My thinking in these instances always was, what the hell, I've never been to Atlanta and I'll bet it's nice.

Along the way, both Bruce and SL got to travel the world on indie rock tours as well as assignments for real magazines paid for by record labels back when such things actually occurred—before budget cuts, file sharing, MP3s, and bloggers obliterated these promotional extravagances. One such indie rock tour took place in early 1993 when myself and five other gentlemen piled into a small van and toured through eleven European countries in nine weeks. We were all issued a detailed tour itinerary from the booking agency responsible for this jaunt. Each page was a new day, a new town, a new venue, and just maybe a new adventure. The back of each page was blank. As we rolled through this tour, I got in the habit of jotting down notes about each day, which I figured, when coupled with all the photos I was taking, would put together a nice little picture to help my brain keep these memories sorted out. Someday in the old rockers' home this would bring a tear and an ever-so-slight smile. Not long after we got going, these notes and this tour itinerary turned into something of a journal.

Back in Los Angeles, following the tour—and a short time after my girlfriend decided it was time to leave Hollywood, leave me, and get back to Ohio where everything made a bit more sense—I took a look at my scrawlings on the backside of the itinerary pages and found myself somewhat amused. Thumbing through the pages, I sat back and asked myself: "Could there be a book lurking in here? Do I have a worthwhile story to tell?"

Convinced that I did, I began pounding it out, night after night, and in a few months it had a beginning, middle, and an end. I finished the draft sometime in 1994 and then pondered what to do. A few of my friends had parlayed being rock critics/music writers into the publishing game, but mostly we're talking about music bios, ghostwriting, tell-alls, or analytical music think pieces. In other words, the same subject matters as the magazine articles they were writing, only many times longer—and with a bunch of photos. One of these folks made an introduction to a notable publisher who specialized in books about music and musicians. They reviewed the book and informed me that, while it was well written, it had no star power and wouldn't attract an audience. They wanted sex, drugs, and platinum-selling rock 'n' roll.

I refused to accept that and knocked on some more doors, but soon found that the publishing business as a whole was in agreement—unpublishable. I put the manuscript on my nightstand under a CD of William Burroughs bedtime stories and forgot about it for years and years.

The clock rolls forward even farther, and in 2005 I decide to euthanize SL Duff once and for all. In the nearly three decades that I'd manhandled the word processor, the chore of writing about music had soured for me. The pay hadn't really improved, promo items were becoming non-existent (you want me to download it, burn my own CD, and then write about it??—again, this was 2005. No iTunes for me yet). Trips on the label promo budget had vanished, the music one had to write about was more fleeting as the one-hit wonder became the norm and the artist with a multi-release career became the oddity, and the editing my work was being subjected to became more nonsensical. Sound bites were preferred to developed opinions. Meanwhile, I had set up a Pro Tools studio in my house, and the thought of writing about music I wasn't terribly interested in as opposed to spending my time multi-tracking just seemed pointless.

The clock limps forward yet again, and now as we scrape into the Twenty-Teens, we live in a world where nostalgia for the 1990s is a real thing. At the time the first draft of this piece was typed, *That '70s Show* was a hit television program. When the real 1970s were happening, we had *Happy Days*. The twenty-year cycle had caught up with me. The Flannel Channel is real, and we have a Mudhoney triple play coming up right after this break sponsored by your favorite energy drink.

My book was now capable of informing of a lost time, when indie rock could survive on the road with a real, functioning indie label back at home that was working a catalog and had a staff of just-out-of-college go-getters. They would peddle vinyl records for a slim profit and CDs for something hefty. No one made much money, but no one cared too much because everyone was inspired by what they were doing—or at least that's how we remember it now.

So it's 2014, and SL Duff is sitting at the Mac typing a foreword to the book he'd forgotten about. My wife—who, truth be told, is the culprit who snuck the manuscript off to a publisher when I wasn't looking and hence pulled the stake from the chest of this dormant vampire, informs me that SL must remain deceased. Since his previous departure, Bruce Duff has asserted himself in a variety of ways into the social consciousness, and the intrusion of SL Duff would only serve to "dilute my brand." So my nom de plume is anti-brand, my ego must bow to my options. My brand? That's what Nabisco has, not me. It is a different world from the one that birthed this od(d)yssey.

With that said, my new friend, let me gently take your hand and guide you into a forgotten time, before laptops, cell phones, texting, tweeting, Blu-rays, Bluetooth (teeth?), going green, MP3s, streaming media, digital recording, 9/11, the TSA, etc. We're going back to

an era when the A&R exec (should such a creature still
exist by the time this downloads on your tablet) would
actually listen to the first ten seconds of your best song
and glance at your photo taken in front of a brick wall
before dismissing you as not having a single and/or being
video-unfriendly. Nowadays he/she skips that step and
goes straight to your paltry four-digit Facebook friends
tally. Hopefully you're reading this before Facebook is
just another chunk of nostalgia, rolled up like a dead
fish in yesterday's papers. Buckle up...it's the law.

THE SMELL OF DEATH

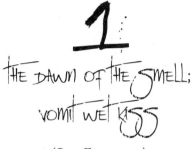

1

THE DAWN OF THE SMELL; VOMIT WET KISS

(San Francisco)

THE SUN WAS SETTING over the San Francisco skyline, making a Hallmark-perfect postcard, just as my Toyota minivan crossed the Bay Bridge. My girlfriend at the time (long since departed) woke up at this moment, having slept through most of the boring journey up the I-5 from Los Angeles to San Francisco. I usually felt relieved driving across the bridge. It meant the dull drive was over and the fun would soon commence. This particular crossing, though, filled me with a vague dread, the roots of which I could only guess at.

I was playing in a rock 'n' roll band, and my van was packed to the gills with rock gear—amps, guitars, cords, pedals, and silly clothes. My girlfriend had come along figuring that since the band was only doing one show, we'd have the following day free to goof off in the city, seeing the sights and shopping. But she, like the couple of other people that tagged along on this particular outing, was also curious to see the underground star we were opening for, the notorious GG Allin.

The band I was in at the time was the Jeff Dahl Group, consisting of Jeff Dahl on guitar and vocals, Amy on lead guitar, and Del on drums, while I played bass and sang vocals. Dahl had been around for some time, singing lead in various popular underground punk rock bands with names like Angry Samoans, Vox Pop, and Powertrip. Now, he was fronting his own marginally successful independent recording group. This particular pilgrimage to the City by the Bay took place in 1987, and by then I'd known Jeff for about four years. We'd met in 1983 when I was the bass player of the campy death rock band 45 Grave, which featured members of Vox Pop, Jeff's band at the time. He'd abandoned live performance and recording in the mid-eighties, got himself a respectable job in the tape library of Warner Bros. Records, bought a house in Woodland Hills—an upscale suburban area of the suburbs—and settled in with his wife, Sylvia, whom he'd married right out of high school.

By around 1986, Jeff had gotten the rock 'n' roll bug again. He started taking guys into the studio to make demos and singles and returned to doing local shows. I was tapped as the bassist, and I played with him for a solid three years. This trip to San Francisco was in the middle of my tenure. Even at that time, I knew the band wouldn't last forever because Jeff was planning to sell his house and move to Phoenix. He'd begun to really hate L.A.—the crowds, the filth, the general animosity that buzzed through the air like a sixty-cycle electronic hum—

and he was thinking about bailing out and moving on. Still, he was enthused about his ongoing recordings and shows at the time, and virtually ecstatic about the opportunity to open a show for one of his heroes, GG Allin.

Allin was lionized by many punk fans and underground music lovers who claimed he was the last true rock 'n' roll outlaw. It wasn't exaggerated—Allin spent a large portion of his adult life behind bars for a variety of charges involving lewd conduct, violence toward fans, and public misconduct of almost every kind—the list goes on. He went to jail shortly after the San Francisco concert on what many said was a trumped-up charge involving sexual misbehavior with a groupie. Allin claimed she was a scorned fan who wanted sexual favors. When she got them, the cry of rape went up. Whatever the case, he spent three years in prison, which promoted him even further to martyrdom. He subsequently vowed to kill himself onstage upon his release. He also swore he'd take several audience members with him. This, coupled with the notoriety that already surrounded his stage show, guaranteed every performance would fill to capacity or more. Allin didn't make good on his suicide promise. Instead, he ended up going out just like a regular rock chump, overdosing on heroin following a New York performance in 1993.

In 1987, GG really hadn't yet reached the level of celebrity he would eventually attain prior to his death, when even mainstream publications like *Spin* and

Creem were devoting considerable editorial space to his shenanigans. Still, he was notorious, reviled and revered, and this concert, held in a tiny watering hole called the Covered Wagon, would be filled way beyond a reasonable capacity.

Besides playing in bands and holding down a job in a music business PR firm where I hocked stories of mediocre metal bands to mediocre metal magazines, I also moonlighted as a rock critic, writing for magazines such as *Rip, Creem, Metal, Music Connection, Billboard,* and anyone else whose check would clear the bank. I received tons of promotional records and tapes for review. One that caught my attention a year or so earlier was *Hated in the Nation,* a collection of GG's work. Fast, basic, and vile, Allin got under your skin with blunt songs like "Drink, Fight & Fuck" and "Needle Up My Cock." His music, rude as it was, was surprisingly listenable, but it was his stage show that garnered him so much attention. Along with the *Hated* tape, I received a copy of a then recent live review of a GG show at The Cat Club in New York, culled from *The Village Voice.* The article described Allin stalking the stage, dressed only in a jockstrap and cowboy boots, smashing the microphone into his face until it formed a mask of blood. He would shove the mic up his butt and then into his mouth. He peed and shit all over the stage, throwing feces at hapless crowd members. According to the review, this all took place within his first song. By the end of his second song, he was physically evicted from the club. So it seemed to go at GG Allin shows, and following similar publicity across the country, these grotesque shenanigans were what the fans came to expect—and they shelled out good money to experience first hand.

I MET UP WITH the rest of the band at sound check at around 6:30 p.m., where we found that the Covered Wagon was reasonably preparing for GG. They had taken huge, industrial-strength garbage bags, slit them open, and used them to cover every inch of the stage, the wall behind the stage, and the sound booth—any area that could possibly be a target for Allin's self-generated shrapnel. Dahl was running a well-tuned, professional rock 'n' roll machine, too, and we knocked through our sound check without a hitch, stashed our instruments, then hung around to see GG's. A few minutes later, Allin entered, right off the Greyhound bus that brought him to San Francisco. He's bearded and disheveled, strongly resembling the infamous 1969 *LIFE* magazine cover of Charles Manson—the same picture which is, as it turns out, painted on the back of Allin's leather jacket.

Dahl immediately jumped up from the table where we were sitting to greet him. He'd met Allin years earlier at the notorious L.A. punk club Cathay de Grande, a hole-in-the-wall that had become home to bands too crude, ugly, and non-conformist to play the more upscale venues. Allin seemed cordial enough, shaking Dahl's hand and smiling.

He and Dahl were working on logistics involving an Allin recording session set to take place in a week or so back in L.A. in which Dahl would co-produce and our band would provide backing tracks. At the time, Allin had no steady band—he toured Chuck Berry-style, by himself. He would send tapes ahead to each city he was booked to play, to local musicians he'd been set up with who would learn his songs, show up at the sound check and gig, and be his backing band for the night.

The local guys filling that position tonight were onstage, plugging things in, doing regular musician stuff, trying to look cool, but ultimately incapable of disguising their nervousness. Allin got onstage, shook hands with his temporary band, and launched into a perfunctory version of "Bite It, You Scum." It sounded decent enough, and getting worked up, Allin suddenly jumped offstage and lurched through an Iggy Pop/Jim Morrison-style convulsion. (Keep in mind this was only a sound check.) The band, mouths gaping, stopped jamming and just stood there. Allin snapped to attention and begun hollering at them.

"No, no, no! Never, ever stop playing! No matter what I do, whether I'm singing or not, whatever I'm doing, you just keep playing the song. Okay?"

His rock 'n' roll spaz attack is merely a test for the band—if they can't make it through that, they will surely have a heart attack when Allin begins unveiling his typical showstopping antics. They tried it again, and the band gets it right this time. Jeff and GG confabbed a little more, and then we all adjourned for pre-gig rituals. For us, this merely meant pizza. GG, as we would learn when we returned to the club, had a more specialized diet.

We all piled into my van and headed to Divisadero Street, looking aimlessly for a pizza joint that would please everyone. We spot the marquee above a place called Rocco's, and it proudly proclaims, "Johnny Thunders eats here." Thunders, late guitarist for the seminal New York Dolls, was a true rocker and a lifelong drug addict. He's a hero to all concerned. We figured if it was good enough for Thunders, it was good enough for us. We entered Rocco's, ordered a king size, and made moderate pigs of ourselves. Upon leaving, we walk out the door under the marquee, inadvertently turning the wrong way. When I look back up at the marquee, I notice that on the opposite side it reads, "William Burroughs eats here."

"That's just too weird," I note. Thunders on one side and Burroughs on the other: the greatest junkie guitarist outside of Keith Richards and the greatest junkie author, both scarfing at the same San Francisco pizzeria. "What gives?" I say to myself. I had to find out.

"You're the reporter," shrugs Amy. "Get to the bottom of this great mystery."

Upon re-entering, I approach and query the two gentlemen behind the counter. "What's up with the sign out front, fellas?"

They begin smiling and laughing, extremely friendly, but they don't answer me. "Gentlemen," I try again, "what's the deal with the marquee...the references to Burroughs and Thunders? Do you put China White in the pizza dough or something?"

Still, they laugh, smile, wave, nod, but no answers. They talk amongst themselves, straight-up Italian, and I realize they're not comprehending my question. I begin to point. "The sign, guys. The sign. Why does it say what it says?"

"It's always been, since before, since before we buy here. Since when this was ice cream store. You like, you like the sign?"

"Yes, the sign is good. Do you know what it means?"

Again, the blank, well-meaning smiles. I smile back, wish them well, thank them for the good pizza and inane conversation, and exit once more.

"Well?" Amy asks.

"They don't know what it says, they think it's about ice cream. They're very happy about it, though."

UPON RETURNING TO THE Covered Wagon, we go behind the stage to some ramshackle office space that doubles as a microscopic backstage area on show nights. The club staff—which includes a soundman, lighting guy, door person, booking agent, waitress, and bartender—the nine members of the two bands, and ten or so band guests are all vying for standing room in this ten-foot-by-eight-foot office. Allin, in possession of a bizarre star-quality charisma (and well aware of it), is the center of attention. He quietly sits down at the office desk and begins his pre-gig eating regimen. Flanked by two groupies—one a spaced-out looking hippie-junkie and the other a dead-ringer for Marianne Faithfull at her 1965-most-gorgeous—the singer nonchalantly opens the wrappings of two huge, greasy cheeseburgers and begins eating them as if he's a trash compactor. He eats them one following the other, and, upon completion, washes the whole mess down with a full bottle of Crisco oil. His intention is obvious—the fans expect him to shit on stage, and they will get their money's worth.

The feeling of dread I'd had a few hours earlier was becoming more ominous, but I shrug the whole debacle off as another phase of punk rock anarchy. I'm just a bass player. I needn't concern myself with all of this too deeply. If some New Hampshire misfit wants to crap onstage while his two-hour old band rams through three-chord ditties and a room full of punters pay fifteen dollars for the privilege of observing this ceremony...hey, that's cool. This is America, right?

A half hour later, around 9:30, we play a perfunctory thirty-five minute set of Dahl's fast, hard-assed songs, tempered with the usual Dead Boys and Stooges covers that we all love so much. The crowd is appreciative, but toward the end of our turn, it is obvious they are getting antsy. Like us, they've heard the music, they've read the write-ups in the fanzines, but they've never actually seen a live GG Allin gig before—and they are beginning to get impatient.

Following our set, I move my huge, cumbersome
SVT amp out of the way, when Allin, still dressed
relatively normal, approaches Dahl and asks if his band
can use Jeff's guitar amps. Jeff agrees, but looks a little
wary. He just got an endorsement from Carvin, a feat
unheard of for a band even remotely connected to punk
music, and this was the first gig he'd brought them to.
They were brand new.

THE COVERED WAGON'S FLOOR plan is a little awkward.
There's a tiny stage in the far corner of the room, which
itself probably has only about a 120-person capacity.
Directly stage left is a narrow door that leads back to
the tiny office/dressing room, and to the left of that is a
larger door that leads to the bar and an arcade. After our
show, my girlfriend and I go into the bar, where I meet
up with Alex, a long-time musician friend I've known
from bands in my hometown of Riverside, California.
Alex moved to San Francisco in the early eighties, and,
freed from the neurotic control freak he called Mom,
finally seemed happy. He showed up to visit me at the
club with his fiancée in tow, and the four of us begin
knocking back beer and updating each other on our
lives.

During this socializing, Allin and his band hit
the stage, blasting "Bite It, You Scum." We raise the
volume level of our conversation to talk over the music,
but I begin to lose interest in reminiscing and become

anxious to see GG in full flight. I walk over to the door that separates the bar and the concert room, which looks sideways at the stage. I stand on my toes, but can't see a damn thing. The room is electrified with a sort of paranoid, negative energy, the air hanging like Louisiana humidity—heavy, sweaty, and dank. I know I need to see what's going on as quickly as possible, as it's already a good ten minutes into the show, and Allin's performance probably won't last much longer than that. I'm unable to press forward, as the whole club now is sardine packed, shoulder-to-shoulder.

"OOOOHH!" The cry goes up from the whole crowd, as the wall of people in front of me slam suddenly into reverse, backing quickly. "He's throwing shit!!"

Basic confusion and nervousness seem to permeate the air, but my curiosity is still unchecked. A girl right next to me is standing on a chair she pulled from the bar. She yells down to me, "Hey, you want to see?"

I nod and step up onto the chair as she steps down. As my head rises above everyone else's, I'm stunned by something I did not expect or even think about. Never mind what Allin's act would look or sound like, I hadn't taken into account the inevitable smell. It's not so much an odor as an assault, an almost physical presence that literally knocks me back, causing me to momentarily lose my balance. The air is thick from sweat and heat. The smell of shit, piss, and vomit that hangs in that humidity is worse than any outhouse, barn, or slaughterhouse imaginable. It has other aspects and aromas unknown to me. I'm horrified, yet curiously spellbound at the same time. Even with the height the chair affords me I can't really see GG, as he seems to be on the ground grappling with someone. Every so often his head appears amidst his band members, who are standing as far to the corners of the stage as possible. I finally catch a glimpse, his jockstrap pulled sideways revealing his mini dick (which many say was the root of his psycho behavior). His body is covered with red and brown smudges.

The audience is heated and angry, riled up by GG's antics and clearly verging on a riot. The garbage bags, and Dahl's brand new amplifiers which stood before them, are caked in a messy combination of shit and blood. The heat and the smell are unbearable—I feel myself getting slightly woozy, so I climb off of the chair and return to my friends. The show is over moments later.

Following the triumphant concert—no one is seriously hurt and Allin manages to avoid incarceration (although self-inflicted injuries from the show would require him to check into a hospital a few days later, and, for better or worse, force our planned recording session to be cancelled)—we wander back to the dressing room to see what kind of scene is going down. Allin, clearly exhausted but still up for partying, is reclining in the office chair, his face a myriad of blood, various other bodily fluids, vomit, and crap. The Marianne Faithfull look-alike perches herself on his lap, throws her arms around his neck, and sticks her tongue down his throat, giving him the conquering hero's triumphant celebration smooch.

Dahl and I, both big fans of the vintage Faithfull, stand there silently watching in awe. Dahl later titled our first LP together as a band after the incident: *Vomit Wet Kiss.* Meanwhile, Del is packing up equipment in the quickly evacuating club. He's always eager to get moving. I mostly had my gear stored already, and I was standing in the middle of the venue, surveying the carnage. Del tapped me on the shoulder, and pointed toward the front door where the hippie-junkie chick was skipping schoolgirl-style out of the club, carrying the case containing my Fender bass. We both bolt after her, and I catch up with her easily.

"What the fuck are you doing?" I shout, grabbing it roughly from her. She daintily clasps her hands to her mouth and begins giggling, then continues skipping down the street.

"She's as high as a Mr. T kite," laughs Del, shaking his head. I thank him for being observant and saving my axe, and we walk back to the Covered Wagon.

Back at our hotel, we all gather in my room and hang. Conversation naturally revolves around our bizarre evening. Amy and her friend Mary, who'd come along with us, driven by the same curiosity as everyone else, seem to be in a mild state of shock and disbelief. These are hardened punk chicks who'd thought they'd seen it all, but they weren't quite sure what the hell they'd seen tonight.

"The weirdest thing of all, for me," I say to no one in particular, "was that smell, that fucking smell. I can't get it out of my head, I swear I can smell it right now!"

The guys all nod and the girls shriek, "Eeeiiiooow!"

It WAS LIKE THAT for days. Every time I stopped to think about GG's performance, I could smell that smell, that odor from the bowels of hell itself. It haunted me in a way. I know that sounds silly. Everyone's smelled something unpleasant, I'm sure. Certainly anyone who's ever changed a diaper, had to crap in the woods, gone to a Porta-John at a rock festival, or gotten hold of some bad guacamole has smelled foul fecal matter. It really isn't a big deal, just part of the reality of being human. This pungency was different than all of that, though. It carried with it an additional weightiness, only amplified by the crowd-generated humidity. It was, I came to believe, the smell of anguish, self-immolation, hatred, lack of belief in anything, and disrespect for everything. It was the aroma of not just the product of the bowels, but the bowels themselves—the human body turned inside out. It's what a soul smells like on its way to meet the devil himself. It was the Smell of Death: final, brooding, unforgiving, uncaring.

Not to be melodramatic or anything (not me!), but this smell, this feeling, and the underlying apprehension that accompanies it, is the essence of what is on the heels of every musician traveling on a low-budget van tour. It's as if the modern independent econo-musician is stalked by specters: unnamable illnesses a step behind, venereal diseases to the right, psychosis, loneliness, and paranoia to the left. Dead ahead: a skanky bar in Any

Town with Your Band's Name on the tiny, battered marquee—misspelled.

Having recognized the admittedly over-analyzed odor as the calling card of the Grim Reaper himself, I acknowledged that fact and stored it away in my mind for future reference. Flash forward five and a half years and this knowledge would become a part of my daily reality for two and a half months—once again as a member of Jeff Dahl's band—as I took part in a six-man expedition across Europe in a van designed to seat five.

2

WHAT IS A PER DIEM? CROSSING THE SIX-INCH CHASM

(Hollywood to Amsterdam)

B Y 1990, JEFF DAHL had left Los Angeles for a quiet little no-place called Cave Creek, Arizona, about forty minutes outside of Phoenix. He'd made a killing on his Woodland Hills home, and was living the life of Riley, running his fan club, planning tours, making records. He'd broken up the original Jeff Dahl Group when he left town, which was only logical.

During this time, Dahl became somewhat of a cult hero in certain European countries and Japan. He didn't mean much of anything sales-wise in the U.S., but the export business on him had become rather brisk. He'd mounted a small tour of the U.K., utilizing an English band as his backing group—again the Chuck Berry method, then he pulled an ex-Angry Samoans drummer and ex-Powertrip bassist as backup players, and toured the European continent for a month as a trio. He followed this with a Japanese tour featuring a Japanese band. His international fan base increased exponentially as a result, and his career continued to blossom.

As for the original group, Del had disappeared. No one knew exactly what had happened to him. He had been growing pot out of a makeshift greenhouse in his closet, and word was he was sure the feds were onto him. He had purchased an RV and vanished from taxable society. Amy and I played together in another band called Sister Goddamn with the ex-singer of former teen punk stars The Adolescents, but eventually she sadly wandered into drug addiction and left the state for parts unknown. I played with lots of ex-members of this band and that, all of them musicians whose most successful days were probably behind them. Logically, it would seem like my own best days of big crowds and decent pay were on the fade as well, but what was I gonna do, become something respectable?

I'd also left the PR firm and started working for a small, upstart, indie label called Triple X Records who were largely known as the record company that discovered Jane's Addiction. Just prior to my employment there, as coincidence and fate would have it, the label had become the recording home Jeff Dahl, as well.

Along with numerous other duties (when you work for an indie label you usually wear a few hats), I'd begun producing records for the label. Among the bands I flung out to an apathetic world were The Ultras, whose shtick was an unlikely combination of hard-edged glam-pop and Aleister Crowley do-what-thou-wilt Satanism—long before Marilyn Manson would think of it. I'd also secured a job at Triple X for The Ultras drummer, Jeff

Zimmitti, which pretty much coincided with the band's
inevitable break up.

A prototypically suave Sicilian, Zimmitti fit in with
Satanists and accountants alike. He was basically a quiet
guy who could adapt to almost any situation. He was
dark, with movie star good looks, but had a certain
sullenness that kept people guessing on what was
really going on in his head. A bit of a pretty boy, he
was constantly rethinking his look, from brooding Nick
Cave look-a-like, to New York Dolls androgynous clone,
to forties gangster in sharp suits and spats. He was quiet,
but a character nonetheless. His mature countenance
obscured the fact that he was only twenty-three.

Zimmitti–Z for short–had begun a dialogue with
Dahl that he kept under wraps. Eager to see the world
and get the hell out of his desk job, he'd slowly convinced
Dahl to take him along on the next tour. It was shaping up
to be quite a lengthy expedition–nine weeks in Europe,
plus a week in Japan. Since my desk was next to Z's, my
big ears caught wind of this. I rationalized that if anyone
deserved to hit the road with Dahl, it was going to be me.

Dahl remained loyal to his players at the time, and
John Duffy, the ex-Powertrip bassist, was still in the bull
pen. Dahl told me that he wasn't sure if Duffy could
leave town for that long. If he couldn't, I had the gig.
The owners of the label were shaky about Z and I
taking a two-month-plus leave of absence, but we began
working on ways to make it happen, training temporary
replacements, delegating authority, that sort of thing.

The tour was set to commence in late January of
1993. By the fall of 1992, it was confirmed. I would
be a part of it. Jeff would return to a quartet format,
adding lead guitarist Ratboy, who'd played on Jeff's most
recent LP (the one the tour would promote?). Ratboy
had been a longtime member of the L.A. drunk-rock
band Motorcycle Boy. Rat had recently quit the band
and relocated to New York, where he formed his own
band, worked in a record store on St. Mark's Place, and
was dating a girl named Lizzie who was also in a band
(wasn't everybody?). Rat was originally from Switzerland,
the son of a French mom and an Italian dad. He spoke
fluent French and English, a little German, and some
sketchy Italian, abilities that would obviously be an asset
on the road. Having moved all over Europe, he claimed
to be an expert on looking like a freak but got through
customs borders unscathed.

His nickname derives from his face, which is made
up of a series of rat-like features. His smallish frame is
exaggerated by an absolute lack of both muscle and fat.
His head had a certain rodent shape, accented by the
fact that he had virtually no chin. Rat sported a stylish
rock-dandy look—vests, ruffled shirts, caps, bolo ties,
and skin-tight pants. Lurking just below the age of thirty,
he was vaguely ageless. It wasn't that he was eternally
youthful or anything, rather that you couldn't estimate
an age on him by virtue of his appearance. He'd lived a
hard life in some respects, surviving hand-to-mouth and
from scam to scam in Hollywood, New York, London,

and Paris. If you looked close, you could see that in the lines around his eyes, but, for the most part, he looked young and lively.

Dahl's recent bands had been of the dressed down T-shirt and blue jean variety, which he was comfortable with. Jeff was a glam fan raised on Alice Cooper, the Dolls, and Mott the Hoople. With this lineup, the band would definitely veer into frilly glitter territory. Dahl easily rolled with that, too. In the trendy in today/out tomorrow music business, the way a band looks can be as important as the way it sounds. A glam band traipsing through punk rock Europe could be interesting from a sociological standpoint. Or, it could be a death wish. This was starting to sound like an adventure.

DAHL HAD GROWN UP in Hawaii, and was the lone rock rebel in his school. He played drums in the loudest band he could find, and won the heart of his future wife, Sylvia, by being the only kid freaky enough to come to school with Alice Cooper makeup on. He had enlisted in the army right out of high school, which he didn't talk about much. It was obvious his need for order and respect of discipline had stayed with him from that experience. He liked to be in control, and he liked things to run smoothly. This usually meant everyone in the band doing things his way. He never raised his voice, and he hardly ever made serious demands of his players. He would demonstrate a song in its most basic form, and allow the player to put his or her spin on it. Things had always run smoothly for me while working with Jeff. Rehearsals were orderly but fun enough. Shows were usually decent with adequate pay, and any recording royalties would be split evenly amongst us musicians. To my knowledge, he wasn't in it for the money. He truly loved rock 'n' roll, and felt that he could help carry on the tradition of his favorite artists: the Dolls, the Stooges, MC5, and Alice Cooper. We had always gotten along well, but it was a very low-key friendship.

Jeff is a year older than me. His real name is Jeff Dahlby, but he'd shortened it when he released his first record, a 1978 single titled *Rock 'n' Roll Critic*. He had an average build, stood about five foot eight, and had a strong German nose and chin that were buried under a huge, frizzy afro. His hair was always changing color, and whether it was black, red, blond, or a combination thereof, it never looked quite right. Still, with his fans, his mop had become sort of his trademark, and each year it seemed bigger and more preposterous.

During the early punk rock years, Jeff had been quite a wild man. He had a reputation for being able to put away more beer than just about anyone. When I'd go see his band Powertrip, beer seemed to practically seep from his pores, as he alternately guzzled it and sprayed it at the audience. He kept himself going through the endless drinking bouts with healthy doses of speed. When he dropped out of the scene in the mid-eighties, he quit drinking and using drugs, with the exception of the occasional puff of pot. He kicked his habits so suddenly that, years later, when I went to his house for an aftershow party, he offered me a beer from his fridge, claiming it had been there from the day he decided to quit. I was impressed. My willpower is not nearly as strong. He still needed something to go overboard on, though, and he replaced his drugs and drinking with running, bicycling, and swimming, all performed to the maximum. He began participating in triathlons, grueling athletic events that involved a mile swim and miles of running and biking in the same competition. He was clean, lean, and mean.

BACK AT THE TRIPLE X office, Dahl begins to prepare both me and Z for the road ahead. Now that I have secured the gig, I begin inquiring as to what to expect in terms of travel, comforts, and naturally, money.

"The last tour was five weeks long, and by the fourth week we were into profit," Dahl reports. "So, we really only made money for one week. But, this tour is just over nine weeks long, not counting Japan, so we should turn a profit around halfway through."

Seems logical. Z is handling a lot of the logistics between the label and Dahl, and one afternoon I ask Z what our per diems will be.

"I don't know. What's a per diem?"

"A per diem," I explain, "is a daily allowance that's doled out to everyone on the tour for day-to-day kind of things, such as cigarettes, food, candy, and chips at roadside markets and gas stations, and for barhopping after shows, etc. Important stuff. Usually on a small tour like this it's around ten bucks a day."

"Really? Yeah, we should get that. I'll check on it."

A few weeks pass and I still haven't heard a firm answer to the question. In fact, as we get closer to the departure dates, the subject of money seems to get hazier. Apparently, Dahl and his European agent, a guy named Camille, who works for a Netherlands-based talent agency called Paper Clip, are still ironing out certain details. Since this is Dahl's third time over, Camille is trying to get him better guarantees and lodging. Around Christmas of 1992, information comes in that could cancel the whole tour: we have lost all of the German dates.

Germany is Dahl's biggest market. The band was going to play there for almost a fourth of the entire tour. Camille had, apparently, been squeezing the German promoters for bigger pieces of pie, and they finally decided to pull out altogether. At the eleventh hour, another promoter, Powerline, agreed to work with Camille to piece it all back together. This meant that, until the last minute, we wouldn't have a confirmed itinerary or a completed budget. The word finally came down that there were to be no per diems, at which point, I give Dahl a call directly.

"How can we survive on the road for two months with no per diems?"

"Don't worry about it," he replies. "Everything will be provided for. The venues will put us up in hotels. The hotels will provide breakfast. We'll get a rider that will provide us with snacks when we get to the gig for sound check and a meal before we play. We'll get all the beer you can drink at the gig."

"What about just day-to-day, you know, when we're traveling?"

"If we stop somewhere, and you want, say, an apple, we'll have money in the budget for that."

My experience on the road is not anywhere near as extensive as Jeff's, but I'm not really buying this. An apple? Why would I want an apple? I'm going to want the immediate gratification that roadside garbage and nicotine provides, usually a bit pricier than an apple. I know that over a period of two months, we're going to need some pocket cash. I mean, we'll be seeing the sights and chasing European women, right?

"There really won't be that much time outside of the shows and travel," rationalizes our leader. "On the last tour, Duffy and I were fighting over who would get the Woolite so we could wash our socks in the hotel sink. That's what we did in our spare time!"

Now, I refused to believe that I was going to spend two months in Europe solely driving, playing bass, and hovering over a sock-filled sink. There had to be a solution.

Given that Jeff is a Triple X artist, and that The Ultras, Sister Goddamn, and Motorcycle Boy all have

CDs out on the same label, I suggested that we take a load of CDs along, sell them at the shows, and split the money as per diems. Z, who deals with a lot of our sales outside of the U.S., works it out with Peter, who owns the label, and we pack up fifty copies of Dahl's latest album, *Wasted Remains of a Disturbed Childhood*, and twenty-five of each of the releases by the other bands. Figuring we can sell them for the equivalent of fifteen dollars apiece, this will likely add up to some decent cash.

Like the Lemon Pipers, money fuels my music machine. I'm still uptight about the budget, so I convince Dahl to manufacture more shirts and caps than he originally planned. Merchandise can generate healthy income on the road. Since we'll be out for two months, and since Jeff usually comes up with great looking merchandise, I assure him it's money in the bank.

We are getting closer to the start of the tour, and rehearsals are set to commence five days before our departure. We've all been working on the songs off of cassettes Jeff made. These three rehearsals are just designed to tighten us up. Z and I went to Phoenix to play a warm-up gig with Jeff a month ago. No one is too worried about the musical side of things.

I TAKE MY MINIVAN down to LAX to pick up Ratboy and Dahl. Both of their flights are late, so I keep driving back and forth across the L.A. airport hoping one of them will arrive. I eventually settle in at Tower Air, which is the airline Rat was supposed to come in on, the cheapest flight he could find. He'd gotten on in New York, while the flight had originated in Tel Aviv. Two hours late, he finally comes marching through the terminal, loaded down with an unbelievably huge folded bag and two guitar cases. Walking quickly while still trying to maintain that ever-present style, he takes a violent spill when one of his Beatle boots fails to connect properly with the floor. The nearby crowd scatters as his guitars, behemoth bag, and cap fly in opposite directions. I shake his hand, help him collect himself and his belongings, and we head out to fetch Dahlby.

"I couldn't believe my flight," says Rat, shaking his head. His accent is a combination of dialects from everywhere he's lived, but the Swiss and the French stand out the strongest. "You know how there's a double window pane for the windows at each aisle? There was no inside window on mine, so there was just a quarter inch of cheap plastic keeping me from being sucked into the abyss!"

REHEARSALS START OUT SHAKY. Z has difficulty keeping an even tempo with the fast music. Dahl is visibly worried, but I keep reassuring him that I'm confident he'll get it together. Although, the truth is, I have no idea whether he will or not. I'm just sure there isn't enough time to get another drummer, much less secure a passport and a round-trip ticket to Amsterdam with only two days notice.

By the final rehearsal, it's still rough, but it's beginning to resemble music. *It'll be fine*, I think. Surely, it'll come together once we start performing every night. Dahl announces that, on top of the CD sales, there will be a hundred dollar a month payment that will serve as our per diem. This works out to roughly three bucks and a chump of change per day. Ever the optimist, I'm unwilling to look at the dark side as we all prepare to launch the longest tour of our lives. I am sure we'll make money on the road and at the gigs. Everything's gonna be just fine.

The night of our last rehearsal, a Sunday, Jeff and I go back to my apartment. My live-in girlfriend, Gina, whom I'm ridiculously in love with, is cooking up a Cajun feast, and has invited a few of our friends over for a bon voyage. Gina will miss me, but she has all of the added responsibilities of managing our empire during my absence. Involved in the music business herself, she finally has a job she really likes, working at a big management firm that handles heavy-duty rock stars like Faith No More, Rage Against the Machine, and L7. In spite of it all, she hasn't complained or made any fusses. She always encourages me to do what I want and to take my music as far as it will go.

Gina dishes out the vittles and we all sit down at the dining table, but Dahl declines to join us. He sits across the room, eating only a salad. He seems uncomfortable socializing with anyone, and he's shyer than I've ever seen him. I figure he's probably just nervous and anxious.

WHEN JANUARY 19TH FINALLY comes around, we all board KLM airlines and head to Amsterdam, the city where the tour will begin and end. Since it's an international flight, the smokers—myself and Z—will be allowed to partake in the joys of tobacco at will. It's a back-of-the-bus scenario, but we don't mind the ghettoization. It's a long flight. Better being in the leper colony of nico-heads than getting nerves because we can't smoke on this ten-hour rocket ride.

Once in Amsterdam, we breeze through customs with relative ease, considering we have six guitars, three large crates stuffed with hats and shirts we intend to sell, and five bags of luggage between us. We are all pretty groggy upon arrival and stumble sort of haplessly toward the exit. A spry young man with wavy red hair approaches us.

"You must be the Jeff Dahl band. I'm your tour manager, Simon Easton," he introduces himself. He looks at me and asks if I'm Jeff, and I point out Dahlby. His famous frizz is tucked in a ponytail, which makes him somewhat incognito. We run through the remainder of the introductions and head for the van.

It's cold and rainy out, but the van is nearby. It's a new Renault rarin' to go. I naïvely expected the kind of van one tours the States in: a big cargo-style Econoline with a backseat and plenty of room to stretch out in the back with the equipment. It hadn't occurred to me that the antiquated back roads of Europe would never accommodate a big American road hog, and indeed, the European-style van was a much different design. It's tall rather than wide with plenty of room in back for whatever we needed to store. The front has the driver's seat and a wide passenger seat, big enough for two. The back comfortably sits three across, but there's no place to stretch out and get any real rest.

Another thing I didn't consider was the fact that this type of van could be a stick shift, which was a problem because I never learned how to drive anything but an automatic. This characteristic would provide us all with significant moments of tension, as I had agreed in advance to take up the slack driving—and had even obtained an international driver's license, as had Dahl. Z didn't even bring a license, and Rat didn't want to drive. This was sure to get interesting.

We stashed our luggage and instruments and put them in with the rented backline equipment—amps and drums. I hop in front with Simon. The rest of the guys pile in the back. As Simon pops a Doors compilation into the deck, we head off. The backseat starts to nod off one by one as Morrison sings us lullabies.

"Cancel my prescription to the resurrection..."

Simon is mercurial, enthused—a veritable bubbling spark plug of positive energy. He's English but has been living in Holland for some time, working as a club DJ in-between road stints. Though only twenty-two years old, constant roadwork and party favors have aged him beyond his youth. We chat about what is ahead and Simon's past experience while we begin rolling north— considerably north—to our first destination, Groningen.

"I've been a tech before," he relates. "I tuned guitars and was a keyboard tech. Mostly, I've worked with this Dutch band called The Soft Machine." (Not to be confused with the English prog/psyche/jazz group of the same name.) "This is my first gig as a road manager, and I'm really into it. I'm going to make things run really smooth for you guys, no problem."

"When I was back there in seminary school..." The tape rambles on. It all seems to be tying together somehow.

"I'd like to get into management." Simon leans toward me when he talks and manages to not disturb the band members sleeping behind us. "I'm keen on having a go at it. I'm good with people, and I think I've got what it takes to bring people together and get people to rally behind a band. I'd be good at that."

Very English. I decide I like him.

I start to feel my own head bob up and down—getting sleepy...sleepy...

"Carry me caravan take me away. Take me to Portugal, take me to Spain..."

13

DUTCH DENTAL HYGIENE AND SURREAL LUGGAGE

(Holland and Belgium)

WE ARRIVE IN GRONINGEN a little before 6:00 p.m. Everyone is still groggy, but we're ready to begin our lengthy adventure. Simon hands out printed itineraries, delineating our fifty shows through eleven European countries: Holland, Belgium, France, Spain, Italy, Czechia (Czech Republic, formerly Czechoslovakia), Switzerland, Germany, Denmark, Norway, and Finland. Like Jeff's shirts and caps, the itinerary is headlined "Jeff Dahl Euro-Tour '93." We check into our hotel and everyone quickly proves that while we are musicians, we're also tourists: we all line up to buy Groningen postcards.

We have three rooms tonight. Dahlby rooms with Simon in order to discuss what his responsibilities will be and to get organized. Dahl is bound to be concerned about keeping our bankroll safe and sound. On his last tour, someone got into Jeff's hotel room in Toulouse, France. They walked away with his passport and all the cash they had earned so far. Needless to say, this put a damper on the proceedings. When Jeff told me his last tour had turned a profit, it was partially untrue. An unknown third party had liquidated a lot of the cash. There wasn't any evidence of a break-in at his hotel in Toulouse. It must have been some kind of inside job, probably someone from the hotel. No doubt money will be kept under close watch this time.

Z and Rat take one room. They actually were roommates in Hollywood for a time, so that leaves me on my own, for one night anyway. Tomorrow night our party increases to six strong. Our merchandising guy will join us. No one really knows anything about him, except for Jeff.

My room is interesting, different than what I'm used to in the States. There's a small closet, a small sink, and three single beds crammed into the remaining space. There's no toilet or phone. That means my Fender Jazz Bass gets its own bed.

Everyone except Jeff reconvenes in the hotel restaurant for a deluxe meal. We eat like pigs, and generally begin to get acquainted with Simon. After dinner, we're supposed to go to some bar/club where Jeff has agreed to appear solo and acoustic, unplugged. A guy named Theo, who runs a punk rock record store in town that carries a lot of Jeff's releases, set up the gig.

Groningen is pretty far north, as far as you can go in Holland before you dump into the North Sea. Needless to say, it's mid-January, and it's cold for us California and Arizona residents. After dinner, we hike the three or four long blocks to the club.

The streets are narrow and made of stone. Most of the traffic is comprised of bicyclists. They outnumber drivers throughout the Netherlands. As we cross a tiny bridge, a small car slightly clips a rider who tumbles over, losing his balance. He yells at the driver and chases him down the street. The driver stops, gets out of his car, and approaches the biker. They start punching each other in the face. After each one receives a few blows, they stop hitting each other, and start talking. By the time we've past them, they seem to have worked out some sort of agreement. Still, the negotiation style is interesting—hit first, then talk. Future politicians, perhaps?

We enter the club, which seems to have no discernable name, although the motif is early cave, with the roof designed to resemble stalactites. It's quite small. The bar itself occupies almost half of the space. Jeff will play to his fifteen or so hardcore fans in a little room off to the side where a lone mic and a small practice P.A. system await. The rest of us negotiate for free beer, and drinking begins in earnest.

Most of the people here are thirtysomething guys, and they have a few other similarities amongst them. They are all punk rock fans, and most of them are involved with sidecar motorcycle racing. One fellow corners me at the bar and talks my ear off in a drunken slur-blur about this sort of racing. He's a sidecar rider, as opposed to a driver, which seems simple enough, provided you don't fall out.

He explains there is a certain strategy to it, balancing and weight shifting and countless other scientific variations that I couldn't be less interested in. Theo shows up, a Frankenstein-like chap, closing in on seven feet of Netherland monstrosity with sunken cheeks and dark, scary eyes. He gives us shirts and sweatshirts that promote his record shop, and pays Jeff some cash on a Dahl video he's been selling. I'm in the video, so Jeff kicks me some cash. I'm already liquid, and I haven't played a note yet!

Besides the previously mentioned affinity for punk rock and sidecar bikes, these guys have a nearly inhuman tolerance for beer—Euro-beer is stronger than the Ameripiss we Yankees swill down on a daily basis. I'd been warned that European standards of hygiene were less stringent than in the U.S., but these guys smell like they haven't touched soap or water in this decade. Never mind that, they probably haven't even owned a toothbrush. If you put all of them together, you might just barely get a complete set of teeth, but individually their mouths looked like bowling lanes with spares ready to be picked up. Simon opines that it has to do with no fluoride in the water, but he's English, so his dental observations and opinions must be taken with a grain.

"I'm pretty nervous. I've never done this before," Dahl confesses to me in private prior to his solo venture.

"Don't worry, man," I reassure. "It's definitely a Jeff Dahl crowd in the house tonight."

He plays Johnny Thunders' "You Can't Put Your Arms Around a Memory," and a few of his own toned-down numbers. They're warmly received. We bullshit with the locals a little more, then bail back to the hotel. I check my watch and it's only 10:00 p.m. Not really much of a night out. We haven't even been here a day, yet been up for two. I figure it's the jet lag and everyone's pretty shagged. We all go straight to bed like good little boys.

Somewhere around 3:00 a.m. the evening's beer consumption sends me to the halls trying to remember where they hid the toilets. It's dark, and I use my cigarette lighter to find my way. Some geek in tight red pajamas and another guy in a floor-length nightgown, complete with matching stocking cap, approach me from the other direction. It turns out to be Rat in the PJs and Z, always the fashion plate, in the Ebenezer Scrooge get up.

"We both sprung up in bed at the exact same moment, looked at each other, and said, 'I gotta piss,'" reports Ratboy.

The need for meaningful conversation immediately subsides, we finish our business, and head back to our rooms. Thing is, I can't go back to sleep. I lie in bed tossing and turning for hours. Finally, at 8:00 a.m., I surrender and get up. Z and Rat tell me that they also couldn't sleep. In fact, Ratboy has already been out and located Groningen's Red Light District, if you can call it that.

"It's hysterical. It's one little street, and there's big, fat, ugly whores in the windows reading books and looking totally bored."

It doesn't sound like much, but it still merits a firsthand look. It's cold out, but we came prepared with hats, wool and leather gloves, leather jackets, sweatshirts, and thermal underwear. We stroll the streets. Z and I, the resident amateur photographers, snap pictures at anything and everything—interesting buildings, uninteresting buildings, and angry prostitutes who don't want their pictures taken shaking their fists. Dahl and Simon join up with us around 11:00 a.m. We get a tourist guidebook from the hotel and see what there is to see. We're all art enthusiasts, at least to varying degrees, and Groningen has a number of museums, so we go check 'em out. A few are closed, but we find two that are open and make the most of it. They're actually pretty lame, but we're having fun anyway, charged with energy and excited to be in a foreign land. Dahl and Rat have been all over Europe before, but it's a first for me and Z. Everyone's having a blast.

This town would not hold up over a Californian fault line. The whole place is made of bricks. A number of canals go through the city, with brick bridges traversing them. It's as foreign as anything could be to a guy who grew up in Southern California. It's beautiful, and the Dutch people, at least the ones we've encountered on the street, seem very friendly. Most of them speak a considerable amount of English. So, it's no problem getting directions, picking up things in stores, and ordering beers in bars.

At 6:00 p.m., we show up at Vera for our first show. Volunteers run it. That's common in Europe at the local club level. It keeps the music scene healthy, vibrant, and

enthusiastic. They treat us like kings and make sure to
satisfy all our petty needs. Dinner is served right away.
Our rider includes beer, juices, chocolates, fruit, and
enormous quantities of bread and cheese (the latter
being European for breakfast and lunch). Z and I should
have put cigarettes on the rider. They're expensive in
Europe. We'll end up plowing through the numerous
cartons we stowed in our gig bags. You learn as you go.
We also should have asked for some hard liquor. We'll
develop immunity to beer over the upcoming weeks.
Like I said, live and learn.

We have yet to play the whole show straight through.
Tonight's the big night. The hall is medium-sized with
a collapsing stage and a full-blown sound system. They
also have a closed circuit video system to tape the band.
We'll get a dub at some point. (By the time we get to
Japan, the Groningen tape will have made the bootleg
market.)

Right before we go on, Dahl and I sit at a table in
the club's showroom. A guy walks in carrying a huge
blue duffel bag. He's got long, surfer-blond frizzed hair,
and he looks spaced-out. Dahlby jumps up and rushes to
greet him and shake his hand.

"Tim! Great! You're here! I was starting to get
worried about you."

Tim is our Mystery Man of Merchandise. He has just
come in on a train from Amsterdam. It turns out he
is the brother of one of Jeff's friends in Los Angeles,
a lovely redhead named Brigitte. When Dahl would

come to L.A. for business, he would frequently stay at my house, and Brigitte would inevitably pop-up. Jeff always assured me they were just friends, as if I would judge someone else's infidelity. If they were just friends, I always felt I should get close to her, in a Biblical sense. She was smart, savvy, and sexy. Alas, I had no such luck.

Her brother is another story. Tim's thirty-two going on fifteen. Back home in The Valley he has his own place, but his folks cover the rent. Basically, he does odd jobs, takes care of a condo for someone, plays lead guitar in a heavy metal band, and chases girls half his age. He's the polar opposite of everyone else on the tour, but he has a job to do. It would be unfair to pass judgment on him too early, but it's obvious that right out of the gate, no one in the band aside from Jeff has much of an affinity for him.

The show turns out to be an hour and a half long, including the encores. Dahl likes to milk the crowd for the encores, and that's where most of our cover songs go, tunes by the Stooges, Dead Boys, Lords of the New Church, Flamin' Groovies, and, on some nights if the crowd really wants more, an audience participation version of "Louie Louie." I don't think any of us would try this at home. There are a few clunkers in our set, but nothing major. The energy we crank up more than makes up for a couple of minor mistakes. All and all, it's a hit. We're all feeling pretty confident about the upcoming forty-nine shows by the set's end.

Following the show, I'm talking with one of the volunteer girls who works at Vera. She tells me there were

136 paid customers, but we played to close to 200, as the volunteers get a number of their friends in for free.

"How was the show?" I ask.

"You guys were good. You'll see on the video. You should definitely keep an eye on your merchandise guy, though."

"Why do you say that?"

"Because he slept through most of the show at his little table. Some salesman."

Okay, the guy's jet lagged, we all are, but she's right: we gotta keep an eye on this guy. This ain't just a free vacation. He's gotta earn his keep, and Dahl needs to sell all that stuff or he'll be in hock up to his 'fro. The Vera crowd was one of the most enthused and high-energy we'd play to for a few weeks, and we sold them a total of one hat.

Back at the hotel, Rat's hanging out in my room, and Tim, my roommate for the evening, is unpacking a few of his things from what is easily the largest duffel bag I've ever seen.

"Aw, you know what I forgot to bring?" Tim asks no one in particular. "Toothpaste. Can I borrow some of yours?"

"Go ahead, but pick some up tomorrow," I request. "Say, Tim, I couldn't help but notice, unless I'm wrong, you don't have a jacket packed in with all that crap."

"Yeah, you're right. Aw, I won't need one, I've got plenty of sweatshirts."

"In the middle of winter, in Europe?"

"Yeah, yeah, I'll be fine."

"Wait 'til we get to Finland," Rat points out.

· ●.

THE BEASTIE BOYS ARE on the tape deck, and we've substituted the lyrics: "No...sleep...'til Eeklo!" Eeklo, Belgium, is our next stop, and for the next few days we'll crisscross the borders of the Netherlands and Belgium. The European borders, for the most part, are open now, so it's like driving across state lines in the U.S. In many cases, it's even more lax.

Eeklo is a pretty, but very small, very boring town. It's rainy and cold, and the unfriendly innkeepers at the Savage Claw, or whatever the hell hotel we're staying at, scrutinize our passports for what seems like decades. They then shuffle us off to the undesirable's quarters, 'round the side and all the way in the back.

The rooms are awful, among the most claustrophobic and mildew ridden we'll have to endure. Dahl points out that the pillows smell funny. Well, we won't be here long.

The gig is in a hall where we have to go down at least seventy flights of stairs, lugging our amps and drums. At home, we all use bigger, meaner amps than these rented jobs, but they're plenty big to be dragging down all these steps. I'm one of those people who'd rather have a needle poked in my eye than make two trips, so I end up carrying too much and drop my amp down a few steps. Although it's in a flight case, I'm sure this Trace Elliot amp was not designed to bounce down stairways.

The club is cold and dank, with a backstage that's down even more stairs. Once we reach it, one of the workers, again a volunteer, unlocks an office and gives us carte blanche to the telephone, so everyone calls their girlfriends/wives, except for Dahl, whose motto is: "I'll send her postcards and call her maybe once. She knows what I'm doing."

I call Gina, who's at work at the management company. She can't talk for more than thirty seconds, because she's supposed to pick up the phones. After the initial "hello," she even seems kind of annoyed that I called. She does say that she's been going out every night and having a blast—so much for missing me. I suppose I shouldn't make anything out of it. I want her to have fun and do well at her job. Rat's wife, Lizzie, is in the middle of contract negotiations with one of the bigger U.S. indie labels, and she's constantly consulting with him about this clause or that. They end up talking for a long time. All and all, I'm glad we'll be long gone when the club's phone bill arrives.

Backstage, some blurry-eyed Eeklo native starts slurring in my ear. "I'm Boeff, from Eeklo. Whuz happening? I need to get some of your shirts for my friend who couldn't come. Can I have them for free?" This guy is relentless, and for the rest of the evening he attaches himself to us like a leech, constantly drinking and haranguing us for free goods, which are not forthcoming.

Two other guys, Eric and Charles, drove all the way from Rosny-sous-Bois, someplace in France, to see the band.

They get records signed by everyone and are amazingly friendly and down to earth. They're true hardcore rock 'n' roll fans, the kind that don't care what kind of hardships they have to endure to see their favorite bands. They say they'll go to the Paris show, and, in fact, by the time the tour ends they plan to see us a total of five times.

The organizer of this event, on which we are the only band, hands me twenty or so drink tickets for beer or soda. "I'll be sure to give the rest of the band and crew their share," I tell him.

"No, those are just for you. They have their own, too."

Well, I guess I'll start drinking a case or two. Hell, I could even go for an apple. After the show, which seemed to be predominantly attended by guys, I survey the area for local talent. The prettiest girl in the whole place, a lovely young lass with blue eyes, straight dark brown hair, and an anachronistic brown suede fringe jacket, approaches me.

"Can I have your autograph?"

I can't help but laugh, a non-star like me signing anything but a check. "Sure, of course. I've got a number of drink tickets here. Would you like a beer or something?" I hand it to her, as the inevitable boyfriend walks up, puts his arm around her, and shakes my hand. Fuck it. I'll give him a drink ticket, too. I make my way to the bar and start drinking Duvel, the strongest beer in Belgium—personally endorsed by my good friend Boeff— and give out drink tickets to one and all. The fellow who organized the show is next to me.

"So, how'd it go?" I ask. "Attendance seemed a little lacking."

"Well, yeah. It's a small town. It's hard to get people in, but that's okay."

"You made a little money then?"

"No, we never make any money, ever."

"How do you stay in business?"

"We're not in business, strictly speaking. Everyone that works here are volunteers, and the whole concert series is funded by the local government to give the kids something to do if they want. It doesn't need to make money."

Wow, imagine that. It's a cultural thing. We're presented as recreation, art, and culture, musicians from afar. Back in the U.S. of A., this would never happen. No one thinks of rock music as anything but a nuisance. No civic group would ever put it on just so kids would have a place to hang.

Back at the bar, I can no longer give away these drink tickets. It seems everyone has had all they can handle, band and fans alike. It's time to take the equipment up the seventy flights of stairs into the cold Eeklo night.

Simon commandeers the van back to Holland where we're to rock a place called Uden. Rat is sitting next to me, fairly miserable, as he's contracted pink eye. Maybe he picked it up off one of those smelly pillows. We've been out for almost half a week, and still no one is sleeping right. My eyes are black all the way around, but at least they're not pink. We talk about the girls, or lack thereof, at these shows.

"I'm telling you, if you want to meet chicks," advises Simon, clued in to all the sagely ways of the road, "the thing to do is to hang around the T-shirt stand right after the show."

"I've been there all night, and there haven't been any girls hanging out there," Tim moans.

"That's because you are there," sneers Rat.

"No, I'm serious. If you want to meet girls, if the band comes down, the girls will come down. You'll see. That is, if there are any girls at any of these shows. Maybe not with you lot."

"Thanks, Simon."

It was true enough. The female species was in short supply at Euro-Dahl events. We seemed to be consistently playing to older punk rock guys who were losing both their hair and their teeth. If there were any girls on hand, they came and left with a guy. Perhaps one of us would find ourselves chatting up one of these ladies while Mr. Boyfriend went for a piss, but that was about it. Contact with the opposite sex seemed to be strictly limited to conversation. There were just no single girls coming in.

"No one got laid on the last tour," Dahl flatly announces.

"Of course not. You guys were too busy washing your socks," I counter.

"I'll tell you, I'm not used to this," says Rat, with one hand over his oozing eye. "In Motorcycle Boy, we didn't have to do all of this courtship bullshit. I'm not used to all of this talking and chatting with these stupid girls. I don't want to talk. We would just have girls around after we played...who knew or cared where they came from. We would just pick one each and pair off and go fuck somewhere. None of this talking."

"I've never had the insta-fuck luxury," I tell. "It seems like I've always been in bands that mainly drew guys. I guess it's just the kind of music I play. Gets to be a drag, sometimes."

"No doubt," laughs Simon. "You guys just don't know what you're doing. I guarantee you I'll get laid, and I'm willing to bet it's before the end of this week."

"What shall we wager, our per diems?" laughs Z.

"No, no, just a gentlemen's bet. You'll see. I'll get laid before the week's up."

The van rolls along, and I fall asleep, my head bouncing against the backseat passenger window. My sleep habits are still all fucked up. I can't sleep at night for more than about three hours. I'm beginning to look like Vincent Price. I've been having ridiculous surrealistic nightmares. The one I slip into during this drive is a recent, recurring dream.

I keep dreaming about luggage that mutates into clothing—that my leather hanging suit bag can be zipped a certain way, folded, tugged, emptied, and turned into a leather motorcycle jacket. It's actually pretty cool, and maybe I kind of wish it were real, but I keep dreaming this pointless dream over and over. It takes place in the van—that's roomier and actually luxurious in my dream—imaginary hotels, and surreal backstages. The dream isn't exciting or unpleasant, but every time I have it, it jerks me awake.

"Luggage again, McGruff?" asks Z, reacting to my jactitation. McGruff is his nickname for me, based on a crime fighting cartoon dog from a public service television commercial.

"Yeah. It turns into a leather jacket now. I wish I could explain..." I fall back asleep, for a while anyway.

UDEN IS A SMALL town built around a town square. Quaint shops and winding streets expand from the humble center. We are staying at a rooming house. The remaining occupants are all GIs stationed in Holland. Most of them are from the South and Texas. They seem excited to have some Americans to watch television and shoot the shit with. They're a coed group, and I get the feeling that more than a little hanky-panky goes down behind closed doors. We invite them to the show at a proper club tonight, but they aren't familiar with the venue. They take the address, but I'm pretty sure none of them will show up. It's far too removed from their daily routine.

The guy who runs this little cottage for wayward soldiers and rockers has volunteered to do our laundry. You can't ask for more than that. So we sort it out, and it's a surprising amount given that we're only on our fifth day. As he toils over our dirty socks and crusties, we adjourn to a nearby arcade.

It turns out that Simon isn't only an expert driver, navigator, negotiator, mediator, and equipment fixer, he can also whip everybody's ass at any and all games, be it pool, pinball, video games, or foosball. Of course he always wins, and after awhile, it gets a bit depressing for everyone else. If I take on anyone else for pinball, my favorite brand of arcade time wasting, then I pretty much always win. Variety and unpredictability are not part of this scenario.

For some reason, I decide to get to know Tim, as he will be around for our duration here. So, we take a walk through the bustling streets of downtown Uden. Tim has done his homework, and he already knows a few key things about me: he knows I work for a record company, he assumes I know everyone in the record business, and he knows I write for rock magazines. He starts telling me about his band, how they have management, how he writes the music, how numerous labels are interested, and how everything will be taking off for them as soon as he gets home from Europe.

"You know, I haven't talked to Jeff about it yet, but I tell ya, my band would really be great opening for you guys in Japan. We're the type of band the Japanese would really eat up. I know they would."

"What type of band are you?"

"Sort of like Aerosmith, with a little Rush mixed in. I add a little more technical angle to it, as I've been to G.I.T., so I like to really play some guitar."

G.I.T. stands for the Guitar Institute of Technology, a place where lots of guys go to learn to play like whoever the most shredding guitar player of the week is. Moms and dads send guys and girls from all over the country out to Hollywood for holing up in cheap apartments and hanging around G.I.T., which, when they get the tuition bill back home in Omaha, sounds like an official university, a place of higher learning. It's a place to take guitar lessons and learn all about music, and there's certainly nothing wrong with that, but the thing is, a certain style of guitarist always seems to emerge from the school—cold, unfeeling, technically proficient, theoretically learned, fast, whiz-banging, jazz fusion meets metal jack-officers. Tim seemed to fit the mold. It was in direct opposition to the kinds of things the members of this band stood for, and the kind of street musician/garage musician roots most of us had.

Tim also had an amazing appetite. At this juncture— the beginning of the tour—he was more or less the same size as Jeff and me. He seemed to eat non-stop. "I'm on vacation," he would say, which certainly was his attitude, especially when it came time to load equipment and sell merchandise. In Holland and Belgium, there are a lot of walk-up stands that sell fritters, what Americans call French fries. Tim stopped at three separate fritter stands during our walk and ate three orders all by himself.

He was indeed on vacation. Nothing wrong with that, in theory. Tim was trying to be nice to me, but I could see we had virtually nothing in common, except that we both had long, dishwater blond hair, we both grew up in California, and we both played in some sort of band. That wasn't going to be enough to form a lasting bond, but I guess it would have to be enough to tolerate him for nine weeks.

When we return to our Uden outpost, we find our laundry done, and our whites all turned to this weird bluish-gray. Since our host can't really speak English, it doesn't make sense to inquire about what the hell happened. He makes up for it with a huge spaghetti/salad/garlic bread feast.

The gig tonight is in a proper rock club, right here in central Uden. We learn that the building directly next door, which is ominous, dark, and with no signs of people coming or going, is a whorehouse. It doesn't seem to be a very functioning whorehouse, still, that's the word, and we keep our eyes peeled. Nothing much seems to happen, no one goes in or out, both literally and figuratively. No one's buying sex in Uden.

Our show is on a bigger stage than usual, and the setup at the venue is pretty happening. The P.A. and lighting guys come in to start their evening's work already roaring drunk, hooking things up incorrectly, causing mind-numbing bursts of ear-shattering feedback, then falling down laughing about it, and blowing up overhead lights.

The audiences are getting a bit stranger, as well. A Dutch beauty that was tending bar prior to our performance comes to dance in front of us while we're playing. She looks like a budget version of Uma Thurman. This is enticing at first, until her boyfriend

joins her, a regular Thor meets the son of Frankenstein.
Together they cavort, and we are again reminded that no
females attend a Jeff Dahl show unescorted.

The drunken techs decide to spice up the show,
cranking on a fog machine. We didn't even know
they had one. Still in the grips of pink eye, Rat's eyes
immediately turn bright red, and he is temporarily
blinded.

"Turn that fucking thing off!" he shouts, stumbling,
trying to find his microphone, but unable to locate
exactly where it is. "Fuck!" he hollers, stumbling
sideways into the mic and knocking it over while the
stage becomes more engulfed in smoke. At this point,
Rat can no longer see his guitar neck and is playing
random noise. He's in so much agony, the music doesn't
even matter to him.

"Man, you gotta turn that fog machine off. I've got
Blind Lemon Ratboys on up here," Dahl instructs over
the P.A. The drunks, still slobbering and guffawing, get
it together enough to can it with the smoke, and things
return more or less to normal. We finish the show.

The highlight of the performance every night, for the
backing band anyway, is our cover version of the Stooges'
"Dirt," a simplistic blues-riff with a slow, three-chord
turnaround for a chorus. It's dirge-like, slow compared
to the remainder of our set, and Dahl holds down the
three chord mantra like clockwork, allowing the rest of
us to go off into a sort of free-jazz, epileptic fit. It's quite
cathartic and is played like the frustration release that it

is, allowing us to stretch, bend, and extrapolate in our own modest way onto the Thelonious Monk, Roland Kirk, Ornette Coleman stratosphere. We play it as sonically tone-bended and mutated as we can, given the abilities of our pudgy, little, non-G.I.T.-trained fingers.

Backstage there's a bit of a gathering with our agent, Camille, who is in attendance for the first time. Along with him came Daniella, a shorthaired, kitten-featured manx of a lass whom he claims is his girlfriend. Though judging by the way she gravitated toward that pink-eyed little Rat, I'm not sure I would want her to be my girlfriend. Rat is intrigued by her, and he seems to like the attention. He sits close and talks in quiet tones with her. Their heads nearly touch to insure privacy. Camille observes this out of the corner of his eye, frowns, and continues to talk business with Jeff. Camille tells Jeff, so we all can hear: "This is certainly the best band you've brought over. That's made a big difference, and the feedback I'm getting from the promoters is very positive." Dahl is already talking about doing summer festivals with another band, one that he does side projects with, but Camille is encouraging him to stick with us, that he should build on one thing, get to know it better, and expand the fan base. Rat, Z, and I say nothing. Selling CDs to make ends meet and living off of three dollars per day makes us think it's best to not volunteer for too many Jeff Dahl tours.

Z isn't paying that much attention anyway. He's sitting in between two Dutch girls, kissing one of them.

Z—the quiet one, the shy one, the good-looking one—is making friends and influencing people. The girl he's smooching gets a little hot, and starts hugging him real hard. The other girl rolls her eyes and looks a little embarrassed.

"All right, rock stars. It's time to lug your gear out. C'mon, I'm a tour manager, not a humper, off your bums, then."

Yeah, yeah, yeah, sure. Z takes the girls' names for the guest list at an upcoming show. I hope it's not within the next two nights, because Z's girlfriend from L.A., Rita, is hooking up with us for a few days. She's visiting family in England, taking the train over to see her man, and she doesn't like to share.

9

IF THIS IS ROCK 'N' ROLL, WHERE'S THE SEX AND DRUGS?

(Still in Holland and Belgium)

I T MIGHT EVEN BE fair to say that I, and perhaps we, was/ were getting into the groove/grind of it all.

Morning: up and at 'em with a hotel-supplied Euro breakfast, which was usually a buffet with a variety of fruits, breakfast meats (if we were lucky), cereals, milk, juice, Euro coffee, maybe some pastries, and of course bread and cheese. Shower, if feasible, pack, and pile in the van.

The Rides: both long and short, were handled as best we could. Music from our limited cache (by this I mean Simon's limited cache—we had tons of music between the band members), books, magazines, jokes, stories, sleeping.

Get to the Town: look for the gig, potentially get lost, look for the gig some more, find the club, load-in (frequently up or down a number of stairs), and set up. There was usually beer and snacks waiting for us. Good European beer, always welcome. Jeff asked for chocolate—good

European chocolate (it is from the heavens). And, lest we forget, bread and cheese.

Sound Check: which could double as a rehearsal touch-up if need be. At this point, things could become more varied. Maybe we'd look around the town if there was time, maybe fall asleep somewhere in the club, or maybe take a look at the support band, or maybe walk or ride back to the hotel if they had a television or some other diversion.

Dinner: sometimes before our set, sometimes after, usually at the venue. The rider said no pizza, so we usually got a meal of some sort, with salad, bread, meat, and veggies. Fine and dandy.

Then: we rock, we pack, we split. Repeat.

Following our Uden blowout, I finally get my first full, normal night's sleep. I wake up feeling alive, full of spunk and enthusiasm. The rest of the guys seem to be coming around as well. As we head back to Belgium in the Renault, I notice Z and Rat have mastered the art of sleeping in the crowded, four side-by-side backseats of the van, whether it be with a pillow between them, folded over their laps, across each other, against the windows, or a dozen other variations. They're aided by a double-sized pillow, which they lifted from the Uden hotel. Dahl notices the extra linen.

"Hey, man. If I get back to the states and we get a bill for that pillow, I ain't paying it."

No one bothers to reply. I change the direction of the conversation. "So, Tim, how're we doin' on CD sales? We movin' anything?"

"We sold two Jeff Dahl CDs last night, but we didn't sell any of the others, none of your stuff."

"That's cool, of course people are going to buy Jeff's first. Well, at least we have some sales, so we can split some cash up."

"We're not splitting up the sales of my CDs. That's my money," Dahl says without blinking.

"Hang on. We agreed that we'd take all of these CDs on the road and sell them for our per diem money, so that everyone would have some pocket cash."

"That's fine. That's what you, Z, and Peter came up with, but this is my tour. I bring the crowds. I'm who they're coming to see. When Sister Goddamn CDs are sold, you keep all of that money."

"Frankly, when Sister GD CDs sell, I'd rather split the money with everyone, so that we all have money, like I said. That was the original idea, which was a good one, and a fair one. Why do you want to change it now—now that we've gone to the trouble of getting all of these discs over here?"

"That's the way it's gonna be. When you sell your CDs, you get the money. Rat gets Motorcycle Boy, you get Sister Goddamn, and Z gets The Ultras. I'm covering a lot of expenses on this tour, including hotels and food on our days off, so that's the way the CD sales are going to work."

From the get-go, we brought twice as many Dahl CDs as any of the other titles. We three were handicapped out of the gate. Z doesn't say anything, but I know what he's thinking. The Ultras, with their androgynous, glam-boy look are going to be the hardest to sell to the party-line punk rockers, which will make him the most cash poor. Of course, he doesn't say anything about it out loud.

The band sits shoulder to shoulder in the backseat of the van. Simon has been the only driver so far, and Tim has managed to commandeer the double-wide shotgun seat. When we argue, there is nowhere for us to separate from one another, no way to put any space between us. This means that we all just clam up, look straight-ahead, and ride on.

●..

TONIGHT IS THE NIGHT Rita will join our entourage, and Z is excited, though as is his style, he barely shows it. We are in a tiny but lovely old Belgian village named Kortrijk, which none of us can spell or pronounce, so we call it "Coat Rack." Tim takes a nap at the hotel, Dahl stays in to write songs and brood, and the rest of us head out to the local pool hall to spend our downtime in this picturesque little town. We drink beer or cappuccinos, depending on whether we want to get wired or relax. I notice some handbills for an upcoming local appearance with Little Richard, so we at least can be confident that the Coatrackians know how to rock.

Our gig is again at a volunteer youth center, in what appears to be a church recreation room of sorts. Two hardcore punk bands open for us while we are more or less imprisoned backstage where it is pretty cold and pretty boring. Cold and boring is becoming the norm—beer to drink, cigs to smoke, bullshit to exchange. The performance itself is pretty lively, with Dahl really connecting with the crowd and Z getting those tempos up to and past their designated speed. Rat and I share stage left. (I'm actually in the middle, creating still more confusion as to who the hell Jeff Dahl really is.) The human rodent and I develop a stage rapport that relies as much on comedy, and some sort of latent sexual angst, as it does on cliché rock moves. Whatever. We become foils for each other, switching rolls as jester, straight man, fall guy, jealous lover, showboating upstager, whatever might or might not be appropriate and/ or amusing to us at the moment.

For the first of two encores, Dahl somersaults back onto the stage from the side. Not to be outdone, I try this ridiculous move where I thrust myself back onto the stage using my bass as a sort of pole vault. Leaping over the headstock, and landing as if coming into home plate, I thought it was a cool idea. But I really didn't execute it right, and as I land, the metal tuning pegs on the headstock grind into my rib cage. It must have looked pretty klutzy, but it seems our audience is looking at Dahl and ignoring the rhythm section, so I get away with it. As I check my Fender's tuning, I notice that I bent my G-string tuner by attempting this stupid little stunt. It didn't work, no one noticed, and I screwed up my instrument. What a fuck up! I can play "Dirt" out of tune and get by, since I have no other bass with me, so that's just what I do. While Dahl and Rat are tuning, I take the mic.

"Like to send this one out to our tour manager, Simon. Simon is God!"

Simon really has been doing a bang-up job, keeping us a little under budget (so he says), driving all the time, playing table games with us, fixing things, telling us endless jokes that we can't remember even five minutes after we hear them, but that crack us up anyway. Perhaps God is a bit much, but if someone has to fill those holy sandals, it seems like Simon's the cat.

"Simon, bad news," I say as I approach him after our last encore. "I fucked up my bass. It doesn't tune anymore. Can you make it well again?"

"No problem. I'll just get a pair of pliers from the sound man and put it right." He does, and it is. All is well.

The hotel we're staying in is really fancy: pillars, a huge ornate front door, fancy cable TV, twentieth century telephones all over the place, plush drapes, and unusually huge beds (for Europe) that make us feel like kings. Following our last four shows, we've been accumulating our rider beer and stashing it in the van, where, even during the day, it's cold enough to keep the brew more or less refrigerated. It's a Sunday night, and nothing sounds better than gathering up a few sixers and vegetating in front of the color TV.

As we enter the hotel Plasky, the night watchman stops us in our tracks. "What's that, in that crate?"

"Just a spot of beer, friend," says Simon, smiling ever so friendly.

"You can't bring it in."

"We can't take beer into our own rooms for a nightcap?"

"You can't bring it in."

"Simon, the man says no beer," I interject. "We'd better just take it back out to the van."

Once outside, we fill our luggage bags with the bottles and head back upstairs, where Simon and I smoke cigarettes, drink ice-cold beers, and watch the European version of MTV's *Headbanger's Ball*, with tonight's guests, everyone's fave raves, Def Leppard. Z paces the floors, waiting for Rita. She should have been at the show but didn't make it. Now, it's hours later and she still isn't here. My man's getting a bit worried.

· ∴

"MORNING," I SAY IN my best Monty Python fake English accent.

"Morning," Simon answers, ever cheerful, as he sits at the Plasky's communal breakfast table.

"Have some bread and cheese, dude," Dahl offers. Z is walking down the plush spiral staircase from our rooms with the lovely Rita in tow. She had gotten in after the rest of us crashed out.

"You can't believe what I went through to get here," she growls. Rita has the gruffest voice of any girl I've ever known. It was not very feminine, yet on her, with her bleached blonde hair, sarcastic wit, and jaded attitude, it was fitting and somewhat sexy.

"I guess I got on the wrong train at [blah blah blah blah] and no one would help me. I showed them my ticket but these people will deliberately fuck you over [yada yada wank wank blah blah]." As she talked, my mind drifted to the thought of my own girl back home. What was she doing? Was she missing me? Or was it actually better for her with me out of her hair? I'd left enough money for my share of our bills and then some. She had our huge Hollywood Hills apartment to herself. Was she lonely or finally free?

"...and finally I got someone to tell me where this fucking hotel was, and get me in a cab here, that must have been after two in the morning, and you guys were already all asleep. Are you rockin' or what? What's up?"

"We are a regular ticking time bomb," says Rat, barely above a whisper, his first utterance of the day.

THERE ARE NO SHOWS for a couple of days, but we're to go to Brussels for a Dahl acoustic performance and an on-air interview for BRT Radio. Upon arriving in Belgium's capital we all agree on one basic thing: Brussels sucks. It's ugly and dull, and since we're here on a Monday, everything is closed. It takes forty-five minutes of driving up and down one-way streets and trying to extract directions from the locals to find the hotel, another half an hour to actually park. Our rooms are small and musty, it's raining out, everyone is restless and antsy. Z and Rita are anxious to do something—anything—since their time together is limited. I take the opportunity to change my bass strings and practice a bit, Tim takes this opportunity to show me what an ass kicking, popping/slapping, super-funky bass player he is, naturally with my bass. This makes me want to cut practice short, even if it means walking around in the rain and going nowhere.

We all walk to the radio station, just for something to do, where we find there was no acoustic performance scheduled after all. We wait around for the interview to start. Jeff, Rat, and I will do it while Z and Rita wait in the station foyer. The interview girl shows up, an attractive redhead who seems to look down her nose at us lowlifes, anxious to get us in and out (of the studio that is). At the last minute before we begin taping, Tim asks if he can sit in. Rat and I look at each other with apprehension, but Dahl says it's okay. We set our three chairs in front of the big interview microphone while Tim sits to the side. We clear our throats and wait for the red light to indicate taping has begun. Ms. Interviewer raises her hand to count us in, "five...four..." Then Tim starts asking questions.

"So, do you live around here?"

Dahl, Rat, and I stare in disbelief. He's actually used this lame line on girls at the gigs, but now he's interrupting our interview and wasting our time.

"Have you had this show long?" he continues.

"About three years. Ready...four...three..."

"What do those switches do?"

"Tim, do you mind!?" cuts in Dahl, trying to save face. "Just be quiet, okay?"

She proceeds to ask unbelievably standard formula questions. The whole procedure takes five minutes. I say about five words and Rat says none. Tim talks more than the two of us combined, thankfully not on the air. We leave the station as quickly as we can.

"What a waste of a day," Z says.

Rita chimes in, "You mean, that was it?"

"What can you do?" asked the ever-tolerant Dahl.

That night, all of us except Jeff, who chose to stay in the claustrophobic cubby hole of a hotel room, go get some grub in downtown Brussels, a sort of poor man's Times Square. We get some good beefsteaks, which sort of makes the day seem better. Various members of the troop are beginning to catch colds. Z in particular is losing his voice, and he begins to sound as raspy as Rita, making them an almost comical couple.

Rita departs the next morning. We head back to Holland again, where we're to record a live performance for a Dutch radio broadcast. She will hookup with us again in France, down the road a bit. Meanwhile, Rat is almost over his pink eye, but now has a bad cold. Z has completely lost his voice. Tim has the sniffles. Simon, Dahl, and I hold tough against the invading illness. Vitamin C and DayQuil packed from home, combined with Dahl's trusty Fisherman's Friend throat lozenges (used by all touring punk singers in the know) allow the three of us to stay well for the time being.

We show up at N.O.B. Studios, a big complex in the woods outside of Hilversum, a studio once favored by seventies progressive rock bands like Genesis and Van der Graaf Generator. We're set to cut three live tracks in a room, mic'd with everything separated and mixed through a thirty-six channel board direct to two-track tape. I'm enjoying being in a pro studio environment with all the classic gear. It's a nice diversion from our rock/rinse/repeat. Despite sniffles, scratchy throats, and cold medicine grogginess, we cut six songs in the allotted time. We are a rock machine.

Following the late afternoon session, we have to hightail it to Rotterdam, where we are to play that evening. Riding along in the van, I ask to hear the cassette of our afternoon session.

"Okay, this time, but I hate listening to live tapes in the middle of a tour. We'll be getting tapes all over the place, and I don't wanna hear them."

"What are they for?" I ask. "Aren't they made to be listened to?"

"Yeah, but not on the road, not in the van. When I get home, I'll listen to everything and analyze it. I can send you out copies then, if you want."

"That's all well and good, but if we listened to the tapes now, we could hear how we're playing, what we're doing, and maybe improve right now, as we're touring."

The van grows quiet again. No one else has anything to add.

By the time we get to Rotterdam that evening, everyone is getting a bit edgy and bored. The club is downstairs below a bar, with a low ceiling and a P.A. that accommodates only one microphone. None of us seem too interested in the gig. Mostly, we just sit upstairs, look at the girls hanging out at the bar, and play foosball with the locals. We have no contact with these women. We just look at them. We're not even working up to a good stare, that's how lethargic we're becoming. A pretty Indonesian girl parades around the bar like a regular baton twirler, causing Simon to fall madly in lust. The chase is on.

"Oh, I fancy her," he smiles, then lowers his head back down to devote attention to the highly competitive foosball showdown he's engaged in with Ratboy. "I'm getting a bit horny. Did I tell you my maximum? It was five girls in one week on the road with The Soft Machine."

"That's impressive," deadpans Rat.

After the show, I'm standing alone in the bar, completely uninspired to do anything but stand around and wait, when Simon tells me we're "all in," ready to go. As I hop into the back of the van, I see the Indonesian girl is sharing the front with our fearless English navigator and Tim, who's tired from a day of doing next to nothing. A girl who we don't know is actually riding in our van, right alongside us, a band that has played mostly to guys and a few of their dates for the past six days. At the bar only fifteen minutes ago, Ratboy had chuckled under his breath,"We're such losers."

Back at our quaint, yet ornate, digs I'm sharing with Simon, Dahl is teamed with Tim. Z and Rat score the single rooms. We've been taking our turns with the singles so that everyone gets their fair share of privacy, allowing time for relaxation, reflection, meditation, or good old-fashioned masturbation. Simon and I are playing host to his new love interest, Vanessa, but when I walk into my room with my bass, Tim is already sitting—shoes off—on my bed.

Simon was correct in pointing out that the merchandise table was the hot spot to meet people. Whether just browsing or curious, whether true fans of the band or tourists, most everyone at a show drift by during the course of the evening. However, this was not helping Tim make friends and influence people. His pickup lines might work on the sixteen-year-old Valley girls he lures into his web of slacker-evil back at home, but here they just don't fly. His oft-used *Do you live around here?* line has already become a comic catchphrase for the band. Rat, Z, and I would ask, straight faced, any pretty girl on the street or at a roadside stop if she "lived around here." Now, Simon had made the effort to drag some ne'er-do-well vixen back to our micro-rooms, and, if at all possible, Tim was going to horn in on the action.

I sit in a chair, unable to stretch out on my own bed because of Tim. Seeing as entertainment is lacking and I'm reasonably bored, I decide to sit back and see what happens next. I organize a soundtrack for the proceedings by hooking up my two battery powered porta-speakers, which plug into my Sony Walkman. A compilation of funky seventies hits start making the air move a bit.

"Nice of you to drop by, Tim," Simon says sarcastically.

"My pleasure," Tim returns, equally mocking.

"So what do you do, Vanessa," Simon offers as a combination icebreaker and timewaster.

"I'm a student here in Rotterdam. I hate it. School is so stupid and pointless, but what would you expect in a town as boring and ugly as this."

"You're a regular ray of sunshine," I impose. "What are you studying, if I might ask?"

"Religion and Philosophy."

"That figures, I suppose."

"That's great," Simon says with a smile, trying to salvage a quickly backsliding situation. "School can be such a great time, all your chums, hanging out and getting abuzz everyday. Just a big party, can be."

"Not here. The people are so stupid, these are the descendants of those who nailed Christ to the cross."

"The Dutch did that?" Tim sincerely inquires.

"Not literally. Figuratively."

"Religion and Philosophy, Tim," I point out.

"The Bible tells you one thing but means another. It tricks you into thinking everything's all right, but it's not. Between the lines, it's telling you, *We will get you. We will kill you in your sleep.* All religions do that, they wrap you in a blanket of security while sneaking up behind you with a dagger. Remember the Manson murders in California?"

"These guys grew up there. They can probably tell you all about it," Simon motions toward Tim and me.

"Not me, I'm too young," lies Tim.

"Spare me," I say, hoping Vanessa will resume her paranoid tirade. She does.

"They took Charlie as a religious leader. Followed him and killed for him. They'd all still do it, too. They're not reformed. His followers are like sheep; in a way, it's the perfect religious sect. The Catholics would kill for that kind of control. But few Catholics would kill like Charlie did."

"Remember," I say, starting to get interested, "Manson didn't kill anyone. He went down for being a ringleader. He didn't really kill anyone personally. Just like Hitler."

"They're sensitive about Hitler around here, McGruff," says Simon, referring to the fact that Rotterdam was leveled during the war.

"I'm not. You could blow this place up again, for all I care." A brief silence hangs in the room like musty air. How in the world is Simon gonna turn this mess around? Does he even want to, with this sullen Indonesian Squeaky Fromme? Our Lady of Hopelessness and Despair continues.

"That music you play, that punk rock, I remember when it first came out in the seventies, and we called it New Wave. Some of the New Wave bands were definitely trying to achieve that level of mind control, to harness an army of marauding killers."

"Like who, Kajagoogoo? The B-52s?" I ask.

"This chick's whacked, man," figures Tim.

"Now, c'mon. Everyone's entitled to an opinion," defends Simon.

"Yeah, especially if they kick down a little trim in the immediate future," countered Tim, visibly riling Simon, who was looking less likely to succeed with every passing moment.

"The German industrial bands, they had their audiences turning into the new Hitler Youth." This girl is relentless. Our door flies open to reveal our leader, Mr. Dahl, slightly pissed off.

"You idiots have woken the whole floor up. You can hear your bullshit about Manson and Ohio Express all the way to the lobby. Cool it!" He shuts the door and shuffles back to his room down the hall.

"Well, that's put a damper on things. Goodnight, Tim," Simon says without a smile. After Tim departs, Simon goes out somewhere with little Miss Medusa, and I just go to sleep.

FOLLOWING ONE OF THE best days of being a happy-go-lucky tourist in the beautiful town of Utrecht, hosted by our tour guide, Simon, we end up at Tivoli, a big ballroom with full concert sound and a full lighting system. The show is crowded. Apparently, there is a Dutch equivalent to the previously referenced Guitar Institute in this town. A large percentage of our audience happens to be guitar students who stand with their arms folded and stare at our fingers. Not too inspiring. They all have that familiar deadpan *I can do better than that guitar player* look.

After the show, the place turns into a big dance hall, cranking out everything from old disco to new rock to some pumpin' R&B. Simon, Rat, Z, and I make regular pilgrimages from the dressing room, where the supply of free beer continues unabated, to the dance floor, where the supply of girls increases exponentially with the amount of time our show has been over. As I dance, I become aware of a sharp, nagging pain in my rib cage. It's been bothering me off and on all day, and the only thing I can figure is that I must have bruised or cracked a rib doing my aborted bass pole vault routine in Coat Rack. Even though it's unabashedly un-punk rock, the dancing is a nice release, a bit of exercise, a way to clear my head, something mindless to do.

After a few twirls to Gloria Gaynor's "I Will Survive," I head back for what must be my tenth or eleventh beer. Seated on the folding chairs, amongst a few other hangers-on, are the two girls Z put on the list back in Uden. Z, seemingly aware of this, is nowhere to be found. I chat with them for a minute, and the shorter one, whom Z had made lip contact with a few days earlier, asks me if I might like to score some hashish. Given that virtually anything that is fun and illegal in the States is legal here, and that I've had absolutely no recreational drugs yet on this tour, I decide that this situation has got to be turned around immediately, certainly before we get stuck in France. Dahl glances over at me with a look that says, "Hash sounds like a good idea." So it's on a hash pilgrimage I'm a-goin'.

"It's really close by," says the short, slightly plump brunette whose name is Joannie.

"Let's go, then."

Utrecht is a toned-down, prettier mini-Amsterdam, with winding stone streets flanked by parallel canals and canal walkways. Like a lot of European towns, it all spirals out from a cathedral located in the center of town. Leaving the club, we start walking uphill a bit.

"It's about a block and a half," says Joannie, who I notice is having more than a little trouble coordinating a smooth walking style, although she insists on moving along at a quick clip. Four blocks later, I ask if we're almost there. "Almost, but I really gotta pee. Let's go down here, to this club that's going on. We'll get a beer, too. I know everyone there. It'll be free."

Leaving the main street, we walk down a stairwell to a path that runs along the canal. There is a whole separate series of shops, bars, and whatnot along this lower level. We enter one that is an all-ages rave—a techno dancing, strobe light flashing, bass-speaker booming, shoulder-to-shoulder happening. The air is laden with tobacco and hashish. The floor is wet with beer. She heads for the toilet while I think to myself: *Damn, look at this crowd, young crowd, mixed crowd. This is what's happening. Rock 'n' Roll is dead here, these kids want Techno. They want to shake ass, get high, get laid. The same things rock fans wanted before they had to veg out in the retirement home.*

Oh well. I try to figure out how to get a beer. I line up at the bar, but learn I need a beer ticket purchased from a booth at the far end of this sardine can. My thoughts return to hash, and when Joannie emerges, I grab her, and we head back to the street.

After five long blocks, the pain in my ribs evolves from creeping ache to sharp, stabbing pain. "I thought you said it was nearby. We've walked half a mile...make that three-quarters of a kilometer"

"Right up here, don't worry." Three more blocks, over to a side street, up an alley, and around a bend. Wherever we are, there is no sign of human life. We approach a metal garage door, chained and bolted from the outside, and Joannie starts pounding it with her fist.

"Call it a hunch, but I would say no one's here."

"No, no. They're here. I promised you some hash."

"Yeah, but it's bolted shut. There's no one here." I lean against the wall and let her pound for a few more moments. Then, we begin our half-hour hike back to the club.

"I hope you know how to get back. I'm completely lost." I'm one of those people who can get lost anywhere. I can get lost a few blocks from my home. She starts walking faster and faster, meaning, I suppose, she's gotta piss again. Long city blocks are flying by, and sure enough, she starts moaning about her bladder.

"We must be almost back to the club, just go there," I instruct. "You can make it."

We turn a corner and see the Tivoli marquee. "Let's run!" I shout, trying to garner some excitement from all of this. We start running, and within ten strides, Joannie trips over her own feet and hits the concrete, hard. I turn to look at her sprawled on the sidewalk, seemingly unconscious.

"Shit!" In no time, a crowd gathers. Great, I've killed someone on foreign soil. The authorities will haul me off to some underground dungeon at any moment now. I can foresee it: endless days of dark cells, ambassadors, arguing diplomats, and quagmires of red tape. I bend over Joannie, not wanting to say anything out loud, and give myself away as a slimy American in front of this mob who'd love to lynch me just for the hell of it, American or not. I get her on her feet. Her head is reeling; a sizeable golf ball begins to emerge from her forehead.

"Wow..." she finally says, looking up at me as I try to steady her. "Good thing I'm very drunk right now, this is going to hurt tomorrow."

"Okay, folks, show's over. The little lady's just fine." She heads back into the club, as I remain outside for a minute to catch my breath and make sure the lynch mob disperses. I turn and notice two drop-dead knockouts standing by me, smiling, appearing as if by magic or hallucination. What on earth do I have to lose?

"Excuse me, but you girls wouldn't know where to get some hash, would you?" They nod, each grabs a McGruff arm, and it's off on a wild goose chase, number two. I can't believe my fortune. Unlike Joannie, they speak virtually no English. I'm unable to negotiate anything from them—hash, romance, ménage à trois, anything. I merely get led around by them as they hang onto my arms. It's fun for a while, but by the time I get dropped off back at Tivoli, I've spent an hour walking around the city in search of hash and am empty-handed. I've probably gotten more exercise than I've had in months, though.

Back in the dressing room where the endless flow of fine bottled beer—Oranjeboom, my favorite—continues unabated. Joannie's tall friend with mousy brown hair and pointed features, looks bored and fed up with her drunken comrade. Z still avoids the two of them like the plague. I grab the tall one, "Let's hit the dance floor!"

Her name is Martie. She talks about her job as a bookkeeper and her upbringing in, of all places, the Inland Empire area of Southern California. I'm amazed to meet a local who has spent time in the same part of the world as me, and we hit it off pretty well. At least she's smart, friendly, speaks so I can understand her, and doesn't act like she's roaring drunk. We hit the floor where we are dancing next to Ratboy and our agent's girlfriend, Daniella. Those two are getting oh so cozy, dancing something like Lambada, "forbeedin" dance of Brazil.

Dancing is great, and proves to be a dependable outlet for the boys in the band—get the show over with and get the hell out and dance. Though I never spend that much time dancing at home, and probably won't spend that much time on the dance floor when I get back to the U.S.A., here it proves to be my one reliable release. Dancing becomes the physical expression of all that is pent up inside me—the day after day on that damn bench seat in the back of the Renault.

Our Utrecht hotel is an Ibis, the European equivalent of a Holiday Inn. It's nothing fancy, but you know you'll get a tub, shower, toilet, two beds, a TV, a phone, and room service if they take your credit card. Jeff loves the orderliness of it, the fact that all Ibis' are essentially identical, and wants to return to it now. He has been tolerant of us wasting time and having fun, and now we got to get moving. None of us, including Simon, want to go. We're all just having a blast. This is probably the first opportunity we've been afforded to really let loose and party with the locals. Only Tim, who's getting nowhere with the girls and who can't hold any more beer, is in agreement with Dahl. Still, he's the boss, so we do the usual gear hump to the van. Once we've loaded the equipment, I perform the nightly ritual known as the Idiot Check, one last pass is made over stage, wings, and backstage, to see if we've left anything behind. When I get back outside to the van, Joannie and Martie are rammed in the backseat along with the band. I hop up front with Tim.

"These girls insisted on coming back to the hotel and partying with you, McGruff," laughs Simon.

"They want Z," I counter. "I'll sell the fucker into white slavery and turn a profit on this expedition yet."

"This is a nice hotel we're going to," said Dahl. "We don't need another loud party to get everyone else in the hotel pissed off at us."

"Don't worry. I'm going straight to bed. It's been a long day, and after my mile hike, I'm knackered," I say, truthfully.

Tim doesn't miss a beat when it comes to honing in on girls, once they've been rounded up. Back at the hotel, he heads straight to the elevator with them, leaving the rest of us with tons of luggage and all of our guitars. "Where are those chicks ending up?" I ask Z and Rat. "Not in our room, I'll tell you that," Rat assures.

"That one Joannie has been bugging me about you all night, Z. You gotta be the one to get rid of her."

"Nope." Z was traditionally a man of few words.

"I just really want to get some sleep. My fucking ribs are killing me, especially after that walk. I swear, I think I've got a cracked rib."

"Get that tall girl to give you a back rub, McGruff. I'm sure she's got something good for all your aches and pains, and I don't mean Advil." The Rat had spoken.

As fate would have it, I was rooming with Tim tonight, and to little surprise, a mini-soirée was underway as I arrived. Even more beer was a-flowin', and Tim was trying his best to get close to Joannie. He peeled off his shirt for added sex appeal, which gave me a sudden, queasy, claustrophobic feeling. From the bathroom, I heard water running.

"What are you doing in there?" I yell through the door. Martie replied she was taking a bath, and suddenly I could see a light at the end of the tunnel.

"Well, you better let me in so I can make sure you've got everything under control."

"She's fine. She doesn't need you," snapped Joannie.

"C'mon in, the water's fine," I heard from the other side of the door. Joannie suddenly jumps up and stands between the bathroom door and me, arms outstretched. "Where's your drummer? I want your drummer."

"He's gone to beddy-bye, like a good little drummer boy."

"Well, you can't come in here until your drummer comes over here."

"Look, this is my hotel room. I can go anywhere I please. I'm sorry our drummer doesn't want to visit with you at the moment, but I have no control over that. Now, step aside."

"No!" was the petulant reply.

"Alright then," I pick her up and throw her over my shoulder. As she pummels her fists against my back, and aggravates my aching rib cage, I toss her on one of the single beds, and instruct Tim to deal with her as he sees fit. I go into the bathroom and lock the door behind me.

There is one obnoxious, florescent light that glows overhead. Martie has hung her black dress over it to tone it down. Admittedly, I'm drunk and exhausted. She looks pretty good amidst the bubbles (where did she get bubbles?), smiling and winking at me. I take my clothes off and slide in behind her. The water is warm and perfect. She leans against me gently, and we just sort of drift off. For a moment it's quiet: no music, no talking, no van engine running—just dim light, steam, and two bodies clasped together in warm water. We scrub, play, fondle, kiss, and all the other things drunk people do when they're naked together in a tub. Eventually we tire of all this. When she stands up to grab her dress, it falls off the light into the draining tub, soaking it. She hangs it up, puts a towel around herself, and goes out to the bedroom. I stay behind to clean my contact lenses, brush my teeth, and shave.

A few minutes later, feeling relaxed and very unwound, I walk over to my bed, where Martie is sitting and watching Tim fuck Joannie in the other bed. They don't make much of a show of it, trying to be subtle as it were, but the fact that they're about eighteen inches from us makes the act difficult to conceal. Martie is visibly excited. Her nipples look like they're about to explode under her black bra, her sole item of clothing besides the towel loosely draped across her lap.

"Ho Hum," I yawn, pulling back the covers. I'm very tired, sobering up a bit, and not really feeling like going the distance with this girl, who, truth be known, wasn't even invited here by me. Wearing my sweat pants, I climb into bed with the intention of getting some sleep. Martie throws the towel aside and snuggles beside me, wearing only her bra. Shoving her tits into my chest, she grabs me hard and starts kissing me. I'm not very responsive, as if to say, whatever special something we had in the tub is lost in the bed.

"Duff, Duff, I love you," she babbles drunkenly.

"Shut up. You don't even know me. You're wasted. Go to sleep."

"No, Duff. I'm serious. I've never met anyone like you before. I love you. I really do."

"If you say that again, I'm going to hurt you. Now, shut up and go to sleep."

She grabs my cock through the sheets and gives it a few strokes. She then drops off to sleep, almost instantly, and snores loudly. Hmm, guess that doesn't say a fuck of a lot about my cock, which even by the strict standards of American hussies had always been well received.

DREAM SEQUENCE

I'M LOOKING IN THE mirror, and I'm fully made-up, drag queen style, with rouge, lipstick, eyeliner, and mascara. Wearing Martie's soaking wet black dress, with my leather jacket draped over my shoulders and my untied Doc Martins, I head down to the Ibis lobby, where Rat and Z await.

"Dig your makeup, man," says Rat.

Though it's daytime, a scythe that is the moon hangs surreptitiously above our huge, deluxe tour bus. As I climb onboard, I notice Simon is handcuffed to the steering wheel, his mouth sewn shut with big, metallic wires. "I'm feelin' funky, baby," says Rat, as he turns on the radio. It blasts some heavy, nasty rap.

"Didja fuck 'er, fuck that skanky bitch/ Didja ram 'er, Didja scratch that itch/didja plug 'er, then leave her in a ditch..."

"Rat, turn that off. It's awful. Do we have any Ramones? Where's Dahl?"

"We killed him, and Tim is no more. It's our tour now."

Rat is suddenly dressed in a toga with a laurel leaf headpiece. He dances up and down the aisle of the bus, which seems to stretch for miles. The miles of aisles are lined with barnyard animals—pigs, goats, cows, chickens, and what have you—like a rock 'n' rolling Noah's Ark. Rat babbles in tongues. Z follows him around with a fruit basket, as he tells everyone to bow to the great Caligula, though no one else is on the bus.

I take off my leather jacket, unzip the proper zippers, and it turns into my overnight bag. I open a side pocket, and pull out Martie's head, which someone has neatly severed and packed away for me.

"Oh, I'd like some head," laughs Z, followed by Rat. Soon all three of us are chortling uncontrollably, save Simon, whose mouth has been sewn shut.

END DREAM SEQUENCE

THE PHONE RINGS LOUDLY, it seems to literally leap into bed with me. Simon's cheerful limey accent chirps through the receiver, awakening me from my death sleep. "We're leaving in five minutes. Cheers."

There's a knock on the door. "Boy, a hot dog stand would clean up around here," I say to no one in particular, remarking about the sudden traffic. "Tim, be a guy and get the door." I roll over, notice I'm alone in bed, and scream as I'm reminded of the pain in my ribs, which now really, really hurts like a motherfucker. Tim answers the door and it's the two girls, with tea, coffee, rolls, toast, and jelly. "How nice," I say, as I dig in. Small talk is exchanged, Tim is still even feigning romance, but I want to eat, pack, and get moving. Joannie mentions she saw Ratboy in the hall. "With his hat and sunglasses," she opines, "he looks like a real pop star." An amusing comment, I make a mental note of it, though I'm not sure why. Perhaps it will be of some use in the future.

Down in the lobby I say goodbye to Martie while the rest of the band has their eyes glued to me, grinning. I walk out to the van past their snickers, while Tim stays behind and milks a long goodbye out of it. We load the van, climb in, and Simon backs the Renault right into a BMW parked next to us.

"Simon, what the fuck are you doing?" shouts Dahl.

"Let's just get the fuck out of here," I suggest. "Hit and run, it's an American tradition. No sleep 'til Lieden."

As we pull out, Martie and Joannie are walking across the street to the train station to get back to town, the opposite direction from where we're going. We never offered them a ride anyway. "Look at them," chuckles Dahl. "Talk about going home with your tail between your legs."

"So, McGruff, did you fuck her?" inquires Rat.

"No, I didn't. Besides, a gentleman never tells, so don't ask again."

"Oh, you fucked her. You dog, you McGruff."

"No, I really didn't. We just took a bath. Very therapeutic, like you suggested."

"Well, I fucked mine," boasts Tim. "And I'll tell you what, when you were still in the bathroom after yours came out, she walked up to me while I was laying in bed. I pulled her towel off and gave her pussy a lick."

"Man, you don't know where that pussy's been," admonishes Dahl, who was beginning to take more and more of a fatherly tone with Tim. "I hope you at least wore a rubber."

The van got very quiet, and Tim failed to respond.

NEXT WE ARRIVE IN Leiden. Leiden, Uden, Eeklo, all these towns are becoming difficult to differentiate from one another. We get to the hall, and despite a crippling hangover, I settle in for a few hours of Funhouse pinball with Simon, who brutally beats me every time. A friendly blonde girl who books the venue walks up to me, and asks: "Are you the bass player for Jeff Dahl? You've got a phone call, a Dutch lady."

What the hell? I pick up the office phone. "Duff, it's Martie. Duff, I hate to call and ask you this, but I honestly can't remember. I must have blacked out. Did we, uh, well, you know...?"

"No, we didn't. Do you still love me?"

"What about Joannie? Do you know?"

"That depends on how much anyone cares to believe Tim. I would say the answer in that case is a probable yes. You may have done things with him for that matter, but I can't say for sure."

"Oh, my God."

"Look, don't worry about anything. You just got a little drunk. You're fine. Watch what you drink, and don't go to see any rock bands for awhile, okay?"

I hang up the phone, notice my trembling hands, and wonder how on earth I could give advice to anyone about drinking.

The Leiden gig is succumbing to a stronger punk vibe then the previous few nights. The band plays with extra venom. Following the gig, Simon and I are hanging out at the T-shirt stand, rapping with a guy named Big George who is, once and for all, going to score me some hash. I get a sizeable bag for ten gilders, about seven and a half bucks. Meanwhile, a tall, very politically correct Leiden punker is scrutinizing our shirts and caps, which, unfortunately, haven't been selling well. The Iron Cross insignia is used quite a bit in Dahl's design. He always liked the look of it, and felt it gave the merchandise an American biker feel. The Leiden punk is not in agreement.

"This is very bad. You'll see. These symbols still carry a lot of weight, many bad feelings."

"I just sell the shit. I don't design it," Tim says with his usual lack of eloquence.

"This is very bad. The Germans are not going to like it. You play Germany?"

"Yeah, we're going to Germany, for quite a while," I answer.

"No, the Germans won't like this. They might get violent. They're Germans. They will get violent. Maybe you should not sell these things in Germany."

"We're in business here, friend. We've gotta pay the bills all the way across the continent. We have to try and sell these shirts everywhere we go."

"Very bad. The Germans will be angry. I see bad things ahead for all of you. The gutters of the streets will run red with your blood."

It suddenly grew silent. I looked at Simon. He looked at me. We both looked at Tim. *The gutters of the streets will run red with our blood.* Darkly poetic, yes. Exaggerated? One would hope so. Food for thought nonetheless.

WE GO FROM LEIDEN to Goes, pronounced "goose," where we play another small hall to an enthusiastic audience of guys and a few of their girlfriends. The only girls who approach us are very homely and seemingly desperate, so obviously the pseudo-orgy in Utrecht was an isolated incident. At the club, we get an excellent home cooked meal of Indian food that at least makes the night worthwhile. Leaning back, full, content, and picking my teeth, I look over at the dressing room wall and notice some superb graffiti that says, "We have ways of making you rock." Clever, four stars.

Simon relays the details of an adventure he has kept under wraps. "You know that blonde booking agent at the club last night in Leiden? She met me back at my hotel room after you lot were safely in bed. She was hot and ready to fuck, no doubt about it."

"How'd you get her in and out—of the room that is— without any of us seeing her, especially in the morning?"

"Oh, for fuck's sake, I didn't let her sleep through to the morning. I had a go at her then told her to leave. Must've been about four in the morning by then. She didn't want to go, and tried everything to get me to let her stay. When I finally got her out the door, she suddenly went down on me, right there in the hall outside my room. I went, 'alright, fair enough,' leaned back, and let her blow me." Road romance, the stuff dreams are made of.

We end up extending our stay in Holland with a visit to Apeldoorn, a bigger, college town, meaning people under thirty and even some girls might be at the show. The gig is more or less the same as any other, except that tonight the soundman has some sort of deep-seeded grudge against music and takes it out on us with an offensive monitor mix.

Tim has been imbibing on the backstage beer a lot. No one's really keeping an eye on him. Following our rockage, Rat and I stumble to the club's bar to hang out and see what the available girls look like. Rat's funny about girls. He talks about how he'd like to get some attention, how he's not used to being in a band like this with virtually no female appeal, and so forth. Should a girl actually go after him, it becomes instantly obvious that, despite the talk, his girlfriend is first and foremost on his mind. Nonetheless, a cute, bespectacled brunette resembling a young Diane Keaton is chatting up Rat. She asks him about Tim, of all things.

"Is that blond surfer guy with you guys?"

Rat confirms that he indeed is.

"He's really revolting. He was following me around, a footstep behind, leering and drooling. He comes up with these horrible lines to try and talk to you."

"Let me guess, *are you from around here?*" laughs Rat.

Some guy walks up to me, dragging behind him a girl with short, curly, brown hair and a moronic smile.

"My girlfriend, very naughty!"

"Well, spank her once for me, pal."

"No, really naughty!"

What is this leading to, something sacrificial?

"Her name is Hette."

"That's Naughty Hette, I presume."

She hands me a Jeff Dahl shirt, which means they actually bought one. In sign language, she asks me to sign it. Having no marker, I invite her backstage for the ritual. Another couple and Hette's bragging boyfriend follow, but only Hette is brave enough to cross the proscenium into the musician's netherworld: the backstage. I locate a marker and sign the damn thing, while her boyfriend keeps peeking through the door to see what's going on.

"Christ, he tells me your naughty, sends you off alone with me, then watches us like a mother hen." She smiles, but I can tell she has no idea what I'm saying.

Back at the bar, Rat says the poor man's Diane Keaton wants to go dancing, which is quickly becoming our pastime of choice. We plan to go to the center of town, actually a pretty happening little strip for Holland, when we suddenly realize how much tension is in the air amongst our provincial six man society. Dahl is uptight, worried about getting back to the hotel, worried about the equipment in the van, worried about whether his troops are getting too out of control. Tim is drunk, woozy, and looking to vomit at any moment. Simon and Z are playing it cool. They tell us to head to the disco, and that they'll catch up in a taxi after they put Tim and Dahl to bed.

Flashing lights, drinks clanging, an evenly mixed crowd. Here we go, now we're having fun. The four of us guys and this girl hit the dance floor. We're now at a point where dancing is just a physical release. We don't need to be dancing with girls; we're just as happy dancing with each other, giggling and drinking. Z busts some killer moves. Simon does the James Brown shuffle. I show off my locker-funk steps. Before we know it, we're in the middle of the dance floor with the remainder of the crowd spreading away from us, as if we are diseased or something. We don't care. The more they react, the more we overdo it, making rude faces and doing outrageous moves.

Soon enough, we've worn this poor girl out. She can't keep up anymore, and bids us farewell. We stay on. Just before the joint closes, the DJ plays the original Stooges version of our encore blowout, "Dirt."

"Yeah!!!" we all shout in unison, hitting the floor, doing the slow motion Iggy snake dance in a tribal circle. By now we are the only ones left dancing. The groove trudges and lurches along. His Majesty Iggy Pop coos, "Can you feel it, can you feel it when you touch me? Can you feel it when you cut me? I'm alive, I'm alive."

For just a lightning's flash of a moment, we do feel it. We're alive.

5

WEAR A HAT, GO TO PRISON—THE AUDIENCE HAS LEFT THE BUILDING

(France: Part One)

"I HATE FRANCE," RAT declares with the blasé frankness, which was becoming his trademark among us. Acting as our official backseat travel guide, he comments as the highway slices its way into the land of French bread, French fries, and French kisses. "Look at it. It's disgusting. It's filthy. Look at the cranes, everywhere. I remember this from when I was a kid, cranes all over the place, constant rebuilding, but nothing ever seems to get finished. The people, of course, are so rude and unfriendly, that's pretty well known. You'll see. You'll hate France, too."

"I don't much have any use for it myself," adds Simon. "Mind you, I don't think I've ever been laid in France. If I get laid this time, it might boost my overview."

"I miss the sheep of Holland. At least they were fun to drive by and wave to. Hello, little sheep," Ratboy giggles. He soothes himself by clutching the pillow he lifted in Uden. It's sometimes spread across his lap and Z's, sometimes pried in between them, sometimes fondled as if it were a giant breast, sometimes lightly gripped like a security blanket, but always within reach, just in case.

Simon hits the buttons on the tape deck, and the familiar opening salvo of Nirvana's "Smells Like Teen Spirit" scratches its way out of the Renault's tiny, no-fidelity speaker system. "Nooooo," goes up the cry from Z and Rat. "Not again!"

"Watch it, he might put on The Doors again," I warn. We are a day shy of being two weeks into the tour, but already our tape supply has become redundant. Part of the problem is that Simon is always driving. A traditional rule of the road states the driver may lord over the music selections, since he's going to have to maintain consciousness and be responsible for everyone else's ass. Fair enough, but between us we've brought along a ton of tapes. Simon, who has far more commercial taste than the rest of us, seems to burn along on the same handful of options over and over again. Rat and I brought an assortment of blues and funk. I'd brought along some newer rock, metal, and even some dance music. Z brought along his cherished Frank Sinatra and swing bands. Dahl has some vintage Queen, classic punk, and obscure garage bands from around the world. Tim, probably for the good of all, had forgotten to pack any tapes; obviously he kept them with his toothpaste and jackets back at home. Whatever the case, at this moment we are listening to the singularly most overplayed and overexposed song in the world for what seems like the eight-millionth time. "Oh well, whatever, nevermind."

Whenever music played that he really hated, Dahl would take his long, Air Force issued overcoat and pull it up over his head. Simon swore that underneath the coat, out of view from the rest of us, he had his fingers pushed hard into his ears, so as to keep each and every offending note at a safe distance.

Meanwhile, back on the road into France, Simon attempts to beg off driving.

"You know, it'd be really keen if I didn't have to drive all the bloody time. If one of you lot could take over, that'd be really great. How 'bout it, Ratboy?"

"Why me? I specifically asked not to drive."

"You've got a license. Z doesn't and fucking McGruff can't drive a stick shift, can he?"

Dahl must be able to tune into the conversation through his carefully shielded ears, 'cause the coat comes down, revealing the beret that keeps his frizz in place. As he pulls the protective sound barrier away, his bare wrist reveals a bracelet on which the word MASTER was engraved into the metal. And so, the Master speaks.

"You know, Simon, I don't have a problem with driving, but it does bother me that you're so tired all the time 'cause you're staying up late chasing ugly girls around. If you at least were scoring some good-looking girls, I might feel different about it. I know that last night after you took me and Tim back to the hotel you went back out, and I would imagine you were out late."

It was true enough, but I personally was thankful for my lengthy respite from the hotel in Apeldoorn. I had drawn a short straw, once again, and had been paired with Tim, who, thanks to his beer consumption, had spent the hours I was away violently throwing up. By the time I returned at around 3:00 a.m., he was done puking and had given himself over to a grotesque, guttural moaning that conjured the devil himself. He still looked pretty green this morning, but, after a good barfing, was fit enough to hit the road leading to France. He'd been quiet most of the ride, until now.

"I think we'd better pull over somewhere. I'm not feeling so great," he sheepishly announces.

"Oh, for fuck's sake. You're not gonna be sick again?" asks Simon.

"Uh, I uh. I just think we should pull over."

"Don't tempt the fates, Simon. Get us off the road," implores Rat.

We pull into a roadside truck stop, and Tim disappears into the men's room. Several of us could use a piss, but it's best not to risk it, when barf might be flying like shrapnel. Z and I walk out to the van and enjoy a cigarette. We've almost puffed through the cartons we stashed in out gig bags, and, noting the going rate for cigs as we hit these roadside stores, we begin watching our diminishing supplies. Simon hits me up, but he still has plenty of tobacco and papers to roll.

"Give us a fag then, darling."

"C'mon, man. We're getting low," I bitch back.

"Oh, c'mon. I don't want to roll one. We're gonna have to move out as soon as Tim gets done heaving. You know we can't smoke in the van."

I give him one of my precious remaining cancer sticks. We watch as Tim emerges from the can and enters the snack shop. He comes back to the van carrying potato chips, chocolate chip cookies, a ham sandwich, and a soda.

"I guess you're feeling better," Dahl says.

"Well, I gotta eat."

This seems to be the truth.

THE DRIVE SEEMS TO take forever, one of our longest treks so far. Ratboy complains about the cold. The driver's side window is down, blowing the crap out of all of us in the back seat. He claims he needs the air to stay alert. Rat and the rest of us are fairly sick of the music, which has returned to the land of the Lizard King. "Oh show me the way to the next whiskey bar," Jimbo intones.

"Okay, Simon. You win. I'll drive," Rat says. "But when I drive, the van will be the way I want. We're going to turn the heater on and we're going to listen to music I like. It's not going to be cold, with the fucking Doors on. It's going to be warm and bluesy."

Rat has spoken. He is true to his word. Soon the heater is blasting, and Lightning Hopkins is sending me off to a pleasant nap. Rat takes us past Paris and into the twilight. Simon regains the wheel for our arrival into

Orléans, home base of Joan of Arc and site of the most ornate cathedral we will see in all of Europe. Extremely grotesque and monstrous gargoyles line every possible corner. Are they keeping the demons out or in?

In Orléans, we are to connect with our French promoter, Geordie. She'll put us up for the night, and then she'll travel with us from gig to gig in her territory. It's somewhat unnecessary, as Rat speaks perfect French, but apparently she's a big Dahl fan, and wants to see all this pants-wetting excitement first hand. It turns out this is the first nationwide tour she's ever promoted. The notion that anything *might* happen is established.

After we cruise up and down narrow streets so tight they barely accommodate a bicycle, let alone a van, we finally find Geordie's address. Her apartment is at the top of a fifth floor walk-up. The debate rages as to whether or not we should carry our guitars up right away. The paranoids among us prevail, and we climb the five flights of stairs with six heavy guitar cases in tow.

"Jeff!" beams Geordie, as the door flies open and her arms hug the tragically shy Mr. Dahl. She's five-foot-six with black hair, large features—especially her nose—and teeth that would be the envy of the Groningen motorcycle club. While she does in fact still have them all, they've turned to a blue-black that invites a certain queasiness. She greets us all and invites us in.

A good half of her tiny living room—sitting area would be more accurate—is occupied by record racks containing endless LPs and singles of American sixties garage rock, plus every band—such as Jeff Dahl—who emulated that period of musical primitivism. From the 13th Floor Elevators to The Standells to the Chocolate Watchband, it's all here. Being an avid vinyl collector myself, and lover of all things Nuggets, I dive into the makeshift record store with delight and thumb through the platters. Tim bends over and whispers in my ear. His breath is still an unpleasant mix of today's ham and last night's upchuck.

"Is this the whole place? What do ya think?"

I break from my record trance and survey our surroundings closely for the first time. There is a single-bed futon by the records, a small couch, and a door, presumably leading to more rooms.

"Two of you can sleep here," she says, indicating the microscopic futon. "And one of you here," as she motions toward the couch. The door leads to a couple of single beds, which would sleep two more of us. One of us would take a floor spot, and Geordie herself offered to sleep on the floor. Much like when a stalemate froze the air in the van, the room goes quiet.

We all pile into the van and head to some guy's house who Geordie has arranged to cook dinner for us. As we pull up to our chef's apartment, he is outside moving his van.

"This guy, look at him," says Rat, leaning into my ear so only I can hear. "He's so French. You can't believe how many of them look just like that."

With a husky build, a mop of brown hair and a pullover sweater—he's named Claude no less—he does in fact seem the archetypical, young French guy. He invites us in, where his girlfriend barely notices us, glued to her snowy black and white TV, watching a documentary about French singing legend Edith Piaf. It's almost too pat. He serves us spaghetti and wine. We eat until we're contentedly full, then layback. Simon, Z, and I have after dinner smokes and reassess the situation. It is decided quietly, almost utilizing nothing but eye contact, that whoever wants to hang with Geordie is welcome to do so, but the rest of us will get a hotel.

Dahl and Tim decide to stay with Geordie, while the remainders find respite in yet another Ibis. We grab a bottle of Cuervo tequila we got backstage and about eight beers to chase it with from the van, and retire to our rooms. Simon is excited to find the Super Bowl on television, live no less. Z, Rat, and I are truly unconcerned with sports, so we locate some broadcast pornography, a staple of Euro-TV that truly puts American puritanical standards out to pasture. Two rooms, two TVs, no problem. Pass the tequila, son.

THE NEXT DAY IS Monday, the typical European day off, and we have the day off as well. Z and I have decided to take the train into Paris and do the tourist thing. Simon is going to come along to take pictures and make a day of it, but probably, truth be known, to make sure us two knuckleheads don't get lost on the train system, lost in Paris, or lost in insanity. Z will meet up with Rita again at The Louvre around lunchtime.

Following a pleasant train ride with a fellow named Sebastian—who gives us a map and recommends some places to go shopping—we hoof it over to The Louvre where Rita meets us on the front steps. The Louvre is huge beyond description, and filled with all of the most amazing, timeless, and world-famous art. Rita takes us through all the really great sections. We probably walk over a mile inside the museum itself. Staring at wall-sized murals—intricately hand painted and incomprehensibly detailed depictions of various Biblical hoedowns—I get a true sense of just how insignificant our little rock 'n' roll contributions to the world of art really are. Viewing these incredible achievements, knowing that my work will involve nothing more strenuous and intellectually taxing than banging out the three notes of "I Wanna Be Your Dog" is a humbling experience.

We depart The Louvre and head for Notre Dame. "You know," I say to no one in particular, "we can sure move along at a quicker clip without Tim along, stopping every five minutes for a new snack."

"Don't remind me," says Simon. "He thinks he's coming back with me to Holland for a few days following the tour. He sort of invited himself to come and stay, to kill time before he catches his plane back to the States. I wanna see my lady, Melanie. I don't wanna have to deal with Tim. I've got to off-load him somehow."

"Oh, Rita. Tell these guys your Tim story!" enthuses Z, who rarely gets excited.

Rita starts laughing with that glorious, hoarse voice. "That's right, the Tim story. When I was with you guys last, I kept looking at Tim and thinking that I knew him from somewhere, and it finally came to me. A girlfriend of mine had dated him once, and was kinda turned off by him. I guess he got real handsy real quick, you know, the gorilla type. I called her in the States when I went back to England last week, and she confirmed that it was in fact the Tim I was thinking of. She reminded me of the whole story. So, she goes out with him once, doesn't like him, blows him off after that. But he keeps calling, very insistent, wants to see her real bad. She keeps saying no, but he keeps calling, and the calls get more and more desperate, and he starts confessing his undying love to her. She tells him to fuck off once and for all, but he doesn't take the hint, and the next thing she knows, she's at home in bed sleeping one night when she suddenly wakes up. She hears a prowler or something. Sure enough, Tim comes in through the bedroom window, and she's up on the second floor! Apparently, there was a lot of screaming and yelling, and she called the police. Eventually, this led to a restraining order against him."

"Wow, the fucking Night Stalker," I laugh. "Our own T-shirt guy. Incredible."

"I knew that guy had a screw loose," says Z. "I wish we could just get rid of him now."

"It's all beginning to come together, if you think about it," reckons Simon. "The way he follows birds around, leers after them, his increasingly compulsive drinking. He could turn into a violent fucker, I bet."

"Oh yeah?" queries Z, the Sicilian in him taking over. "I'll knock his block off. Forget about it."

PARIS IS FOGGED IN by sundown as we make our way to the Eiffel Tower and Arc de Triomphe. We're hungry, but everyone is so low on money we can't afford to eat in a cool French restaurant and get the full Paris cuisine experience. So, we settle for the next best thing—the Paris McDonalds. Hey, it's cheap, and we know what we're getting. And truth be told, it tastes pretty fucking good. No one's complaining. We hit the tourist stops, and on the way back to the train we check out the gigantic Virgin Megastore, where we search out various records, just to see if they're in stock. All of the records we're selling on the road, plus a lot of Dahl's records are here, so we collect them and make our own little display in a corner when no one's looking.

Back at the hotel, I grab a boiling hot bath for what ails me, which, frankly, is a lot. My rib is getting back to normal, but now I've got a bruised foot. I guess dancing, jumping off the drum riser, and our five or six mile walk today aggravated it. A couple of nails on my right hand have split right in two due to aggressive down-stroke picking on the fast punk tunes. Dahl and Rat have similar complaints. The crowning glory is my butthole, chafed and raw as a result of two weeks using sandpaper for toilet paper. The walk didn't help. Let the hot water carry my aches away.

Pass the tequila, son.

⸭

AFTER A THRILLING DAY of laundry, we ride the van across
town for our first show in France. The club is a small,
underground jazz club called Caveau des Trois Maries,
"Cave of the Three Marys." We walk down the narrow,
winding steps and see the smallest of stages, obviously
designed for a trap set, standup bass, and a Ray-Ban
goateed saxophonist. We each have approximately
two-square feet to rock in. The whole place is done in
latter-day subterranean dungeon—quite cool. Geordie
is helping Tim set up the T-shirt stand at the top of
the stairs, where folks come in the joint. She is already
complaining about Tim and his laziness, it doesn't seem
to take long. He's complaining about her muscling in
on his turf, but we want a native on board that can
rap to the locals to help us boost sales. He's also been
bellyaching about not coming with us to Paris yesterday.
We throw it back at him, and claim he could have called
us before he left.

Dahl is content, enjoying the massive backstage
fruit, cheese, and bread spread as he awaits the arrival of
Carol, the widow of the late Stiv Bators. Stiv, one of Jeff's
punk rock singing idols, had sadly left this dimension a
few years back when he was run over by a taxi on the
streets of Paris.

One of the fans films our set. It must have resembled
an early Beatles Cavern show. The band is shoulder-to-
shoulder, delivering a high-energy show nonetheless,

and the room is literally fogged in with cigarette smoke, the underground venue doesn't have any ventilation. Carol and her crew show up right after we hit the stage. The cameras are rolling, Rita is rocking. It's quite a set. Crowded, yes. I bean Dahl on the top of the head with the headstock of my bass and Z clips Rat with an accidentally flying drumstick, but that's rock 'n' roll for ya.

After the show, countless French fans request autographs and ask detailed questions about our records and our opinions on records by other weirdos. Whatever anyone says about the French, one thing's for sure, the fans know their music inside out.

A pretty blonde named Isabelle, who has come along with Carol, starts chatting me up. While she's not exactly Greta Garbo, I find the increasing lack of female attendance at our shows is making my standards decrease. Some guy hovers around her, but with no apparent strings attached. I assume they're just friends. Carol, Isabelle, and the two other guys they came with invite us out for a night of drinking. Dahl begs off, which surprises me given Carol's connection to him, but the rest of the posse, plus Geordie, make it a regular street gang. As we walk side-by-side down the winding streets of Orléans, the eleven of us must resemble a punk version of the West Side Story Jets.

We hit a bar called Paxton's Head, a darkly lit drinking hole packed with bleary-eyed locals, all of whom are whooping, hollering, and spitting with excitement as they drunkenly converse, and slop beer all over the place.

As the eleven of us squeeze in, the entire place goes quiet all at once, and all eyes stare at the wildly dressed young folk who have just entered. A man scurries from the bar, brandishing a bar towel, and rushes up to us, stuttering in French. Immediately, Carol, Geordie, and the towel man are engaged in some sort of heated debate. I consult Rat.

"This guy is saying we can't come in because we are all wearing hats," chuckles Rat.

"No way. Is that a law or something?"

"No, no. I think he just looked at us and that was the first thing he could come up with since most of us are wearing hats. He just doesn't want us in his bar."

The girls continue to make a stink about it. The vibe with the locals is not improving. They sit there staring at us, casually sipping their beers and not talking. The wild reverie that greeted us has been supplanted by grim, watchful eyes.

"Now they're asking if we can stay if we take our hats off," reports Rat. "I think I'd just as soon leave. I don't really care if I get to drink a beer in Paxton's Head or not. This situation could take a turn for the worse at any moment."

"Wait a minute, Rat. Paxton's Head? No hats? Coincidence?"

"I don't know, McGruff. Let's get out of here."

Back out on the street, our friends join us one by one. Carol is fired up and seeing red.

"How dare they! Do they know who we are?" Then she falls about laughing. We all start guffawing and head down the street in search of another beer emporium. We find one, enter, and are invited to stay, hats and all. The increasingly lovely Isabelle is engaged in conversation with your humble narrator. As my beer intake increases, so does her profound beauty. Still, this other joker comes around, butting in just as I begin to get close to my darling new friend. Rat pulls me aside.

"McGruff, that guy's her boyfriend. You're wasting your time."

"Are you sure? They don't act like boyfriend and girlfriend. I think she wants to be my girlfriend, don't you?"

"I'm not absolutely positive, but I'm pretty sure they're a couple. Here, have another beer, talk to the Rat, and forget about her."

We stay 'til closing, head back to the hotel, where I begin to drink myself to sleep, once again. I sit back on my bed and kick off my boots. Simon pops another beer, and Rat is half asleep in a chair.

"Well, Simon. I'm glad you're with McGruff tonight. His snoring has been getting unbearable."

"What, I snore!? That's impossible."

"Oh, of course it is," tosses Simon, "and you don't fart, either."

The latter was true. I had mastered bodily control to the point where I'd eliminated farting from my list of bodily purges. Burping, spitting, blowing my nose, these were all still mandatory, but I'd kicked farting. No one believed me, but no one could prove otherwise. While we're on it, I hadn't thrown up in about a decade, and considered this a point of pride as well.

"McGruff, your snoring sounds like a chainsaw, a power drill. Your bass isn't that heavy," continued Rat. "I've never heard anything that obnoxious."

"Really? Damn. Well, sorry fellas. It must be all the smoke in these clubs. Maybe my allergies. Here, have another beer and it'll seem more quiet."

"No, I'm done for the night. Me and my hat are going home."

*

IN BORDEAUX, WE ARE to play with legendary British punk band the Buzzcocks at the Theatre Barbey. It's a genuine big rock show with a large stage, crew, concert lighting, and sound rigs. Our sound check runs smooth. Afterwards, I go out into the freezing cold auditorium to watch the 'Cocks. I stretch out on four seats, nod out, and sleep through their blaring sound check.

Dinner is served in a cafeteria next to the hall with the crew and both bands occupying long tables. It's straight out of The Last Supper. A huge, mangy looking guy with brown, scraggly hair, scruffy bandana, and a round, rough, unshaven face approaches us and introduces himself as he sits down next to us to eat. "I'm Kike, of The Pleasure Fuckers. I'll be traveling with you throughout Spain. I'm the Spanish Promoter. I'll take care of you. It will be the best."

Who's going to argue with 300 pounds of imposing Spaniard? Kike—pronounced "Kee Kay"—will take over Geordie's duties, who is already acting sad and complaining about the fact that she can't continue on with us through Spain. She knows we'll be back for the rest of our French shows. (Christ, it can't be that enjoyable to traipse over the countryside with the six of us.) However, Kike poses a new threat. Whereas Geordie is thin, and can easily fit in the shotgun seat alongside Tim or whoever, Kike is the size of any two of us. We simply will not all fit in the Renault. Someone will have to ride in the back, up on the rigged second level over the equipment where we've been hoisting our luggage and our beverage stash.

Back at the gig, we play a tight set and have a blast utilizing the large stage for rock show buffoonery. The crowd loves us, and we even get a couple of encores, rare for an opening act. Following our set, Rat, Z, and I make the rounds and check out the women. There are more girls at this gig than at any show we've played, maybe more than all of them combined. Walking through the venue, the younger ones huddle together and whisper to each other as we walk past—who knows what the hell they are saying. Z off-loaded Rita this morning, and is keeping a careful eye on all the young babes. Most of the girls over sixteen seem to be with boyfriends, and none seem terribly interested in us. We head backstage for more free beer and a good, close-up view of the Buzzcocks.

They play all of their hits, and are really quite excellent, but their volume, lights, and overall power causes them to blow out the main fuse to the hall at least three times. Each time, frontman Pete Shelley gets angrier, stomping around the stage with his little bowl haircut and mod suit. The bass player, a big, tall geezer with a shock of Sex Pistols red hair, lankily stalks offstage in his jumpsuit and combat boots. "Fuckin' 'ell," he says. Somehow, the band completes their set on a victorious note, and backstage everyone's up and partying. The 'Cocks bassist sees us stumbling about and invites a few of us into their dressing room for some champagne and reefer.

"You guys did a rockin' set," said the bassman in a thick Cockney accent. We exchanged tour updates, and he said this was the Buzzcocks second recent tour of France.

"We pop over ev'ry few months to make some money. These audiences, though, I can't figure them out. You play your set, walk offstage, and, by the time you take your guitar off and walk back out on stage to see if there's any girls or anything, the whole bloody crowd is gone, like an evacuation or somethin'."

"Really?" I asked. "I thought it was just us! You mean, even with a big, popular band like you guys, the crowd evaporates into thin air as soon as the set's over? I'll be damned."

"I've never seen anything to beat it," he continued, puffing hard on a tightly rolled joint. He passes it to me.

"They just disappear. No one tries to get backstage. No one is interested in meeting the band. They just come to hear the music and then rush back home. I suppose on one hand it's nice that they do appreciate the music, but, come on, it gets a bit boring not ever getting to meet anyone, you know what I mean?"

Oh yes, we know what he means. Social contact. The needs of the human condition. The desire to be attractive to and attracted by the opposite sex. No matter who tells the story, and no matter how many ways you slice it, it comes up the same. It boils down to: Why are there no girls at the gigs? And when there are girls at the gigs, would it be possible for them to be more disinterested in the musicians? This simply would not happen in America. Would it?

6

DARK-EYED WOMAN, BLACK-EYED REVOLUTIONARIES—THE BIRTH OF FACTSHEET

(Spain)

I T'S HIGH NOON AND we're roving the range, flying top speed somewhere in between the breathtaking Spanish Alps and the Bay of Biscay. Spain is the strangest countryside yet: dilapidated houses and shacks alongside newly built hotels, beautiful meadows, and beaches next to random ditches and abandoned construction sites. Rural graveyards with no more than twenty plots line the highway from time to time, with no rhyme or reason. It's sort of like the area in between Tijuana and Rosarito in Mexico combined with Carmel in Northern California, completely disjointed. There is the distinctly pungent smell of sewer almost everywhere. We've only just arrived, but we're curious: will all of Spain smell like this? It's beautiful, though, and compared to the places we've been so far, it has a truly foreign feel. We're finally experiencing something completely unlike the U.S.

This is true for everyone except Kike, who is from here. He snores loudly in the front seat. Simon's at the wheel, commandeering us across the countryside at Mach two, when he abruptly steers the van into the highway shoulder. "Photo op," he hollers to us back seat denizens.

Z and I hop out to take some snaps of the Alps, while Tim runs around, burning off excess energy while trying to butt into our shots, as if either of us want souvenirs of him.

"Move it, Dorkboy," yells Z, whose Tim tolerance wanes increasingly each day.

"What about the Master," mumbles Rat, indicating Dahl, who rides on the shelf in the van's back storage area. The back of the van doesn't get any heat, and he is wrapped in a sleeping bag for insulation.

"Oh yeah," remembers Simon. He yells at the side of the van, "Jeff, you like to pop out?"

"No, that's okay," came the muffled yet cheerful voice behind the van's metallic wall. "Let's just get moving as soon as possible."

"Right. McGruff, my love," says the English redhead, immediately forgetting his employer, "snap a picture of me in front of the mountains."

"Christ, Simon," I grouch. "You've had me take rolls and rolls of photos with you in each one; you're the only person or thing you have pictures of."

"That's all I want. I've seen bloody Europe."

"And you haven't seen yourself? Save on the film and buy yourself a mirror. Give me the camera already."

While I photograph Simon, Kike hauls his monstrous frame from the van to stretch his legs.

"You like Spain?" he asks no one in particular. He then growls a series of garbled sentences that no one understands. This guy is to be our interpreter, among other things.

"I'm hungry," says Tim.

"There's a news flash," Simon cracks.

"Are we gonna eat today or not?"

"We'll eat at the gig, there will be plenty of food when we get to the venue," responds Kike.

Tim didn't give up easily. "What about breakfast?"

"No one eats breakfast in Spain," says Kike. "No one eats breakfast. You want some speed?"

"Oh, for fuck's sake. Don't give him any speed," warns Simon. "Although, mind you, it might cause him to do some work later on. Still, never mind. Right, back in the van. Time to move on."

Back to warp drive in no time. "Play some Dictators," demands Kike in a billowing voice that doesn't invite argument.

"Whose got any?" asks Rat.

"I do. It's in my bag. Must hear some Dictators."

"Your bag is in the back, where Dahl is, Kike," Simon politely informed.

"Dictators. Dictators."

"Breakfast. Breakfast," Tim chanted back. It was to no avail, within five minutes Kike had drifted back to sleep. I settle back with my book. Rat and Z nod off on each other with their sacred pillow. Tim chews his nails. Simon shifts gears and sticks ABBA in the deck.

"Gimme gimme gimme a man after midnight..." Not exactly The Dictators, but what the hell. I've heard this tape so often already that I can sing along with the song's ridiculous synthesizer line. It's pleasant enough driving music. It actually is growing on me. My book is making me drowsy, so I stick it in the seat pouch and lay my head on Rat's back. The three of us sit in a makeshift lump. Tim sits straight up and stares out the window. He's probably uncomfortable with his proximity to us in the backseat, fearing our fagginess will rub off, and he'll soon have to question his own sexuality.

The three of us wake up suddenly and sit erect in the seat. Tim's head spins around in confusion, Simon swerves uncontrollably.

"What the fuck is that?" shouts Simon, regaining control, at least partially, of the van.

"I've never smelled anything like it, not anything living," says Rat.

"Where are we?" I ask, grasping for an explanation of what is without question the most offensive odor I've ever encountered. "Could there be an industrial accident nearby? Maybe it's radioactive by-products or something. We'd better be careful!"

"I think you're right," gasps Simon, choking a little. "We must be driving through something awfully fucked up. Maybe a roadkill dumping ground, shallow graves..."

"This place is kind of Third World," opines Rat. "Maybe there are open septic tanks nearby, like right under the van. Simon, roll up your window!"

Dahl bangs on the wall that separates us. "What the hell is that? It's killing me back here!"

Simon dutifully replies, "We don't know. We're trying to sort it out."

"Check it out. Kike has slept through it all," giggles Z, motioning to the bundle in the shotgun seat.

We all turn to each other, and the realization hits. "Kike!" the cry goes up. He doesn't wake up.

"What? Is it that bastard's fart?" asks Simon.

"No way," I interject. "Nothing human can generate a smell like that. Simon, roll your window down."

It was truly indescribable, but I'll try. A combination of cheese left in the summer sun for weeks on end, sewers spilling onto the city streets, and a million unwashed socks. It was unholy. Its perpetrator jerks in his seat wildly without warning, perhaps regaining partial consciousness at the insistence of his own pungency. He begins flailing his arms, and blowing gobs of mucus from his mouth and nose, loudly sneezing and coughing simultaneously. Huge chunks of snot fly around the van's cabin like buckshot. Its potential targets duck and scream. A general hysteria has ensued, with cries of "stop the van" and "throw him out" being hollered in a panic. This terror has caught on throughout the vehicle; Dahl is now pounding furiously on the wall that separates us.

"What is it?" he cries.

"It's Kike. He farted like a wildebeest from hell!"

"Sorry, got some gas," Kike grumbled, coming somewhat to consciousness. "Big dinner last night.

Steak like you've never seen, to die for, sweet and juicy like teenage pussy."

Thank God he skipped breakfast.

ALL OF OUR DATES have changed in Spain. Kike has put together four shows, and promises they will rock like Satan himself. Our king-sized guide is the promoter, and also the lead singer of The Pleasure Fuckers, a group of Spanish punkers. He gives us all promotional shirts of his band. He's a jovial—albeit somewhat crude—individual. None of us really know what to make of him, but he's part of the team now. We're pretty sure our trek through Spain is going to be an adventure.

For our first date, we drive nine hours to a huge hall called Le Real, located in the town of Oviedo. There are three large bars in the room. They clearly expect a drinking crowd. The stage is five feet high, and a king's crown hangs precariously over the drum riser. As I wearily walk in with my accessory bag and bass case, I pass in front of the triple-stacked P.A. speakers. They happen to go from complete silence to 120 decibels the moment I walk by. I feel like a cartoon character that's been blown out of his shoes.

"Thanks," I sarcastically holler to the soundman, who stares at the soundboard as if he's never seen one before. "Gracias," I correct myself.

I walk down the stage steps, and damn if he doesn't blast me with the P.A. again. This time, I'm at arm's length from the speaker bins. "I'm going to kill you if you do that again!"

Now, two guys are operating the sound system. They grin and fumble with the switches. For the next hour, random shrieks, squeals, honks, and bombing raids will emanate from the powerful equipment thanks to these two semi-comedic would-be sound engineers. This racket puts the whole band on edge. The fact that the food platter we've been patiently waiting for all day has nothing but rancid sandwich meat that looks like it escaped from the race track (horse or dog, you pick) doesn't diminish the situation. Dahl, a strict vegetarian, almost passes out at the sight of it. The opening band—four locals doing their best teen version of Mudhoney—clean out all the backstage beer before we arrive. Aggravation.

After a pointless sound check, we return to our tiny hotel rooms, where, after much needed showers, Kike and the members of the support band—an all female punk affair known as Las Vivores—are meeting us for dinner. Down in the cramped lobby, we shyly talk to the girls—our Spanish is poor. A tall brunette bounds into the room, her beaded necklaces rattling loudly as she walks.

"Hi, guys. I'm Nora." It turned out Nora, the band's singer, grew up in San Francisco. "I though you might like to see this. You guys are in the local newspaper."

The article had Jeff's publicity photo, and seemed to be rather extensive for a club show preview. "Read it to us, translate."

The article was the standard bio with the usual quota of inaccuracies, but one mistake stood out above the rest. The band actually had a name: we were Jeff Dahl Factsheet.

"Are you sure that's what it says? Where would they get that?" Dahl wondered.

"Oh, I get it," says Z. "The record company sends out these little information sheets to the promoters before the tour. They say 'Factsheet' at the top. They just got confused, and assumed that's the name of the band."

"I think it's totally great," laughs Rat. "It's so original."

Jeff Dahl would forever be Jeff Dahl. But for now, Rat, Z, and I were Factsheet, the most rockin' trio, even if only a backing trio, in the whole goddamn world, and without question the heaviest thing to hit Ouledo all week.

"Factsheet—we've come to rock you."

"Factsheet—total rocking destruction."

"Factsheet—we have ways of making you rock."

The slogans began to fly fast and furious. Though no one said it at the time, the fact that the three of us were unified in spirit and in name only served to separate us further from our leader. It was understood that Dahl couldn't join Factsheet.

OUR SHOW THAT NIGHT was more rocking than usual. Maybe it had something to do with the Factsheet vibe, but most likely it had to do with the packed house of rock-starved maniacs, the surreal, blaring sound, the fact that we were joined onstage by the girls, Kike, and a few other geezers we didn't know. They all danced around, bumping into each other and singing in unison to the Flamin' Groovies classic, "Slow Death." To hear Kiki sing the opening line, "I call thee Doctor," with his brutal, guttural tone and strong Spanish accent, was in itself a mind-bending occurrence. It became our catchphrase— but of course you had to imitate Kike and his accent.

Or maybe it just had to do with Z buzzing like crazy on the cheap, low-grade cocaine he got from Nora. Z tries to play it cool, but I pick up on his altered demeanor.

"What's with that swingin' jaw action you got goin' there, Bubba?"

"Ah, I had a little coke. It was bunk. I can get you some if you like."

"That's cool. I hate coke. I especially hate it when it makes you do that thing with your jaw, you know?"

"Yeah, well, it's time to move the drums, so I'm gonna disappear." He chuckles to himself, and somehow manages to dissolve into the woodwork. Simon, dreading having to move the drums himself, is soon seen trying to find him.

THE DRIVE TO MADRID is another long haul. We pull over for gas. When Simon turns off the ignition, it sounds like the engine is still running: it turns out to be the sound of six hungry stomachs growling. Kike is supposed to feed us in accordance with our contract rider, which stipulates food at the hotel in the morning and food upon arrival at the show. This doesn't seem to be happening so far. I figure, in an attempt to skim more profits for himself, he isn't organizing our chow time. I use a little trickery of my own to figure it out.

At the gas station, Kike gets out to stretch and blow more snot from his nose. It seems he has an unlimited supply. Everyone's outside the van except for me and Z. I say to Z, just loud enough for Kike to overhear, "So far Spain seems pretty happening. Too bad Kike can't quite get our rider together, the food thing has been a drag. Other than that, he seems cool. When we make our call into Camille tomorrow, I guess we'll have to lay it on the line."

Kike clears his throat and climbs in the van. "Say, I think I'll take you guys for some lunch. I know a great place. The sandwiches are huge. You have never seen sandwiches so big. We go now. Simon, will you please play that Dictators tape."

We all gladly groove to the Dic's "Next Big Thing," and think about those huge sandwiches. Imagine our surprise, when an hour later Kike shows us a Spanish McDonald's. Hey, who's complaining? Make mine a Big Marcos with Cheese.

On Friday night, we arrive in Madrid during rush hour. The city is the closest thing to a big, overblown megalopolis we've yet to see, sort of Manhattan slowed down slightly by siestas. The club, Revolver, is obviously the CBGBs/Whisky a Go-Go of Madrid, with a funky interior, pool table, DJ booth, two huge bars, and show posters from cool bands all over the world. It's very agreeable to our collective mindset.

Rat and I walk through the club to the dressing room, carrying our battered guitar cases and looking ever so cool. "I'll tell you what, Mr. Ratboy," I proclaim, feeling a slight euphoric lift for no apparent reason, at least not one I can identify. "Tonight, things are going to turn around in the road romance department. Tonight, I'm going to meet a beautiful girl who'll be normal, happy, full of life, and ready to follow me to the ends of this here world."

"Is that right, Mr. McGruff? What makes you say that?"

Clearly, the answer lies with whatever energy is causing this sudden, unnatural state of well-being. A chemical imbalance, perhaps, an errant hormone run amok. "I don't know, exactly. It's just a feeling. But it's going to happen. I know it."

I stop myself from jumping onto the cocktail table and belting out "Something's Coming" from *West Side Story*, but instead opt to relax with a fruit soda in the dressing room, where Dahl patiently gives yet another interview to yet another fanzine. Sound check follows, featuring another stellar drum solo by yours truly. It's getting to the point where the rest of the band is abandoning the check altogether. They've come to realize I'll check all of the instruments to fend off boredom and lessen my restlessness.

Eventually my brothers join me onstage. It takes us a while, but we eventually work out a New York Dolls song we've added to the set. We then lock up our guitars and head to find our hotel, a place romantically called Hotel Paradise. As we pull up to the five-story edifice, no lights are on, except for one lone beacon illuminating from the front desk. The silhouette of a bald head with pointy ears hunches over the naked light bulb. I spot this creature and it sends a chill down to my toes.

"Christ, it's fuckin' Count Yorga!"

Everyone laughs.

"Count Yorga!" Dahl exclaims.

"I didn't know anyone else remembered Count Yorga."

"No, McGruff. You've got it all wrong," claims Ratboy. "That's Nosferatu. Just look at the ears."

"Let's go give a pint and get our rooms," says my roommate for the evening, Simon.

Yorga barely acknowledges us. He silently hands us keys and points a boney finger up the stairs to our rooms. A former ambassador he is not.

Following a short break and a shower, we meet Kike in Yorga's small lobby. Kike has, once again, promised us a feast beyond our simple Yankee comprehension. "You have never had pizza like this!" A native of Madrid, he's accompanied tonight by his wife. We're all a little taken back by her. Kike is a huge, crude, foul-mouthed, unshaven, truck driver of a punk rocker. We certainly didn't expect his wife to be a stylish and sexy beauty, complete with perfect jet-black hair, and curves that would overturn a race car. But here they are, Madrid's fun loving couple, and off we go to dinner.

We walk for many blocks, and Kike assures us that we're "almost there." I flashback to the Dutch quest for hash. Finally, we arrive at a pizza joint just slightly larger than the Renault van. All the seats are taken, but we can wait a half an hour if we want to. Dahl is getting antsy, maybe a little pissed, and everyone looks to be pretty hungry. Kike tries to calm the rising tide of anxiety.

"I know another place, a few blocks away."

Everyone is milling around in the street, waiting for someone to make a decision. Dahl heads back to the club alone, without saying anything. Kike is inside the pizza joint, trying to get the owner to kick people out so that the important musicians from America can sit down, but no one in the restaurant is buying it, and we're getting embarrassed. Finally, we move toward Revolver.

We decide on the Chinese restaurant next door to the club. Securing a banquet table, we settle in. While no one else seems to notice or care, I excuse myself to go look for Dahl. I figure he's probably hiding out or back in the dressing room.

Revolver is an all-purpose club. Although our rock show is in two hours, an entirely different crowd is there, dancing to the latest industrial gothic dance music. Strobe lights flash, music blares, and everyone is dressed from head to toe in black. Most of the crowd has pancake makeup on—heavy, dark black eyeliner, mascara, and eye shadow. Bauhaus and Sisters of Mercy live. Dahl must feel alienated. As I enter the dressing room, he's alone, slumped over on a bench, moping.

"Hey," I shout above the racket right outside the door. "We found a good place to eat, right next door. C'mon."

"No. I'm just going to stay here."

"Man, you didn't eat today. You gotta eat. There's all sorts of veggie stuff on the menu."

"No, really. That's okay."

"Dude, you must be going crazy in here with this noise. I know you hate this music." He nods in agreement. "Well, c'mon then. We'll go have a good time and relax. You'll be glad you did."

He finally stands up and follows me out. I don't know why I insisted that he join us. I haven't pushed him at all over the past two weeks. This is Jeff's tour. Shouldn't he try to enjoy himself? It seems like he just hides himself away all the time. I can't help but feel like Jeff has changed since the times we used to go up the coast and rock the Bay Area. Maybe his time spent out in the Arizona desert has changed him somehow. I must try and sit down with him and talk about it, talk it out. I must remember to do that.

Dinner is pleasant, everyone settles down, exchanges stories, and has a laugh or two. Kike tells a story about getting so sick on tour that he puked in the support band's bass drum, didn't tell them, and then helped them pack the drum, puke and all, into a road case. He is an unending source of amusement and amazement.

The gig fully rocks. Wild kids bang their heads onto the stage and maniacal, Spanish guys leap from table to table. Some very rock 'n' roll (i.e., sleazy) girls are up front, grooving with us and shaking their approval. The New York Dolls cover, "Personality Crisis," is a mess, but "Dirt" reaches heights of free jazz liberation, hitherto unexplored by us. Toward the end of the number, all three front musicians lay on the stage and jam. I position myself stomach down, draped over the monitor speaker, with my bass dangling off the front of the stage. I play it while fans gently stroke the strings along with me. Ratboy is on his knees, serving up a sacrifice to a god only he sees, and Dahl is flat on his back, scratching out power chords while staring, spaced-out, up at the brightly, colored lights. The show finally closes to rapturous applause.

Following the show, we sign a million things, from records to napkins, from jackets to this hippie chick's arm cast. She begins to follow me around like a lost puppy. She's pretty, but certainly not for me this evening.

We stow our gear and off-load to the awaiting van. I survey the club and sit down on the stage beside Simon, who's rolling a cigarette. "Gimme one," I demand.

Simon dutifully rolls me a ciggie and nods across the room toward Ratboy. "Looky there. Rat's chatting up two birds. That's one for him and one for me."

"Simon, what's the matter with you? Rat has made virtually no contact with the opposite sex this whole trip. He finally has it going on, and you want to horn in on him. I just hope you're proud."

"Oh, alright. I didn't realize it was that big of a thing."

He skulks off, leaving me to horn in on Rat's action. The girl with the arm cast slides next to me. I smile and quickly walk away.

"Hey, Rat. What's happening?"

"McGruff, meet my friends. This is, uh, I guess I don't know your names."

Rat was hitting on a girl with a leopard-skin overcoat and a huge black mop of Mötley Crüe teased hair. She was not what I would deem pretty, but she had the flashy/trashy rock chick look that Rat appreciated. She turns out to be Kike's sister-in-law of all things. She speaks virtually no English, but her friend is acting as interpreter.

"Hi, I'm Sonny," she says, giggling just a little, "and this is Zelda." I get a good look at her and most definitely like what I see. She's about five foot four, has jet-black hair in a sophisticated European cut straight out of a sixties Fellini flick—the epitome of style. Sonny has huge, dark eyes, a pronounced, strong nose, and cheekbones to die for. Wrapped in a fuzzy black coat, she is quite cuddly looking. As our pointless conversation progresses, I move closer and closer to her, and find myself becoming transfixed by her deep, dark eyes.

Running back and forth to the DJ booth to request songs, the bar to nab whiskey, and to the girls to laugh and dance, I keep myself busy until departure time. Simon admonishes me for doing exactly what I told him not to do, but I laugh it off. I'm having too much fun to worry about Simon.

Dahl is doing yet another interview, but finally it's wrapped, and we can leave. Kike has arranged for us to hold court at Agapo, a bar across town that he promises we'll like. First, we have to return the van to Yorga's garage below the Paradise. By now, Sonny's hanging on my arm. As I walk out with her, my other arm carrying my trusty Fender bass, we enter the brisk Spanish night wrapped in our blacker-than-black attire. I forgive myself for selfishly feeling like total hot shit. I realize it ain't no big thing, but after two weeks of no kinda thing whatsoever, it's good to feel like somebody; it's good to feel something, anything.

Lost in my own thoughts, I swing open the van door to see something that resembles a college prank. The van—which seats seven uncomfortably—is filled with the six of us, Zelda, Kike, his wife, the guy who owns Agapo, and two other random females including the girl with the cast. I laugh—everyone is laughing uncontrollably it seems—and I shove Sonny by the butt into the van and somehow follow her in. This rolling sardine can wobbles precariously down the street. Simon is tipsy, weaving and snickering at how utterly ludicrous this ride back to Yorga Central is. Once there, we off-load and head on foot to Agapo—all of us, of course, except Jeff.

"Jeff, this night might be the most fun night of the tour, won't you come along with us?"

"Naw, thanks. I'm really tired. I think I'm just gonna turn in."

I expected him to say that, but really wished that he hadn't. Factsheet or not, it was Jeff's show and nothing would be happening without him.

AGAPO IS ONE OF the coolest places I've ever been. It's real small, but packed with nothing but cool, friendly people—music lovers, bikers, musicians. Our host loads everyone up with beer and liquor, and the room is filled with sweet marijuana smoke. Music is blaring—the young DJ is in his booth, located right in the middle of the floor. People approach him and request songs. He grins and nods his head in an ambiguous way that doesn't betray whether he'll play the request or not. The word going around the bar is that the DJ is flying on acid. Whatever the case, he's playing excellent sixties psychedelic music, from Hendrix to Big Brother and Pink Floyd.

"Help me with my drink, little angel," I say to my newfound love. I hold her close, and she looks straight into my eyes, not smiling. She lets her eyes do the smiling. She looks to be nineteen or twenty, all youthful exuberance, tempered by the kind of worldly wisdom a person gets from growing up in a big city.

The DJ kicks in a riff I don't recognize immediately, but by the fifth bar I've got it: "Dark Eyed Woman" by Spirit. How perfect. I look at Sonny and pull her close again, gently moving her to the sensual music.

"Dark eyed woman on a hot summer night / Dark eyed woman are you burning tonight?"

I can't resist it any longer. "I think it's time you gave me a kiss."

Her expression doesn't change. Standing smack-dab in the middle of the bar, she rises on her tiptoes and tightly clasps her arms around me. Her mouth opens, and her tongue slips in-between my lips. However old she is, she knows things about kissing that I sure as hell don't. Her tongue seems to magically wrap around mine and manipulate it in a way that I can only assume she knows the secret inter-connector between the heart, soul, and tongue. My head is reeling. I'm actually feeling dizziness. The kiss seems to last days, nights, weeks, months. I'm sure the tour will be over by the time we've finished this kiss.

My head rolls back. I feel the power of the Almighty himself surging through my veins. I have never, ever been kissed like that before, and I don't know exactly what made it so goddamned special. Best not to overanalyze magic.

"But dark eyed women, we both been there before, yeah before."

I light another cigarette, and Simon comes up to me. "Well, at least you're having a good time, you bastard! I've been chasing around this older bitch, but I think she's giving me the bum's rush."

"Simon, just have fun. Look at these people. They love us. It's not about getting laid. It's about grooving with these totally cool people in this great city."

"Fuck you!"

I glance over at Tim. He's at the bar, drinking alone, talking to no one. Z sits against a wall doing the same. Only Rat and I are having any fun. Sonny and I approach Rat and Zelda, and the four of us dance to Hendrix's "Crosstown Traffic." The girls are digging us, the music is great, the booze is flowing, and the gods are indeed smiling on us. If only it could never end.

Sonny suddenly grabs me by the arm and pulls me toward the door. "I can't breathe!" she exclaims.

We walk outside into the freezing cold night, and she wheezes for a moment. "The smoke, it's too much. Oh, that's much better."

After a minute, she continues. "I was supposed to meet my roommate at another club. What time is it?" I tell her that it's 5:00 a.m. "Oh, I'm so late. She's going to be angry with me. I don't know what to do."

"Where's the club?"

"It's about five blocks east."

"Can we walk?" She nods. "Let's go get your roommate and bring her back to party with all of us."

"Oh, she's a student. I don't know if she'll do that."

"You're a student, aren't you? Hell, we're all students. Take me to her, and I'll make sure she comes back with us. You leave it to me. Now, lead the way, darlin'."

We walk quickly through the cold night, holding hands. We exchange minimal small talk, content to get where we're going. Soon we're in front of another bustling club, this one cranking Soca music at top volume. In we go.

Women bounce around in frilly, very low-cut dresses. Guys dart around in razor-sharp suits and hats. It's like something out of a Carmen Miranda movie, incredible. Tequila literally drips from the humidity in the room.

"There's Elvira!" shouts Sonny, spotting her roommate.

Elvira was pretty, but didn't look as Spanish as Sonny. Turns out she was born in the Midwest, and had been living in Spain for four years. With long, dark brown hair and sultry green eyes, I can see that these two made a terrific twosome of terror.

"Listen, Elvira. You gotta come back with us to Agapo."

"And why is that?" she asks, teasing me.

"Because if you don't come, Sonny won't come, and I'll forever suffer a savagely broken heart. Not only that, but I have the perfect guy for you. He's dark, handsome, debonair, and he just happens to be the drummer in the same rock 'n' roll band I'm in."

She bought it. Much as I like this place, the drinks ain't free. The three of us head back to Agapo.

Elvira and Z immediately hit it off. Within ten minutes they're making out in the same spot where Z had been sulking only a little time before. I return to romancing Sonny, and pretty soon the sun is starting to come up. The bar is still open, the liquor is still pouring, but we're all starting to fade, so off to Paradise we head with our newfound lady friends.

Walking lazily down the street, arms around the girls, life seems relaxed, and the hassles of tour seem miles away. The walk takes a long time, and I'm sure I'm not fully awake, but rather in a semi-dream state, abated by the alcohol consumption, the wonderful music that's still ringing in my ears, and the warmth of the bundle of gorgeousness I have attached to me. Tim left the bar a good two hours earlier, but Simon is still with us. He's walking along, odd man out with the three couples, darting in-between all of us, and babbling endlessly about his aborted attempt at a pickup.

"Fucking bitch was teasing me, she was! She came on to me heavy, grabbing my dick and all. Then when I told her she should come back to Paradise—I thought that sounded good—she winked and said she'd have to bring her husband along. Right, I said 'fine,' and she's started saying something about wanting to be the meat in a stud sandwich. I started getting a knobby just talking about it. Think I'm getting one now..."

"Shut up, Simon," demanded Z.

Finally, back at the Paradise, we all grow silent. The three of us—all of whom live with girls we professed undying, faithful love to back in the States, are now ready to take three brazen Spanish ladies up to our rooms for a night of ongoing romantic contact. The fact that I'm sharing my room with Simon really doesn't cross my mind at this point. We walk up the stairs to the Paradise's front door, when, no, it can't be, motherfucking Count Yorga is still on duty.

"No girls, no girls! You may not bring girls in here!" he proclaims. His ears cast an eerie shadow as he wags his boney finger at us.

This can't be happening. It's not like Coat Rack, where we can merely hide the contraband in our luggage and drag it up to our rooms anyway. These are living human beings we're talking about.

He continues to shake his finger in front of us. His pointy ears doubling as roadblocks to Paradise beyond. Inexplicably, and I'll never understand this 'til the day I die, none of us argue with Yorga. We say nothing. It's been suggested that perhaps Yorga merely provided the easy out, an out that our three increasingly guilty consciences were looking for. But I don't buy it, not for a minute. We say nothing.

We separate from the girls and begin to walk inside, as Yorga holds the door open. The girls stand there with their mouths open.

"Bye," says Rat. "Later," says Z. I say nothing, perhaps still in shock. I look back, and, I might be wrong, but it looked like a lone tear was trickling down Sonny's cheek. I would have been ashamed the morning after, cheating on Gina, but I think I was just as ashamed right now, for the way I treated Sonny. More than anything, I feel instant remorse and anger for not standing up to Yorga— none of us did. Simon, I'm sure, would have if he was preparing to become the meat in an abstract deli platter, but since that was not the case, he probably figured if he wasn't getting any, no one was getting any. Case closed.

"We are such losers," Rat chuckles, shaking his head as we started for the stairs. It was becoming a familiar comment from him, and it certainly was true at the moment. Still, the night was far from being a washout. I'll never forget Sonny, how pretty she was, how she kissed. Hey, I said I'd meet a nice, normal, beautiful girl, and it happened. "Life is basically good," the eternal optimist dressed in white said, perched on my right shoulder. The Devil, dressed in red and hanging out on the left, stopped laughing at me long enough to break down and cry.

IN THE MORNING, COUNT Yorga isn't anywhere to be found in the hotel lobby. Kike's there, grinning. "Ah, I guess we'll all be in-laws by the end of the tour. Ha ha ha!"

We drive onto Barcelona, where we're to play a dump called the Garatge, which means garage. Along the highway, there are more of those tiny graveyards, one every few miles. I conclude that it's sort of a convenience store approach to undertaking. The theory seems to be no one should ever have to transport a corpse more than a couple of kilometers before disposing of it in its final resting place. The problem is, you're reminded of death every few minutes. Oh well, you get used to the Grim Reaper riding along like a monkey on your shoulder, especially on this outing, which Z has christened EuroBlur, a take-off on Dahl's '93 EuroTour shirts.

On the drive, Tim sits by me and reads my William Burroughs book, *The Western Lands*. He laughs at it profusely. I think he may be getting more out of it than I did, which causes me to question my own comprehension of the nearly impenetrable novel. Ah shit, he's just bluffing, I conclude. I borrow a piece of notebook paper from him and scratch out a song about my darling Sonny (maybe it was Sunny) with completed music and lyrics in about ten minutes. I'm still reviewing last night's surrender to prudent hotel rules with some remorse.

"I can't believe we just went into our rooms, letting the whole thing go like that. Damn, she was so fine!"

Rat rolls his eyes. "Get over it. Besides, you have to think, what kind of girl goes back to the hotel room of some lunatic rock 'n' roller the first night she meets him? It's nothing to get a broken heart over, believe me."

What kind of girl, indeed. Sonny's face faded in my mind. It dissolved across a canvas that sprouted portraits of numerous other women, women who have shoved their nails through the ventricles of my wounded heart. Gina, my ex-wife, and all the other would-be starlets and harlots came to mind. Before they settle into my nest and under my spell, these women are known to share their time with the occasional traveling musician. Groupie was the operative term that would tumble from the mouths of those who looked down on such ladies, and, in turn, looked down on me for spending time with girls of such questionable moral fiber. I viewed it this way: these girls preferred the companionship of musicians, and, after all, I was a musician. What was I supposed to do? Chase around girls that were into lawyers or ballplayers or short-order cooks or stock brokers, for God's sake? It all made sense to me.

Once we load-in our gear in Barcelona, Kike takes us to a small diner within walking distance. Everyone goes except for Dahl, who will survive on the backstage platter, thank you very much. The joint is small and homey, and Kike obviously knows the proprietor, who seats us immediately in the back. Menus are distributed, and we begin to order right away.

Waiter: "So, everyone ready to order, then?"

Simon: "I could use a minute, as I haven't opened my menu yet."

Rat: "Yeah, I might like some kind of sandwich. I don't know."

Kike: "I'll have the usual."

Waiter: "Of course."

Z: "I'd like to get this Italian cold-cut sandwich, with a salad."

Waiter: "We can't make that. We don't have all the meats available at the moment. How about a ham sandwich?"

Z: "Uh, no. Lemme look at the menu a bit more."

McGruff: "I'll have the ravioli, with garlic bread, please."

Waiter: "No ravioli. Would you like some mostaccioli, perhaps?"

McGruff: "Yeah, maybe, but I don't see it on the menu. Where is it?"

Waiter: "It's not on the menu, but we have it."

Tim cuts in: "Can I just get a burger and some fries, fritters, or whatever they're called here?"

Waiter: "No, no hamburgers. We ran out. We can make you a grilled cheese."

Simon: "Grilled cheese? That's not on the menu. Where do you see that?"

Waiter: "You're right. It's not on the menu, but we do have it."

McGruff: "Is there anything on the menu that you actually have available for eating?"

Waiter: "Yes, many things."

Z: "Can I get a grilled cheese with a salad?"

Waiter: "What kind of salad?"

Z: "Any kind ya got, with lettuce and Italian dressing. I don't see where it pays to be picky around here."

Waiter: "Excuse me. Let me check on that."

Weary, confused, low on patience, we all lower our menus and frown at each other. The waiter returns.

Waiter: "I'm sorry, there's no more grilled cheese."

THIS GOES ON FOR an indeterminable amount of time. At some point, somehow, we agree on stuff to eat, and eventually it is brought to us. Before Simon, Tim or any of the Factsheet Three eat, Kike is served a huge, double-sized platter full of delicious looking grub, including a char-broiled steak, baked potato, mixed vegetables, soup, salad, pastry, and wine. All of our mouths drop open. Some of us begin salivating involuntarily.

"What's up with that? Look at all that food! I sure as hell didn't see that on the menu. Damn, that looks gooood!" we all seem to chant at once.

"Well, you have to know how to order here," says our well-fed Spanish compadre.

AT THE SHOW, WE play with metal punk ruffians El Legado, whose singer is a bizarre cross between El Cid and Glenn Danzig. Muscle-bound and intimidating, he approaches Dahl: "I sing 'Search and Destroy' with you, no? Ha ha!" he laughs.

Who's to argue? The acoustics in this place are so bad that the sound bounces around like metallic ping-pong balls. I'm so deaf after our gig that my own voice sounds like Daffy Duck inside my head.

Conveniently, all of us who have dined with Kike get the runs, so we all vie for poll position to the one stall in the whole Garatge. Eventually we overflow the lone toilet, leaving the last in line, Simon, to improvise something outside the venue, which none of us choose to inquire about later.

The next morning, Z and I take on the town, eager to spend money in one of Europe's most famous and fashionable cities. We both buy hats, and I get Gina a frilly, floral, translucent blouse. I wonder what's on my mind.

THE FOLLOWING DAY, WE leave civilization and enter a world known as the Basque Country, headed for a town called Deba, (or is it Itziar??) and a rock outpost known as Txitxarro. (I have no idea how you pronounce that.) Kike has promised to finally feed us well. "I take you to a place to get a steak. You've never had steak like this, I guarantee!" Before the proposed feast, we drop our luggage at a farmhouse, which Kike has arranged to be our respite for the night. It's a pleasant surprise. The caretakers—a wholesome looking family, a man, wife, young son, daughter, and a chained-up German Shepherd that barks from the moment we arrive until our departure twenty hours later—show us their home as well as ours for the night.

It's quite charming, a utopian, pastoral setting. It overlooks a gorgeous landscape, a postcard-perfect valley. We all grab rooms, and I hook up the porta-stereo to blast my Deee-Lite tape ("The chills that you spill up my back...I couldn't ask for another"). Simon and I dance in our socks on the beds. At this particular moment, it doesn't feel like a tour, but a vacation in a spectacularly beautiful, secluded farmhouse, tucked away from the outside world. If only that dog would stop barking.

We off-load to soundcheck and eventually to the *restaurant of steaks unlike etc. etc.* Upon entering the restaurant, everyone that works there acknowledges Kike. Regardless of his standing in the Spanish independent recording biz, he seems to be infamous in any place that grills up a decent piece of beef. The food is so-so, but it's location makes up for it. It's situated right in a little cove on the Atlantic Ocean. After dinner, we frolic like young schoolboys in the sand, chasing each other, laughing, and generally acting like geeks. It's so great to blow off some steam. The fact is, none of us, save Kike, have seen this kind of awe-inspiring beauty before. The night is black as satin, the froth of the sea dangles from the sliver of the moon, and it all is framed by rock formations that seem to cradle the whole scene in the very Hands of God. It's sharply cold, but no one notices, insulated by the meat's crunchy gristle and the wine's incubation. To all present, it looks to be a great evening ahead, maybe the best one yet.

The club is setup, shall we say, very uniquely. From the middle of the stage on down, smack-dab through the middle of the club is a wall that perfectly divides the entire venue in half. The folks from Deba gather off to one side and those from Itziar collect on the other. Talk about segregation. Dahl had warned that we'd encounter some of the strangest and perhaps most potentially dangerous guys in this area of Spain. He told us about the revolutionaries—armed rustic guerillas ready to strike the unseen enemy at any moment. We were there to rock them, to give them a form of release from whatever kind of civil war they were locked in. I didn't understand the politics of it all. Dahl just knew to be wary of it, and Kike kept his mouth shut.

At the club, we begin to get a little restless as we hang around downstairs and backstage. The backstage was a brick dungeon with a long wooden table with delicacies served up on it. In the room, there was a closet door that seemingly lead nowhere. Bored, Simon kicked it open and made a significant discovery.

"Fuckin' hell, look at this!"

Behind the door was a room the size of the entire club. Bottles of liquor were strewn in random piles. They appeared to be ten feet high. It made no sense. Why would a venue, dependent on liquor sales for ongoing revenue, store their main commodity in such an impractical, haphazard, and unheard of way? They were mounds of unrelated and unsorted bottles of liquor. They were neither stacked nor organized, but merely arranged in giant, mountain-shaped piles that were taller than any of us. Our mission seemed clear.

"How much do we steal, and how do we load it out?"

"We gotta be careful. Dahl won't approve."

"Fuck it. Load it into everything. Gig bags, drum cases, hell, the drums themselves. We'll drink our fucking per diem."

It is, after all, a musician's God-given right to steal any and all alcohol left unattended at any establishment wherein a musician might be providing services. It's in the fine print. Check it out for yourself sometime, if you don't believe me.

Meanwhile, Z has found another pastime. He calls it cold cut Frisbee. It seems harmless enough: merely take a few slices of cheap meat, find a random object, aim, and launch. Simon joins in and backhands a few choice hunks in Z's direction. Soon the entire backstage area is covered with bologna and salami, garnished with freshly cut Swiss cheese. The circular wedges of pork hang off tables, chairs, instrument cases, and neatly hung coats, which resemble Salvador Dali's soft watches. It seems appropriate. After all, it was Spain.

Dahl enters and flips. "Who fucking threw food all over the place. Goddammit, I hate that kind of rock star bullshit. Who did it!?"

We're all quiet. No one wants to tattle. No one really gives a shit. The people at this club seem a world apart from us, and truth be known, a little misplaced sausage is probably the least of their worries. But Dahl is bumming hard.

"I can't believe you fuckers did this. Goddamn it!"

He storms out of the room, incapable of stomaching our presence another moment. Soon, it's time to rock the good Basque revolutionaries.

"Well, shall we rock?" asked Rat with a smile. "I think it's time. The kids are ready to rock!"

We march up the stairs to the waiting throngs of predominantly male Basque Separatists and deliver our most mediocre performance yet. It feels flaccid, unfulfilling, unrewarding, and forgettable. The best part is walking back and forth onstage—playing to the guys on this side of the wall, then peeking at the guys on that side of the wall. The crowd, who probably don't get much entertainment in these here parts, is appreciative and spirited, and demand encore after encore, to the point of being ridiculous. We actually run out of material and must resort to "Louie Louie," during which Kike and a half dozen other guys jump up onstage and join us.

Following the show, no one in the band or crew talks to each other. Downstairs and backstage, numerous locals have crowded into the small place to party with the traveling minstrels from afar. Pot is passed around, and the numerous running noses and grinding teeth indicate various forms of white powder, affectionately know as Spanish Breakfast, are in circulation. Chitchat goes in one ear and exits the other side. After much consumption and talk, we relocate upstairs and begin to move our equipment to the van outside.

We are amazingly disorganized tonight. No matter how much we talk to the locals, we're not communicating with each other at all. Gear is coming and going with no game plan. No one pays attention to anyone else. Everyone, save Dahl, seems a bit high on something or other, and Dahl is drunk on a highball of anger itself, chased by pure hatred—a hatred for his own band, the Factsheet, those rock star meat-slingers. I'm moving across the dance floor of the club with a mountain of gear, trying to expedite our departure in any way I can. I have my heavy bass cabinet in its rolling hard case with the bass drum and some toms cased up and rolling on top. The whole pile is taller than I am. I roll it quickly across the floor, distracted only momentarily by an attractive girl who walks past, taking no notice of me. My eyes follow her, deserting what I'm doing, until I hit a crack in the floor tiles. My gear topples over, and, before

I can regain control, tom toms are smashing on the head of this poor girl. An innovative icebreaker, wouldn't you say? She rubs her head, and curses at me in Spanish. I apologize, but she walks away quickly.

The other members of the Dahl entourage move stuff around me, pay no heed to the accident, and don't offer to help. They merely carry on like good little zombies.

Outside, it's windy with the stars and moon creating as much light as the club's fading fluorescent lights. I roll my pile toward the steps that lead to the van. A tall, drunk guy approaches, grabs the rolling cases from me, and starts pushing them toward the steps. I yell at him to watch it, but I could just as well be yelling at a piece of wood. Trying to catch the gear, which is about to tumble down the five or so steps, I end up getting sandwiched between the falling drums, cabinet, and the passenger side of the Renault. The bass hits my hip, crunching the bones, and throws me against the van. My head ricochets back and hits the car. Now I'm pissed.

"You stupid fuck! What's the matter with you!"

"What's up, Bruce?" asks Simon, sticking his head out of the van's back door, where he's stashing gear and dozens of stolen liquor bottles.

"This farmhand just tossed my amp down the steps!"

It's safe to say the guy doesn't understand English. He doesn't come after me following the farmhand remark. He just stands there, dazed, staring at me like a freaking moron. I notice drool coming out of the side of his mouth, and he begins weaving on the steps, waving his arms, and shouting at me.

"Bloody, fucking stupid idiot," reiterates Simon on my behalf. "Let's try to get out of here as quickly as we can."

Whatever the guy is shouting, it's starting to draw a crowd. The steps fill with crazed-looking Basque Country killers, drunkards, and anarchists of all stripes. They look pissed off. They all weave and wobble like their de facto leader, and leer at us with expressions of hatred. Damn, aren't these the same characters we were just wailing "Louie Louie" with? The girl who I'd just bonked on the head with Z's ride tom emerges and points an accusing finger in my direction. Tim appears carrying the merchandise, and they all began to grab at it as he hurries past. The whole incident is beginning to resemble a scene from a George Romero zombie picture, with hordes of black-eyed, emotionless stiffs lurching toward us, slobbering, arms outstretched, and threatening. Their eyes—that's the scariest part—they're all black, cold, unfeeling, desperate, and dead looking, perhaps a bit hungry even. They're capable of looking through you and past you, but not directly at you, not so much a mean look as heartless and soulless.

We all finally climb in the van, and Simon revs it up. They seem to surround it. As he starts backing out, they grab on and begin rocking the van as it moves, punching at it with their fists. Kike has missed departure, but we are outta here. Simon guns it, and the black-eyed zombies scatter, as if a bigger fear has come along. We ride toward the moon back to our safe, secluded farmhouse.

"I'm glad to fuckin' be outta there," slurs Simon. No one responds. I decide it's time to clear the air.

"You know, I know we play all these shows, we never listen to tapes, we never talk about the music, but we really played a lackluster, shitty show tonight. I was starting to feel like we were really getting to be a pretty damn good band, and then we go and suck like we did tonight."

"Yeah, and I just wanna say that I was really pissed off at whoever threw the food around the dressing room. That's such petty rock star, Van Halen bullshit. This is my tour. It's my name that's on the line, and I won't stand for that shit!" Dahl had spoken. I had spoken. No one else had a damn thing to say.

Back at the ranch, everyone scatters to their rooms silently, like cockroaches. Simon and I are sharing, and together we make our way to the front balcony after everyone else has apparently turned in. We light up some cigarettes, and turn in the direction of the chained dog that's still barking nonstop. We bust out a newly acquired bottle of rum and begin drinking it straight from the bottle.

"Fucking Dahlby. I pour out my heart about the music, which is by and large his music, and what's he going on about? Literal baloney, that's what. He cares more about appearances than how we sound!"

"I see what you're saying, but I see his point, too," says Simon, working toward a future position in

Parliament. "It's his band, and you lot most likely won't come back over to go through this again. He will. And if he feels it's getting all messed up, well, he probably feels it'll require more repair work from him to get it back up to snuff in the future."

"Simon, that so-called dressing room hadn't been swept since the seventies. What difference could a few pieces of headcheese possibly make in the overall scheme of things?"

"Look, I see both sides. Have a drink." He hands me the bottle and continues. "I'll tell you this. Dahl mentioned to me he's having serious second thoughts about taking you lot to Japan. Me, it doesn't affect me at all. I'm not going anywhere with any of you psychos following this expedition. But you guys, well, I would think going to Japan would be a big deal. He may just pick up a band there, now."

"The bastard! He wouldn't do that to me. We've been through thick and thin, together, damn it! We have history together. We have roots. He's never had a band this good. Ditch us for a bunch of Japs!"

I'm seated on the edge of the balcony, balancing wildly and swilling liberal gulps from the rum bottle. I teeter over the edge, and begin to fall backwards toward the ground, some three stories below.

"Simon!" I shout as I lose my balance. My legs shoot up, beginning to dump me on my descent to the ground below. I toss down the bottle and barely grab the edge of the ledge, saving myself from an inevitable crippling tumble.

"Why'd you throw the bottle? I didn't steal that many. Be more careful in the future," admonishes Simon, who'd had his back turned while rolling yet another hashish spliff, not even noticing my near fatal fall.

"To hell with the joint," I say, starting to lose my grip on rational thought. "Let's sneak down and kill that fucking dog!"

"Are you serious?"

"Why not? I've never killed an animal before, not even a frog, but that bastard deserves to die. He's barked nonstop since we got here, fucking organic car alarm. He doesn't even have a decent watchdog. He's the wolf that cried burglar. Let's kill it! C'mon!"

"You know, McGruff. I have a lot of responsibilities that have come into play since I started this road-managing charade, yet, fortunately, animal extermination hasn't become one of them. I think maybe it's time we get you off to bed."

I suppose he was right. Still, between the warring Basque zombies, my apathetic rock band, and the mindless cretin that keeps making unrelenting noise for no logical reason, I felt the uncontrollable desire to cause harm and pain. It seemed cathartic, purgative, cleansing. Still, no doubt about it, Simon was right. It just wouldn't be polite to kill this nice family's pet, no matter how much it truly deserved to die. Better to just go to sleep. Forget. Dream. Darkness.

Yeah.

7

HE KEEEL you—THE MONTARGIS CHAINSAW MASSACRE

(Back in Fucking France, or France: Part Two)

"FRANCE. I CAN'T BELIEVE I'm still in France."
It was straight from the opening montage of *Apocalypse Now*. I was Martin Sheen. My head hanging off the edge of my bed, upside down, staring at the nothingness of our desolate and boring Toulouse hotel room. The soundtrack still played in my head. It rang in my ears for the nineteen-millionth like that damn Doors tape in the van. Just like Coppola's Vietnam epic.

> *The killer awoke before dawn. He put his Doc Martins on. He went looking for his passport to appease the rude bastard at the front desk and then he...HE WALKED ON DOWN THE HALL...*

Dahl's prediction of a tour plagued with Woolite is slowly coming true. Z and my shared flophouse shit room is covered with freshly hand-washed socks and long johns strewn all over the place—hanging from the ventilators, window sills, draped off the radiator. It's interior decorating at its most slovenly. However, it's functional. Although Tim is rooming with Dahl, he insists on barging in and out of our room.

"What's up? What are you guys going to do? Wanna go walk around? Wanna get some fritters?" And on and on. Trivia spews from his mouth. Z lies on his back on his bed, pulling the pillow over his head when Tim walks in.

"Wow, you guys got a regular Chinese laundry going here. Hey, maybe I'll bring some things over and wash them in your sink, since you've already started."

"No, Tim. Wash your shit in your sink," demanded Z. "Go away. We're tired. We've been doing nothing for so long we're just absolutely exhausted."

Simon bounces in, cheerful again, having survived Spain. "What are you lot up to? In case you're interested, we're going into town, going to run some errands—banking, post office, that sort of thing. Leaving in five if you want to join."

I rise from my lumpy bed and gaze back at it. The outline of my body remains embedded in the worn and faded covers. It resembles a chalk outline of a corpse at a crime scene. Pain runs down my spine as I attempt to straighten my back and fail miserably. The positioning in the back of the van during those long hauls has reshaped all of our postures. But in school, I would also slump, low rider style, at my desk, trying to emulate the posture and demeanor of a delinquent. Years spent playing the low hanging strings of my weighty Les Paul Triumph bass, have also reeked havoc on my posture.

The four of us depart for town. Rat, Dahl, and Geordie, who has rejoined us, stay behind. We queue up in a bank and attempt to exchange Spanish pesetas for French francs. No change excepted, no English spoken, no can do. On to the next the bank.

"Bonsoir," says Z, his accent perfect. Unfortunately, he's exhausted his French vocabulary with the greeting. "Can we exchange pesetas for francs, por favor, pretty please?"

The teller, a chunky woman edging into her forties, smiles a brown smile and lets loose an embarrassed laugh. She calls over another lady, who also doesn't understand what we're asking about. These two women smile and laugh as they stare at us with blank expressions and brown teeth. A third woman joins, at which point we revert to sign language. We point at the pesetas we're placing on the counter, to the francs in the teller's drawers, and hope they realize we want a simple exchange and aren't looking to rob the joint. Eventually, they understand and exchange most of our paper money. We're stuck with the coins, which, for some reason, I have a huge amount of. Oh well, someone will take it, somewhere along the line (wrong). Meanwhile, Z, bored already, returns to our makeshift dry cleaner.

During the course of visiting two banks, we've lost Tim, presumably on fritter patrol and unencumbered with the needs for petty cash. Daddy's money is accepted everywhere, just like American Express. I need stamps for the communiqués I've been darting off to Gina, my folks, and work. I suggest we go to a post office. Simon informs me that he has a larger transaction to complete—for the Master—and it must be done at the nearest Banque of France.

Of course, we're in Toulouse. How could I forget? This is where Dahl got robbed last year. He's gonna want to off-load as much cash as possible to alleviate all financial headaches and conceivable disasters. Whether it's superstition or hard-learned forethought, it's still a good idea. We may possibly be experiencing the height of his paranoia this entire tour. It's doubtful he'll leave his room except to play and possibly go search for the commode down the hall.

"Well, let's go find the bank, and then go to the post office," I suggest.

"To be honest, Dahl said I should go to the bank alone. He didn't want any of you coming along," announced Simon, punctuating the abrupt proclamation with a nervous giggle.

"What the hell's up with that?" I ask, even though I know what's up with that.

"I don't make the rules. Look, tell you what, the post office is right down the street there. You go there, and meet me outside the bank in ten minutes. Then, we'll go find some pinball or something."

"Gee, ya think maybe I can get an ice cream and ride the mechanical pony outside the market, too? What do you take me for, a sap? Never mind, don't answer. Simon, you know I'll get lost. I get lost between the dressing rooms and the stage. You can't turn me loose in war-torn Toulouse."

"Don't be such a baby. You'll be fine. Look, there's the post office. Go right there, and then it's just up that street dead ahead to your left. Take the first right, and you'll see the bank. You can't miss it."

"How the fuck do you know all this? You've never been here!"

"Well, you've gotta know these things to be road manager, don't you?"

Off I go, wary but nonetheless brave. The folks at the post office are friendly and confirm Simon's directions. I walk back out into Toulouse's main town square and head in the correct direction looking for the designated Banque of France. I make the pre-ordained right turn, and there, dead ahead, is a bakery, a butcher shop, a tobacco shop, a photo studio, but no bank. How could I have screwed this up, it was one turn? Maybe it's one more block up and then right. I make the walk and still no bank.

"Excuse me, madam," I say to a well-dressed woman walking down the street. "Parlez vous Englishe?"

"Oui, a leetle."

"Do you know where the closest Banque of France is?"

"Oui. You go straight up zat street, you see? Follow zat a leetle way own-teel you see Bertrand De La Rue, follow zat three blocks, and you are zere. Seemple."

I repeat the directions back and head on my way. Bertrand De La Rue, as best I can ascertain, doesn't exist, as least not in Toulouse. I take a few more turns up and down business streets with a lot of traffic. If nothing else, the law of averages will begin to work in my favor, eventually. No luck. I spot a longhaired, young guy, and ask him for assistance. He speaks English and is friendly. He's my new bro. I appreciate the cordiality, and write down his name to put on the guest list for tonight's show. Following the new set of directions he gives me, I journey to the outer reaches of the town's square, up by a courthouse, and around the back of some horse stables. I'm more lost now than ever and have lost track of the center of town. At least I know my way back to the hotel. I reach in my pocket, pull out the paper I wrote my young friend's name on, and tear it up.

I spot a French cop, and ask for some directions. By this time, I've been wandering around about forty-five minutes, and figure the rest of the guys have moved on from the Banque of France.

"Excusez moi, gendarme. Parlais vous English?"

"A Beet. A teenee beet. Ow can ah elp yiouu?"

"I'm trying to find Hotel Des Arts."

That's a laugh. "Hotel Des Arts." Such a name for that rattrap. "Chambre des Torture Und Artiste Sufferink" would be more apropos.

"Hotel Des Arts? Hmm. Non, non, ah doon beleave ah know eet."

I fumble through eight or nine pockets of my leather jacket, looking for the address to Chez Woolite. Shit! I wrote that geezer's name for the guest list on the back of the hotel address and tore it up in anger.

"Uh, yeah. I mean, oui oui, bon, bon, it's on, shit, uh, it's on Rue, Rue, Rue something or other."

"Ahm eh-frade ah need more details than that, monsieur, American lost man."

He points me somewhere, just to keep me moving, I figure. He then walks away, chuckling. I wonder how Martin Sheen would handle the situation. "Don't get off the boat. Goddamn right. Never get off the boat."

I FINALLY STUMBLE BACK into Hotel des Arts, locating it completely by chance, as the entire population of Toulouse has denied me access to the necessary information. Everyone is sitting around smoking cigarettes and drinking chocolate milk.

"I still hate France," says Ratboy in the nonchalant manner that is his trademark.

"You fucking guys. I told you I'd get lost. If a guy is willing to admit he's retarded, the least you could do would be to allow for that handicap and wait for him. It was just 'down the street,' I recall, some three hours ago!"

"Don't be too mad, darlin'," snickers Simon. "We only just got back. We've been lost as can be. None of these French fuckers will help you find anything, save a rope to hang yourself. To top it off, no one's seen Tim since he went for fritters at the beginning of the day!"

We all have a laugh and all is forgiven. Tim turns up as we're heading out to the van to go to the club,

which is affiliated with FMR radio in Toulouse. Fritter
in hand, Tim hops on board. Off we go, on a wild goose
chase to locate a club that's less than a quarter mile from
the hotel. Even with Geordie, our promoter and guide,
we can find nothing in the maze that is Toulouse.

We finally locate FMR, park the van, and Tim
bounds into the club looking for the deli platter. He's
still burping the last fritter. I guess everyone needs a
hobby. His is eating.

After soundcheck, Dahl and Rat do a lengthy
interview on FMR, while the rest of us shuffle around,
bored. Simon beats Tim repeatedly at Funhouse pinball,
and whips Z time and time again at foosball. I get a beer
and listen to the broadcast in the bar, where the guys
are DJing and playing songs from all the various CDs we
brought along. A tall, late-thirtyish English gentleman
walks by, grabs some peanuts off the bar, and asks if I
mind if he sits down. I gesture toward an empty chair.

"You a Yankee, then?"

"Yeah, yes."

"What brings you to the sleepy town of Toulouse, if
you don't mind my asking?"

"I'm the bass player in a traveling rock band."

"Bloody terrific! What sort of music do you play?"

"Punk rock, more or less."

"Name's Eric, I was importing jewelry across the
channel, traveling all over France, and I came here once
about a year and a half ago and fell for this bird, and that
changed everything. I decided to pack in the importing,
so I could stay with this girl."

"What's her name?"

"Her name's Candice. Her mom and dad are here. She couldn't bear to leave them, so I just changed my whole life to suit her. Love's a bloody chuckle, right?"

"You know it, Eric."

"Now I sell boats, wholesale. Well, it sounds great, but business is slow, times being what they are. Still, as long as I'm around Candice, I don't give much of a damn about money. Her parents, they have a different view, of me laxing about doing fuck all, but if business is down, well then, that's life, innit? Punk rock you say? Prior to the jewelry importing, I helped run an Indian food stand down in Soho, and before that—this might interest you—I was the bus driver for The Clash. I worked for that lot for nine months, great fun it was, too."

"When was this, Eric?"

"Well, back in the day, wasn't it? Late seventies, I should think. Before those guys stunk up the radio with 'Rock the Casbah.'"

Meanwhile, the bar radio is playing one of my songs off the Sister Goddamn album. I don't get to hear my music on the radio too often, and the distraction causes me to drift from Eric's long-winded tale.

"...And Strummer, great bloke, but he'd get excited when he talked to ya, especially when the topic shifted to politics. He'd start spitting all over ya when he got worked up. I don't think he meant to."

Eric is joined by some friends and his precious Candice, who appears to be nothing special, but for every man...I pull out a blank postcard and rattle off a communiqué to my boss back in the states.

> *Dear, Pete. Went looking for Triple X stuff and found some in a few scattered stores. Good thing me and Z have brought some CDs over, that alone has doubled your distribution. I think Rat put me in an ether coma and sodomized me. I can't walk straight anymore. I notice Z has the same problem, but he won't talk about it. Haven't seen Dahl much. Much fear lies ahead. Our merchandising w/ Maltese Crosses causes severe unrest. The gutters of Deutschland will run red with our blood, we've been told. Much love, McGruff. P.S., Please help Gina w/ my estate sale. Top dollar for Voxes and Gibsons. The Yoko collectibles should be worth something. Should I survive, cut me in. I invested in good faith, you know.*

The Toulouse gig is awesome and over the top. This crowd of 300 or so rabid maniacs are more familiar than most with Dahl's repertoire, particularly his original songs such as "Living in Lisa's World" and "I'm in Love with the GTOs." Rat and I clown and goof during the show, striking ridiculous poses and making faces to crack each other up. Z is doing his best, too, to have a laugh. Still, we're working hard, back on track again, and sounding hot. After about three songs, something unusual happens. Actual pretty girls, without guys attached to them, begin to gather along the edge of the stage, just like you hear about with real bands, just like in the movies. Two energetic blondes are in front of

Rat and I—winking, shaking, bouncing, smiling, doing all those things that young girls know how to do that makes guys go into various stages of convolutions and/ or hypnosis.

At the back of the stage, there's a rickety staircase that leads down to the dressing room. We descend and pat each other on the back. The crowd is howling for more, but eventually the adulation begins to wane. We decide to do an encore. As I walk up the stairs and my cap appears onstage, a shriek goes up through the crowd. I quickly duck.

"Wow, did you check that? Screaming?! Just like *The Ed Sullivan Show!*"

I do it again: head up, shrieks, head down, quiet. This is great, more fun than a ham radio. Finally we emerge and do a couple of encores. After which, I walk to the edge of the stage and hand one of the cute blondes my personally embossed guitar pick, which reads "Screamin' Lord Duff." I would never do something so corny or cliché back at home, but things would never be so desperate, boring, and surreal back at home, either. Besides, why be embarrassed? Who from this crowd am I ever gonna bump into on the street?

The blonde grabs my arm and starts yammering in half French/English. She wants to go backstage, and I got no problem with that. "Can I bring my friends?" Of course.

The two blondes descend the steps with two longhair, rocker guys. You guessed it, their boyfriends. They want

to conduct a lengthy, in-depth interview with the legend
himself, Jeff Dahl. I act as Jeff's publicist, which, back at
home, I am.

"Sure, Jeff will talk to you. Take as long as you like.
He loves to talk."

With Dahl and the guys settled in, I begin to
interview the girls, and learn that the one I gave the
pick to is named Carine. She has long, straight blonde
hair, parted to the side with long bangs, straight but soft
features, sort of like Catherine Denueve in *Repulsion*,
king-sized deep blue eyes you could swim in and a body
that any guy would be proud to peak through a keyhole
at. (Did I mention it's been a long trip already?) Though
her boyfriend is ten feet away, she's all over me like
Sunset Strip spandex.

"Brooose, you know, for sure I am not groupie. Nor
my friend. We're just regular girls, our boyfriends write for
punk rock magazine. But, Broooose, we are not groupies."

"I didn't say you were. Have you met the Ratboy?"

Suddenly, there are a few more girls around, and
they all seem to know each other. Geordie comes in
and congratulates us on a great show, and says that
the promoter wants us to eat now. We had chosen to
postpone dinner until after the show, this is one of the
rare occasions we were even given a choice. We mention
that Jeff's doing an interview, and say we'd like to relax a
minute, but Geordie is insistent. "They want you to eat
now. The cook has been working hard, and he doesn't
want it to get cold."

"Yeah, sure, whatever."

"Brooose, you must tell me all about Los Angeleees. It must be sooo exciting. I must know everything!"

A guy runs into the room, waving a long cooking fork, brandishing it like a weapon. "I deed not slave over a fiery oven for hours just to watch mah creation grow cold. You must eat at once."

I invite the girls to join us, leaving Dahl behind with the two fanzine guys. We rejoin in the bar, where a long table has been set for us. Spaghetti, salad, and garlic bread for everyone, at this most preposterous beggar's banquet!

"Brooose, do you like your deenair?"

"Yeah, it's great. Open wide, here comes a bite for you."

With my cap now cocked to the side of her head, she's chewing sensuously on my meatball. Sometimes touring ain't all bad.

"Theese food is okay, but I weesh you could stay longer. I would cook for you all day long. I make fabulous pizza, and breads, and omelets. I feed you all day to make you fat and happy."

Meanwhile, under the table, her legs become intertwined with mine, and her hand caresses my thigh. She talks of all the places we would go and the things we would do, if only I didn't have to ship on out to the next show.

"What about the French Dave Marsh back there?" I inquire, indicating Mr. Fanzine. "Don't you think he would object to your sudden switch of allegiance to the California kid?"

"Oh, no, Brooose. You are soo silleee. It's not like that. I would simply tell him to go away for a few days."

As her hand leaves the general vicinity of my thigh heading north up Highway Hard-On, I realize this fantasy dream date is most likely not gonna make it much past dessert, no matter what she hints at.

"Tell me more about America, Brooose."

"Well, darlin', it's the land of opportunity, where a man can give all he's got just to invest in his own retirement fund, all the time doing a curious two-step with his wicked Uncle Sam. The street where I live is lined with palm trees and for a good four hours either side of dusk, both the setting sun and the full moon sit side by side in the sky, and all the street signs glow with neon. If you're ever in town, you gotta drop in. Can't stay too long, though, it's a small town we got."

Her voice is getting lower, more quiet. "Brooo-ow-ow-sss, it sounds so beautiful, so sexxeee. I wish I could go there with you."

"Honey, I'll take you home in a drum case if I have to."

"Tell me more." Clearly, her hunger for knowledge was insatiable. It was time to up the ante.

"I'll tell you whatever, sweetheart. Why don't you hop in the kill machine we call a van and venture back to the luxurious Hotel Des Arts, where we have the finest in contemporary men's undergarments on display in the celebrity suite as we speak. There, our travel guide—

that's me—will tell you all about the hidden treasures of the utopia known as Los Angeles."

"Brooose," her voice suddenly developing an edge of scorn. "You are like all the rest, you men. You want nothing more than to get me back to some hotel room, and then you'll move on with your band the next morning."

"Well, yeah. I mean, no. I mean, don't wreck the spontaneity of the moment we are sharing."

She is falling back into my web of evil, staring deep into my tired, bloodshot eyes, when this magic moment is broken by the limey accent of our slave driving road manager.

"Romeo, Romeo, time to move your amp now, Romeo."

I dutifully respond. Back in the dressing room, gathering my things, Carine reappears, and begins clinging to me and going through the motions of the long goodbye. "Eh, let's take it upstairs. You know what I'm sayin'?" Her boyfriend's a mere ten feet away, still heavily engrossed in conversation with Dahl, as the two share memories of the late Stiv Bators.

Up onstage, I grab the bag that holds my cables and whatever booze I've managed to steal. Carine is across the stage, vaguely following me around. Though we're in the big showroom for the first time, we're alone.

"Well, I guess I gotta go. Nice meeting you."

She springs up and blocks my exit, and throws her arms around me. "You would leave me without a keees?"

The bag falls to my side, we embrace, and begin kissing passionately. It is not a particularly long kiss. She looks deep in my eyes, draws a breath, and gasps, "If my boyfriend catches us, he KEEEL YOU!"

"Well, what the hell we doing this for, then? Look, you're awesome, come visit me in Los Angeles sometime, but I have a tour to survive right now!"

The duty-bound and the long-suffering rocker, aka your humble narrator, strides up the stairs and out into the Toulouse night. The steel horse, aka our van, awaits ready to whisk us off into a sunset that supports sun and moon, earth and sky. I relate my most recent tale of woe to my fellow travelers. They laugh, and for a couple of days, "If my boyfriend catches us, he KEEEEL YOU!" became our catchphrase of choice.

EVERYONE'S PRETTY EXCITED ABOUT our Paris show. Thing is, it's not really in Paris. According to Geordie, there are no clubs in Paris proper that cater to alternative/indie/ punk, whatever-the-hell-we-are rock. We are instead playing in a Parisian suburb called Issy les Moulineaux, which is akin to playing Jersey instead of Manhattan or Reseda in lieu of Hollywood. It'll do.

Geordie guides us to our lodgings for the evening, a private rooming house she has secured, with four separate bedrooms, all feeding out to a central hall. It's just like The Monkees had, or The Beatles in *Help*. Catching this communal sixties rock band vibe, we all get pretty silly. Rat's running around in his little red pajamas. Tim's serenading us on Dahl's acoustic. Simon's singing along as he shaves. Z and I are playing poker with my newly acquired Salvador Dalí deck of cards, picked up at the Dalí museum on our way out of Spain.

We had taken a special detour to Figueres, Spain, where Dalí's home was now a museum. All of us were fascinated by Dalí, naturally, and had heard this was the best accumulation of his work and installations in the world. As would be our luck, and typical of this tour, we arrive on a Monday and the whole place is closed, except for the gift shop and snack bar. Hence the cards. Six years later, I'm serving as substitute bassist for White Flag on a Spanish tour, and we finally make it to the Dalí house/museum. While it has nothing to do with this story, if you can ever go, go. It is perhaps the most amazing attraction/museum/oddity/rarity on earth.

Back to the card game...We begin talking about the Jon Spencer Blues Explosion, the popular band that's opening for us this evening.

"Spencer's a total critic's darling, ever since the Pussy Galore days," I tell Z. "These French people will know all about him. He'll probably draw real well. I wonder how we'll come off playing after him."

"Like a Top Forty band of old guys," reckons Z.

"We need to do something, something to get an edge. Something to throw the proceedings out of wack."

Z is deep in thought. Suddenly, he utters the proclamation, "Glitter rock."

"Capital idea!"

We run down the halls of Chez Monkee with our concept. Whereas Spencer and Co. will be all dark and trendy and NY noise band chic, we'll be retro-fag. Perfect! Everyone likes the idea, and soon we're crowded in front of the same bathroom mirror, teasing and spraying our hair, applying eyeliner, rouge, lipstick, frilly clothes, ruffled shirts, whatever we can manage. In true glam style, we commemorate the indulgence with a private photo shoot, in the bathtub, no less. Posin' 'til closin', honeys.

Following the crowd's lukewarm response to Spencer's excellent set, we take the stage, all pomp and circumstance. Kicking off with our regular opener, "View from the Gutter," I go right to the edge of the stage and strike my best Mick Ronson pose. Hair flying, guitar in ultra-phallic position, lips in perfect pout, I demonstrate that the early-seventies were not lost on me. I feel a hand slip up my inner thigh, and think to myself, *Hmm, there's something to this. I'm getting an immediate reaction.* Looking down to check out my newfound admirer, I'm staring straight into the demonic-possessed eyes of a bald-headed, toothless, sweating Frenchmen. Ah, the French, they are *soo sensiteeve.* Since The Doors have been our patron saints throughout this expedition, I recycle an old Morrison audience taunt.

"Well, that's Paris for ya. The only people to rush the stage were guys."

So much for Glam.

.

BACK AT THE CRIB, Geordie is in our room, drunk. Rat, Simon, Z, and I are in the house. Geordie is quite giddy. Glances are exchanged sideways amongst the guys to make sure no one's interested in making a move on her, and it's quickly confirmed by all: No!

"I am Number One. You are Number Six." She's babbling lines from the British psychedelic Sixties television obscurity, *The Prisoner.* "What do you want? We need information. INFORMATION!"

We're all in our pajamas, and I put on the ever-reliable *30 Golden Hits* collection by the man, James Brown. We all start dancing on the beds and singing loudly.

"Please, please, please, please, baby please, don't go, oh honey please. Don't goooooo. Huh! (Long pause). I love ya so!"

Down on our knees, pulling hot pseudo-Brownian moves, we are in a place where there's no one to disturb, save Tim and Dahl, and they're just gonna have to tolerate our steam blowing.

Now, remember Claude, the guy who cooked spaghetti for us in Orleans? He's now gigging as Jon Spencer's road manager/driver. He had talked to Geordie before our departure from the gig.

"You know, Claude took the Jon Spencer guys out on the town in Paris."

"That sounds like fun," I mention.

"Well, why don't you guys hit the town? You're back here having a pajama party like a bunch of schoolboys."

"Believe it or not, this has been one of the most fun nights we've had!" enthused Rat.

"I can't believe you wouldn't want to go out on the town in Paris, the city of romance. If you can't scrape up girls at the shows, I know you could at a French bar."

"Well, Geordie," said Simon, who only slightly tolerated her to begin with and admitted in our confidence that he could conceive of no earthly value to her being on the road with us. "Dahl won't let us take the van on pleasure expeditions such as that. That's the rule."

"We could take the night train," she suggested.

"I think that's coming up on the James Brown tape," said Rat, going over most of our heads.

"We can't afford to take trains, Geordie," said Z, slightly huffy. "We've even run out of CDs to sell. We're almost flat broke. Did you see Ratboy trying to work out getting more from the French distribution company, backstage tonight? We need to get more CDs just to afford cigarettes."

"It's so sad," says Geordie, half sympathetic, half frustrated at the plight of being stuck on a beyond-boring tour with a bunch of deadbeats. "When Jeff stayed with me, he didn't want to do anything. It was like having an old grandpa around."

"That's just the way he is. That's the road Dahl," said Simon.

I have to disagree. Jeff seems different to me. I've mentioned it to the other guys and, well, it's not that they haven't noticed, it's just that they don't really give a damn. But I insist it's an important matter for discussion.

"When I was in the first band, it seemed more like a regular band," I said vaguely. "For example, we got some gigs up the coast in San Francisco. We'd drive up in my van and Del's truck, grab a couple hotel rooms, play, go hang in the Haight, and go record shopping or go get a pizza or just go walk around and check out the basic vibe and feel of the city. But, whatever, we'd do it as a band, and Jeff seemed more, well, with us. It didn't seem 'us' and 'him' at all, not at all. I wonder why it feels so different now?"

"Maybe it has something to do with him hanging in the desert for so long," proposed Z. "It must get weird out there, all isolated, just answering his fan letters all the time, that being his major connection with the outside world."

"Whatever, he sure seems different," I add, redundantly.

"Why don't you talk to him about it?" proposes Simon, reasonably enough.

"Yeah, I guess I should. I'll have to remember to do that. Gotta see if there's something wrong, 'cause, bottom line, he's my friend, right?"

"Yeah, whatever you say, Bruce."

"You're the greatest, McGruff."

It seems obvious that they weren't even listening. I deal off the bottom of the deck and ante up for a round of poker. I've got to make some money out here somehow.

FOLLOWING TOULOUSE AND PARIS, places most people have actually heard of, we head for unknown parts, towns French people themselves are unsure about. In Nimes, we arrive at a fairly typical small rock club on time and find no one else involved with the show has arrived yet. There is no equipment, food, drinks—hence, nothing to do. So we sit. I lay across a table. Z sits on the stage. Dahl and Simon sit in the van. Rat sits at a booth. Tim paces back and forth, looking like a junkie waiting for his fix. The boy needs his deli tray. This goes on for an unmeasured amount of time, perhaps ninety minutes, maybe two hours. There is no conversation during this time.

Bored with boredom itself, I muster the excessive energy it takes to stand up and walk out the venue's front door. I look up and down the street. No shops of interest, no movie theaters, no junk food. Even if I had money, there's nothing to spend it on. It's a ghost town with living people. I turn, return to my table, and lay back down.

Finally, the crew guys show up, and begin erecting a massive lighting rig over the dinky stage. "What's with all the lights?" I ask, observing that a performance under them is going to be similar to a tanning salon or being stuck on a rotisserie.

"The rider. It's in the rider," answers a polite, young guy who introduces himself as Richard. "See, right here. It's in the contract rider."

"Richard, no one reads the contract rider. We're lucky if we get half the things we ask for to eat or drink. We never get all the sound and lights. You've got enough lights to do KISS at Madison Square Garden."

"It's in the rider."

Richard and his crew diligently set up their mega-rock lighting and sound rig. They are nice guys, but they are slow...very, very slow, and this setup takes hours. More time sitting with nothing else to do. There is virtually nothing to do in Nimes.

True to following the rider, the letter of the law, they feed us a rich, fattening, mind-numbing meal that is fantastic, consumed about five minutes before we go onstage. Sluggish and apathetic from the pig-out, I turn in a going-through-the-motions performance, peppered with countless mistakes. The rest of the band is equally lax and no one seems to give a damn anyway.

Following the show, Dahl seems a little pissed. I assume it's due to the lackluster Factsheet performance, but I'm wrong again.

"I told Camille no private accommodations, and damned if we don't have them tonight. Why do I bother to arrange these things so far in advance?" he poses with disgust.

Private accommodations mean that the club, promoter, or some fans are going to put the band up for the night. It's a common way to cut costs on van tours, and none of us are strangers to it. Dahl has been through it a thousand times. Sometimes it's pleasant, even homey. Other times it can be pure hell. It's a crapshoot.

"That explains why they were so anal about all the other rider details," I mention. Dahl had promised us no private accommodations. It was part of his deal to make the practically nonexistent per diems more bearable.

While waiting to depart for unknown parts, I mingle with the good people of Nimes, who are, by and large, an unusually negative bunch. I repeatedly hear reports of "I hate this town," "The economics here," "My neighbors," and so forth.

I ask a few of them, "Alright, why don't you leave?" They look at me as if I'd asked, *Why don't you ram an ice pick into your ear?* As much as they hate it, the thought of leaving is completely alien.

Having lost my patience for their logic and lack thereof, I begin a flirtatious conversation with a tall German girl. At this point, I shouldn't even have to mention it, but of course she attended the show with her boyfriend. Knowing this, given my advanced state of hyper-boredom, I decide to try to pick her up, for the simple sport of good old-fashioned home wrecking. If she lives here, she hates it anyway, so what difference does it make?

Geordie overhears my ridiculous come-ons such as "follow me to paradise" and "what say you and I blur cultural boundaries," and she laughs to herself. She can't believe it when the girl agrees to go back to the hotel with me (yes, I know there isn't one), but then her boyfriend comes up and takes her by the arm away from me.

"Hooray for you, Bruce," says Geordie. "At least you're trying to have fun."

I'm not sure how to respond, so I don't. I continue milling about, and I've just about exhausted every possible social encounter available. The club is thinning, and we're still waiting. Finally, at a few minutes before 2:00 a.m., Richard announces we're ready to go. His partner, a glad-handing English bore, is putting up Dahl, Ratboy, and Geordie, while the rest of us are to go with Richard. We grab some guitars and follow Richard on foot to his apartment a few blocks away.

Outside Richard's place, we stand in the street. No one says anything. We just stand there. Time passes. More time. "What's up?" asks Tim.

A guy we don't know has led us here, presumably Richard's flatmate. He says nothing. We continue standing.

Richard comes up and joins us. More standing. I cannot take it anymore.

"WILL SOMEONE OPEN THE FUCKING DOOR!!!" I scream like a complete idiot. Everyone has stopped pacing, the two French guys are both staring at me, while Simon, Tim, and Z gaze silently at the ground. My outburst has instantly turned me into John Wayne Gacy, madman and killer. I quickly try to analyze the situation. Do I quiet down, apologize, and act humble in the hopes that everyone will forgive my petulant tantrum, or do I continue to act like an asshole in the hopes that someone will actually open the door and let us inside? Right.

"What is the deal? Are we going to stand around all night outside in the street drooling like a pack of freakin' zombies, or are we going to go inside and behave in a more civilized manner?"

Richard was getting impatient with my childlike fit, and I was growing tired of his namby-pamby inability to accomplish auspiciously simple tasks in a reasonable time frame.

"I have to walk back to the club to find the key," he says through barely clenched teeth. "I'll run if it makes my guests happy."

I shoot a glance at Simon that says, "Don't let him off the hook. A brisk run will do him a world of good."

Fifteen minutes or so later, we gain entrance to Chez Richard, a mildly grubby crash pad that is actually fairly tidy given the context of being in France. Richard breaks out a bottle of wine, and we start to relax. I apologize to everyone, especially Richard.

"Hey, sorry I acted like a total idiot. I was pissed. Forgive me. I really don't have an excuse." (That is, no excuse beyond boredom setting in at an unchecked rate to an advanced degree. Nothing more serious than spending an entire day doing virtually nothing besides sitting, gazing at nothing, dozing off due to gazing at nothing, and playing bass for a little over an hour. Thank God for that hour!)

Everyone loosens up, and Richard smiles and says all is forgiven, but I can't help but think he thinks of me as a typical, spoiled, selfish American pig. As Simon would say, with his deep London accent, "I can't be bothered."

A girl, who Simon hit on at the club, suddenly wanders around the living room in a halter-top and cutoffs. Simon gets a good look and comes to his senses. Ouch! I wander to the back of the flat, where Tim begins to play Dahl's acoustic guitar. Simon pulls me from Tim's room out into the hall.

"You know, Tim can play rings around the lot of ya, yet you all treat him like shit."

"Yeah. So?" I respond.

"I just think you could give him a break. I know that when he first came out with us he was a bit of a goof, and he realizes he doesn't fit in with you guys, but he's really been trying to get along and fit in."

"Hey. I'm letting him read my Burroughs book. I've roomed with him more than Z or Rat. Lecture them, why don't ya?"

Back in Tim's room, he stops the instrumental workout to lead those in attendance through a rousing five-verse sing-along to the "House of the Rising Sun." Hail, hail, the gang's all here. A Beatles medley follows, and by the time we hit "Patience" by Guns N' Roses, I politely bow out.

DREAM SEQUENCE

I'M IN A CITY I don't know, and judging from the interior decorating and design, it seems to be the early sixties. I'm in a high-rise apartment somewhere, and Jeff Dahl walks in.

"Everything's going to be real cool on the tour. You're going to have the time of your life!" says Jeff.

A woman with her hair pulled up in a bun and a slow-moving, graying, kind gentleman appear through another door. They cordially welcome me into their home. Though I'd never seen them before, I accept them as Dahl's parents. A pretty girl with short, dark-brown hair and a shiny, blue-green mini-skirt/space suit come up behind me. It is love at first sight. What I assume to be the male part of Dahl's secret family enters, three guys of an indeterminate age all wearing brand new, perfectly pressed, sharp black suits. These are the notorious men in black, and it becomes clear that they were not working for the C.I.A., nor secret societies within our country, but for space aliens all along. This sort of unnerves me. I remember feeling both anxious and unpleased that Dahl's sister must be a space alien as well. The next thing I know, I'm being pursued by the men in black. However, the foxy sister decides to save my life. Using her secret knowledge and special alien chick capabilities, she forms a bubble around me so I can float up and out of harm's way. I see no point in continuing this dream, so I wake up.

END DREAM SEQUENCE

WE QUICKLY LEAVE THE next morning. I accidentally leave behind the only lay around piece of clothing I have, my black sweatpants. Not good. French cities are becoming indistinguishable. It's what Z has dubbed the Euro-Blur Phenomenon. After one show, all the Carol Bators crew came back to the hotel with us. Tim and I have adjoining rooms. I told Rat he could bring his French friends up to my room to party, seeing how he was rooming with the Master and a party would not be tolerated. I sat there watching French television while ten people sat in my room and spoke French to one another. It was pretty depressing. I called Gina after they left and had a long talk, pouring my heart out about how much I miss her. I wonder if this separation gets easier over time, if you get hardened to it. She seems to be having fun back home, and is a little drunk every time I call her at night.

Speaking of French television, one night we were in an Ibis after a show, just vegging out and watching it. Dahl was totally happy and in a great mood whenever we stayed in an Ibis. They were regimented and identical to one another; he liked the quality control and loved the uniformity. The odd thing was the French Ibises were all right next to either a hospital or a cemetery. It could have been a coincidence, but after about the third or fourth time we stayed in an Ibis adjacent to boneyards or meat lockers, I was beginning to wonder exactly what the connection was. The familiar Smell of Death was thinly disguised by cheap French perfume, but was still readily recognizable. There was no escaping certain things—

the smell especially. But I was talking about French television. At any rate, we're all in our rooms, when Dahl, who had his own room that night, began running up and down the hall and pounding on our doors.

"Turn on channel three. You gotta check this out!" he shouted and glowed with excitement, and then promptly returned to his nest following the announcement. Channel three was showing a game show that featured large numbers of topless women. It was mildly entertaining, and most of the girls were cute, but after a few minutes I returned to French MTV, hopelessly awaiting the next Leila K video. The following day, Rat expressed to me that he felt Dahl was far too excited about that game show, and we pondered the possible reason for his sudden increased heart rate. Why would a man who had spent his entire adult life happily married be so excited by a few televised titties? And doesn't he have cable out there in Phoenix? When no clear explanations surfaced, we feared a deeper dementia might be underfoot. I lay back on my hotel bed, flicking back and forth between MTV and Breasts of Fortune. Simon took off his clothes, emptied his money belt, and covered his nude body with francs, while his eyes rolled back in simulated orgasmic ecstasy. I could hear Dahl cheering down the hall. Sirens faded in and out of my perception with Doppler pitch-bending effects—far then near, then far again. Were they ambulances, police cars, or hearses, I wondered, trying to remember if we were next to a hospital or mortuary tonight. Of course, how silly of me, it was a hospital. Everyone knows hearses don't require sirens.

IT JUST KEEPS GETTING stranger, and by the middle of the second week of February, we're way up in some mountains heading for a small hill town called Thiers. Our hotel is like a little mountain resort, with a quaint, rustic bar/restaurant. Geordie is hanging in the bar, getting soused by around 4:30 p.m. Rat is on the pay phone with his wife back at home, talking again about her recording contract. Tim is eating the bar's complimentary pretzels. Simon's looking to conquer The Joker pinball game. Z glances at the pictures in the French newspaper, and I check out the jukebox, which has singles by underground bands like The Hickoids and The Mummies. Geordie is getting into the groove of the tour, which at this point can be boiled down to a Zen-like "just be" mindset. Don't look for trouble, don't seek out fun. Just ride in the van and play. She had complained a few nights ago about our not wanting to party with her and her French friends, as if that would be some sort of pleasure for us, and that we're missing out on something really special. Right. Again, she brought up the fact that Jon Spencer's band went out and had fun. I reminded her that for the last few days, we've been in towns so small that we literally were the only thing happening that night. She pouted and looked away.

The gig is in a two-story, small capacity club with no stage. We play right on the floor eye-level with the audience. The soundman is an older guy who encourages us to play as loud as we like in this small room. No problem, friend.

The stage, or rather the corner in which we play, faces a doorway that leads to the barroom. Past the bar are the toilets, and past the toilets a private room, in which we'd stashed all our cases and bags full of crucial musician stuff. I'm heading into the private room when a girl comes down the spiral staircase that leads from the offices and dressing room.

"Hallo, I liked ze ban tooonight," she says in the thickest accent I've yet heard. "Would yew like to smoke weeth me?" she asks, giving me a glimpse of a big fatty she produces from her small bag.

"Yeah, come in here, where it's private."

Inside the room, Tim is hunched over with his face pressed against a wall. I consider this to be unusual behavior, but this is Tim, so I chose not to discuss it.

"You won't believe this!" he says somewhat quietly.

"Let me guess. You forgot you had super glue on your nose when you leaned over to catch that fly that had landed on the wall and licked him up just like a big, green lizard."

"Huh? No, look."

He turns to face me and points to a hole in the wall. The hole peers into another room, but I can't discern what I'm supposed to be looking at. I ask what it is.

Tim pushes me aside and glares through the tiny hole like a pirate through his telescope. "Dude, it's the girl's bathroom! You can watch them squat and take dumps."

"You can't be serious. And your watching it!?! Let the poor girls defecate in peace. Have you been in these bathrooms? It's enough of a chore to take care of business even if you think you have a bit of privacy, much less with some villainous American merchandise hawker peeping at you through a switchblade-chiseled glory hole. I better take a look."

Remembering I had company, I put my bass to bed and tell my smoking companion that we should go smoke in the dressing room. Upstairs, there was some food and beer. We grab a bench. She says her name is Laurence. I ask if I should call her Larry for short. She politely smiles.

Sandwich in hand, Simon sits and joins Larry and me for some serious hash smoking. Rat, who loves being around so many people he can speak French with, comes over and hands Z and me a large sheet of paper.

"They want us to fill these out. They're rock star questionnaires. They're totally hysterical."

They were like the old Gloria Stavers-style *16 Magazine* faves-and-pet-peeves star sheet thingies. We get into the spirit of the thing and complete our factsheets like dutiful schoolboys. All manner of trivia is unleashed. Ratboy cites Lightning Hopkins as his favorite recordings, but "not the songs, just the parts where he talks in-between." Z's favorite song to sing in the shower is the choral section from the fourth movement of Beethoven's Ninth.

Laurence fires up the hash again, and Tim enters sporting a self-satisfied grin.

"He looks 'appy," observes Simon.

"The industrious little tike discovered a free peep show," I inform.

"C'mon, Simon, come have a look," confirms Tim. "You know you want to, you horny bastard."

"I can't be bothered. I'd rather eat me sandwich."

Laurence keeps hanging around, and producing hash. I want to be a good host. I do appreciate her easy-going company and the exquisite hashish, but I'm running low on small talk. Her accent is thick, her English slow and rather painful. Our conversations have to be kept reasonably simple. Ah, I know. I'll discuss something every Frenchie has an opinion about.

"So, Laurence, I've always wondered, we Americans think about this mystery a great deal, and spend no small amount of intellectual energy pondering it: Why is Jerry Lewis so popular with the French?"

"I'm sorry. I don't understand you."

"OK. Jerry Lewis. You know, the funny guy, tall and thin, likes a good cigarette now and again."

She sits there and thinks hard, almost as if she feels sorta bad for putting a crimp in the flow of conversation, what little there is to begin with. She finally smiles and shakes her head *no*. Z's sitting behind her, and appears to be tuning in to the chat.

"He hung around Dean Martin, The Nutty Professor, The Patsy, The Errand Boy, The Bellboy Always Rings Twice, you know, funny movies. Jerry's Kids."

She shook her head again. At this point, I reduce myself to rendering horrible impersonations of the nutty one, to no avail. Z begins to giggle under his breath. "Oh, come on Laurence. You're French. ZZZ-GG-GG-AIR–EEEE LOOOOUUU-EEEESSS!" I spout in the most exaggerated, insulting French accent I can muster.

"Ooohhh. Yes. Oui, Oui! Geeaaiir-Eeee Loooouuu-Eeeesss. Yes, of course," she enthuses while Z doubles over laughing, spilling his beer. She gets flustered by the sudden burst of hysteria directed toward her, stands up, and quickly leaves.

Jeff interrupts his interview and looks over at us, snickering. "You chased that poor girl out of here." He turns back to the interviewer and tells him, "You can't take them anywhere." Three nights later, Laurence turned up again in Lyon, dressed to kill in a black miniskirt. She took photos of the band against a spray-painted psychedelic wall, and says she will paint portraits from the snapshots. Of course, she never did, best to our knowledge anyway. However, it was nice to know that she wasn't offended by our basically good-natured ribbing and that she looked so great in a miniskirt. The morning after the Thiers gig, I woke up in the rustic hotel in a pool of my own piss. This was quite an unsuspected surprise.

"Shit, Z. I wet the bed. I'm losing it. I'm going out!"

"I'll be honest with you, McGruff. It doesn't look good."

"How could this happen? What does this mean? You think someone put the whammy on me?"

"It might have more to do with the amount of carbonated beverage treats you had. Well?"

"Christ, I don't remember. Do you?"

"No. All I know is, my beer resistance has gone up a lot in the last couple of weeks. I'm drinking twelve to fourteen beers a night now, and I don't even get a buzz. No sensory distortion at all."

"Wow."

IT WAS ONE THING when Z lost his voice, quite another when our lead singer lost his. For just over a week now, Dahl has been slugging back the codeine-fuelled cough syrup that is legally available in France without a prescription. He insists on riding in the back of the van, in spite of the increasingly colder weather. It'd been two hours of no tapes playing and no talking when we rolled into Montargis. The place we are playing is a small, eh, recreation center. It's stuck in the middle of a dirt parking lot on a corner near an open sewer. It is the coldest building I've ever been in, significantly colder inside than outside. I run back out to the van to grab a sweatshirt to bear the freeze inside. The place has no stage, no food, and no toilet. The backstage is just a room full of empty beer crates with no chairs or furniture of any kind. The P.A. is two Peavey columns, subpar for even a garage rehearsal. It won't be loud enough, and it will sound bad.

We had all noticed in our itineraries that tonight would be private accommodations again. I hoped it wouldn't be in this barn. I walk outside to warm up and have a smoke, and join Geordie who is standing alone.

"Hi." No answer. "Well, you must be glad to be rid of us."

"Not really. I'll miss you in a way. I wish this little tour within your big tour had been more fun, but I certainly learned a lot."

I didn't press for an explanation, but rather changed the topic to more immediate concerns.

"What do you know about where we're staying tonight?"

"Jeff said he's stayed there before, but he wouldn't say much about it. He didn't look too happy. I can tell you that tonight is your highest-paying French show."

"What?! That can't be, look at this place. They can't get more than 150 people in here, and that right there is probably more than the entire Montargis population."

"The promoter, Jean Luc, is a huge Jeff Dahl fan. He is paying for the privilege of having Jeff perform here in his small hometown. He's promoted rather vigorously— he printed a lot of those huge concert posters—and I think he thinks he has a fighting chance at breaking even."

"Yeah, what do you think? Do you think he actually will?"

A Mohawked guy with jackboots and an old French army coat walks past. Geordie nods to indicate that is Jean Luc. For some reason, we actually bother to do a soundcheck with this awful equipment in this functioning echo chamber. With my glasses on, and my sweatshirt hood drawn tight around my ears, I look about as far removed from the standard image of a rock musician imaginable.

"McGruff, I think you're onto something," laughs Rat, who even in this cold maintains his capped/pointy shoed/vest 'n' ruffled shirt image. "You should look like that for the show tonight, that would be hysterical."

Simon rounds us up, and loads us into the van, trying to sound cheerful as he fills us in on the plan. "Alright then. We're following this Jean Luc character back to his place, which is where we'll be staying. We're going to hang out there and hopefully warm up and get something to eat. We're going to follow him in his car, apparently it's not very far from here."

All seven of us were in the van at the moment: Tim and Geordie sharing the shotgun, Simon in the driver's seat, and the whole band in the back seat. Though he's in a codeine fog, Dahl's cough sounds like a Harley being kick-started. It's unnerving as he sits there with that raspy, throat-tearing cough. It blasts forth at regular twenty-second intervals, but other than that, there is no sound in the van. Rat slips in some Tom Waits.

"We sail tonight for Singapore..."

The sun is almost down, and we're heading out of town into the hilly forests of the countryside. The main road leads to a small road that leads to a dirt road that leads to a glorified footpath as we continue to follow Jean Luc to his home. What sort of digs would the primary punk promoter of Montargis have?

"I stayed there last year. HAAACCK!" spat Jeff, offering no more information.

As we crossed the rickety bridge, the trees and the dark forest grew ominous. I realized we were miles from phones, hotels, and highways.

"Man, this reminds me of the first scene in *The Evil Dead*, you know, where the kids are all going to the mountain cabin, thinking everything's alright when doom waits just around the corner."

"Didn't see it, McGruff."

"Me neither."

"Stop being paranoid. We'll only be here ALL NIGHT LONG," comforts Simon.

"This guy could be the punk rock Norman Bates," says Tim, catching my fever of fear and paranoia.

"I don't know what you guys are talking about," says Geordie.

"This guy is obviously setting us up for the kill," I conclude. "Look, out in the middle of no place, getting dark, back roads lined with creepy trees. This is so far away from the club, or the abandoned room, or whatever it is. He'd have saved money putting us up at the local Slaughtered Lamb, as the rent would be cheaper than the gas money. Heads are going to roll tonight. I'm gonna sleep in the van."

"Do you know how cold it would be in the van? You'd likely freeze to death," warns Simon.

"Bleeeachchaaack," Jeff coughs.

We finally park in front of Jean Luc's house. It's a gray, stone, two-room affair with an adjoining guesthouse. A very severe looking ax protrudes from a pile of wood. Simon, Tim, and I peer into the guesthouse—a cold, rectangular prison cell of a room with three metal bunk beds and absolutely no other furniture. The whole place was straight out of *The Texas Chainsaw Massacre*.

Inside the main house, it's even colder than the club. We quietly gather around a huge mahogany table as Jean Luc attempts to make us feel at home. "You'll like this," he beams, and puts on a CD by some French hardcore band, cranking his huge stereo to the max. Our entire entourage glares at him hatefully.

Jeff: "Please turn it off."

Simon: "Bloody hell!"

Rat: "I hate music like that."

Tim: "How about something to eat?"

Z: "We haven't eaten all day."

McGruff: "Got any booze? That would thaw us out."

Geordie emerges from the bathroom looking slightly green. Clearly, everyone is unhappy and uncomfortable. Jean Luc disappears into the kitchen and comes back with a plate of white cheese and bread, a jar of orange juice, and a bottle of vodka. We hover around the plate like starved animals. In an attempt to show we're slightly up the evolutionary ladder, we quickly organize. Tim and Simon methodically churn out sandwiches, while Z and I bartend for all. Rat raids the sizeable CD collection and puts on a selection more suitable for a volume that allows for conversation and normal brain functions. Now Jean Luc looks uneasy suddenly, says he has to go back to the club, and darts out the front door.

I slam a huge OJ and vodka and feel an immediate tingle, an increasing numbness, an oncoming warmth. Looking around this punk cabin, I begin seeing various objects that indicate our host might be a white supremacist: assorted Nazi books and posters stashed just out of view, skinhead romance novels, that sort of thing.

Alone in Chez Jean Luc, the question arises: "Are we going to actually stay in this meat locker in the middle of wherever the fuck we are all night?"

"I think we should move on, Jeff," says Simon. "Staying here isn't going to do anyone any good. This is miserable."

"That guy's creepy, too," Z opines.

"I know he's going to hack us up in our sleep," I say with my usual paranoia.

"We can't afford to get another hotel out of our budget tonight. I'm not paying for it," said Dahl.

"Jeff, you're on the verge of death now, plus your codeine supply is dangerously low," I point out. "You need to get into someplace warm more than we do."

Dahl started to give in, which meant he didn't want to stay here anymore than we did, but didn't want to look like he was a wuss. "Whatever you guys decide, but I can't pay for hotels tonight."

I wonder to myself, but Rat and Z can probably hear my brainwaves: *How can this tour be so tight? Aren't we making a profit as we roll along, with a lot of fairly big shows and almost no expenses? How could things be so down to the bone?*

"Well, we'll just drive all night to the next hotel, and hope to get an early check in," says Simon. "Is that all right with you guys?"

We all nod yes. We return our luggage to the van and head back to the center for the show, which is a numb, clanging blur of noise, vodka, white light, echoed sound, cold medicine, and beer. The Bators folks show up en masse to bid us farewell and cheer us on at our last big French show.

This is embarrassing, I think to myself. Playing with my big Buddy Holly glasses and a fucking sweatshirt hood to ten people and Carol and her friends screaming like they're watching the Stones or something. It's all too weird, gimme another shot of that cold medicine. I'm not sick. I just want more blur in my Euro-Blur. They even demand encores, which Jeff grants—this is too much!

We say goodbye to everyone, Geordie included, who hitches a ride to the train station and heads home. Off we go on our night ride.

"I can't say I'll miss Geordie," announces Simon with a smile. "Bloody goofy girl trying to tell me how to run a tour. Hah! Well, McGruff, you going to keep me company while I drive? Because you know that lot in the back will be asleep as soon as we hit the highway."

"I'm with ya, bro. Italy or bust."

Easy enough to say, but in a couple of hours I'm bobbing for apples, too. Simon looks knackered as he tries to keep the van on the road, as 3:00 a.m. turns into 4:00 a.m. We pull into a rest stop, get out, and have a couple of smokes.

"Fuck, it's cold," Simon shivers, as we jump up and down to keep warm while we smoke to stay awake. "Maybe we should sleep awhile, McGruff. I can't keep me bloody eyes open. I'm shagged."

Back in the van, we try to sleep, but for me, it's just too cold. Remarkably, Z and Rat are huddled together and appear to be sleeping comfortably. Tim, who really wishes he'd brought a jacket now, is bumming hard, also unable to sleep.

"At least those two are sleeping," I mention to Simon.

"I'm not sleeping," says Z, barely opening his lips. "I'm too goddamn cold to do anything, including opening my eyes."

"Simon, make it warm, I don't care how you do it," pleads Rat through chattering teeth.

"Try turning on the heat, Einsteins," says Tim.

"If we turn on the heat with the engine running, we might run low on petrol," reasoned Simon.

"We could get carbon monoxide poisoning, you idiots," coughed the Master from the extra-ultra-super-cold back of the van.

"Just get some sleep, lads. You won't know you're cold if you're unconscious."

"This is true rock camping," I shiver after a moment of silence. I seem to drift between a very uncomfortable, freezing semi-consciousness and a variety of nightmares involving Alaska, walk-in refrigerators, a couple of ex-girlfriends, and other frigid tundra. I can finally take no more.

"Simon, wake up and drive and turn the goddamn heater on. We're gonna end up like that plane that crashed in the mountains and everybody had to eat everybody else."

"Who would we eat?" asked Rat, sounding like he was getting interested.

"Well, who would yield the most meat?" asked Z reasonably.

"McGruff?" Z and Rat both laugh at the notion of a roasted McGruffwich.

Simon kicks it on down the road, and finally the heat liberates us from such delusions. We drive a few more hours, and prior to getting to the border, we find a truck stop to hang in and thaw out even more efficiently. We drink black coffee until 11:00 a.m., with Dahl, presumably a human ice cube by now, remaining in the van.

"This tour is beyond belief," grumbles Rat. "I'll never do this shit again. If you're going to go out on the road, you at least have to live at human standards."

"Yeah, Dahl digs it. He thinks he's back in the army or something," says Z.

"He said it's going to be great when we get to Italy," said Tim. "Especially for you guys. Supposedly the women are wild there, that's what he keeps saying."

"He just says that to give us hope over the horizon," I opine. "It's always the next country where the women will be an army of Amazonian nymphomaniacs, where the food will be culinary ecstasy, where the locals will finally be nice to us. It keeps the troops going in lieu of money or fame."

"The prospect of pussy," grinned Simon. "I'm just fucking happy to get the fuck out of fucking France."

"Three whole 'fucks' in one sentence, m'man!" congratulates Z. A hideous looking family stares at us and sneers at our English profanity.

"Pass the fucking sugar."

8

REVENGE OF THE SUPERMODELS FROM THE BLACK LAGOON

(Italy)

OUR FIRST DAY IN Italy, land of love and pasta, is a day off, in Milan no less. We arrive at yet another Ibis at about 4:00 p.m. following an extraordinarily beautiful and rather relaxing drive over the Alps. This Ibis differs from the other ones we've stayed. It's nowhere near either a graveyard or a hospital. The sky is blue, with a slight breeze, the sun is shining down and it's comfortably warm. The Smell of Death is nowhere to be sniffed.

Following some well-needed showers, Tim, Z, Simon, and myself take off on foot to explore one of Europe's most fabulous cities. Rat, complaining of low funds, stays behind, and of course Dahl doesn't hit the town with us. A block away from the hotel, we hop on a streetcar, and just start ridin'. Once aboard, we try to figure out how to pay. It seems everybody else has some kind of token, which we neither possess nor have any idea how to obtain. We just play it cool and ride along, going as far as we can until an attendant, conductor, or whatever might come and check in on us freeloaders. We have no map, no idea which way to go, or where we are going, or what we want to do, but I suppose the reality of it is, the farther we can get from the hotel without laying down any cash, the better. Some guy in a black coat who might be an official of some sort, or perhaps just a thug, starts closing in on us, walking down the aisle of the car, so we bail off at the next convenient stop.

We spot a tall cathedral, and figure that's probably the middle of town, although it's still twenty long blocks away. We pass on hailing a cab and decide to just hoof it, enjoying the mild weather and taking in the wondrous sights of old castles and fortresses mingling with turn of the century architecture and somewhat modern buildings. We take our time—after all, we don't have to be anywhere—and drink in the spender of this magnificent city.

By the time we get to the Cathedral, it's almost dark. Next to the monumental building, one of the largest cathedrals in Europe, is a modern shopping mall that spreads out in four directions from a huge, marble-floored center topped with a glass ceiling. Once there, we begin to window shop and see what kind of food is available. We notice Tim has, as usual, disappeared.

"Goddammit, I'm so sick of that guy," grumbles Z. "Fuck it. I'm not waiting for him." Z storms off.

"Well, that leaves you and me, Simon."

"I'm not looking for him. Let's walk over to the cathedral and see if we can pop off some flash pictures."

Sure, we may be badass rockers eleven outta twelve days, but on that twelfth day, we're lame tourists. After taking in the sights—fountain, cathedral, the marble steps, the local girls—we walk back into the mall and see Z walking up, hands in pocket (with who knows what in there), a vision straight off of one of those old Sinatra cover paintings, not a care in the world.

"You see Tim?"

"No, can't you see that I look happy? The guy's a drag. I say we leave him here. I'm not a babysitter."

"Who would sell your Ultras CDs, then, Z?" asked Simon, forever the voice of reason.

Z just grumbles. I deduce from Simon's comeback that he intends on finding the little lost elf before moving on, which is exactly what we do. It takes about an hour, but we finally locate Tim huddled in a corner working on a slice of pizza.

"Well, nice of you to invite us to dinner," says Simon with maximum sarcasm. "We were getting a little bit hungry, we like the way you always think of us."

"Hey, man. I was hungry. I knew you guys would be geeking off, looking at churches or whatever. I'm bored with churches."

Z walks away pissed off again, but I grab him. I don't want to spend the whole night tracking mofos down. I try to get everyone back on the same page by suggesting dinner.

"Let's go eat at that place," I say, pointing to a classy joint in the mall from which rich culinary aromas are emanating.

"McGruff, how much money do you have?" asks tour boss Simon.

"Hell, I don't know. Must be fifty or sixty million lira.

"And how much, would you say roughly, is that in American dollars when you exchange it?"

"About fifteen bucks."

"Right. That place'll cost you at least sixty dollars, probably as much money as all of us have together."

"So you're saying a meal there is what, two, three million lira?"

They bodily drag me off to a brightly lit, walk-up cafeteria, which is nothing to look at but has great food nonetheless. We all order a smallish entree, salad, and some bread, except Tim, who orders a full half chicken. Where the hell does he put it all?

Following dinner, we strike out blind again and just start walking. I'm having fun, but our random approach to Milan will not work all night.

"In a city like this," I explain, "you gotta know what's up. You just can't stumble into some place and expect it to be the place. You know, Milan must have some rockin' hot spots, the places where the wild locals hang and kick out the good times in a major hedonistic way. That's what we gotta find out, and that's where we gotta go."

"Oh, I don't know," says doubting Simon. "I think we can just go about anywhere and have fun. I'm sure we'll find something good."

"What are you so sure about? This is a huge city, with little hideaways all over it. We don't know anything. We gotta track down some locals and get the inside dirt!"

"I like the idea of just exploring. It makes me feel like I'm learning the city on my own. It's good that way. The locals and what they might tell us—I can't be bothered."

"Simon, trust me on this, we gotta get information—information!"

"Well, you can do what you want. I'm just going to walk along 'til I find a place I fancy and go inside."

"No! We need a plan, damn it! We need the inside track. I'm telling you."

"Yeah, Bruce is right, Simon," chimes in Tim.

"You guys are a bunch of grandmothers. I've had it!" Simon shouts, and storms off up the street.

"What's with him?" asks Z.

"Simon, what's up!?" I shout after him.

"Fuck you!" he hollers back.

"I think we may be witnessing a Factsheet overdose, gentlemen," I warn Z and Tim.

"Hey, do you know where the hotel is from here?" asks the ever-pragmatic Z.

"Not really. I just know it's yet another Ibis. It could be anywhere, you know?"

"We'd better stop Simon, then," says Tim.

"Right!"

We all go running down the street, this being our second Monkees/Beatles scene to be re-enacted, and Simon takes off running too, trying desperately to escape the band he's supposed to road manage. We run for a solid ten minutes, until finally Simon, the youngest and by far the one in the best shape, collapses in a heap of exhaustion. "You bleeding fuckers, I hate you!" he pants. I hug him and pull him to his feet, slobbering the saliva that swells in your jowls after a sweaty run. "I'm sorry," I gasped. "Look, let's go get a beer. This evening will turn out great. I know it will. I'm sorry I was whining. Now stop being a fucking cry baby yourself and come on."

What men we were, swearing at each other like truck drivers, running through the streets like cat burglars, hugging each other in the way only real men, secure in their overt hetero-ness, can. How do we solve a disagreement: like real men, we sweep it under the carpet and go and get liquored up!

It's about 9:00 p.m. now, and we sequester ourselves at a round table in a roomy, pleasant local bar, somewhere in Milan. Beers are a handy 6,000 lira, chump change. A few locals come up and chat, recognizing the fact that we're not from 'round these parts. The people are all extremely cordial, and we ask one guy where we should go. He gets out a street map, and totally confuses us. We order a few more beers.

At 10:00, beers escalate in price to 7,000 lira. Inflation is really catching up with us. A girl walks by and sits down.

"You guys gotta be from the States, right?"

"Well, they are. I'm from England originally, but live in Holland now," says Simon, punctuating his facts with that sickening little boy smile he saves for charming the girls. This girl isn't even attractive. We all know Simon isn't the least bit interested in her. It's almost as if he just likes to stay in practice.

"We're on tour, with a rock 'n' roll band, one that you've never heard of," I inform.

"It's nice to meet some fellow Americans that aren't tourists. My name's Marcy. I'm from Cleveland."

"Cleveland rocks," says Tim.

"Say, Marcy. We're looking for a really great place to go and drink and hang out, someplace with some local color. What do you recommend?"

"Well, there's the Diva, that's gotten pretty popular. Drinks are pretty cheap there, for Milan. Wait a minute, I know, what am I talking about? You want to meet some girls?"

We look at each other and shrug, playing it cool.

"What kind of girls?" asks Z, giggling at the silliness of his question.

"Let me tell you, you want to go to Hollywood."

"You can say that again," I said, feeling instantly, suddenly homesick.

"No, Club Hollywood. It's the spot. Every model in Italy goes there, all the girls that do the French *Vogue* and *Cosmopolitan*, Gaultier runway girls, swimsuit models, you name it. Supermodels."

"Really? That's cool and all, but I can't imagine those kind of girls being even slightly interested in the likes of us," I say, ever the voice of reason.

"Are you kidding!? A bunch of longhaired rock 'n' roll guys—from AMERICA. They'll be all over you! A lot of the girls are from the States. They get fed up with the Italian guys. Those girls get so bored, sick and tired of the same old male models, who are all just a bunch of swishy homos anyway. I can see it now, when you guys walk in, it'll be all over!"

"You're serious? You're not putting us on?" queried Simon, thinking, as we all were, that it was too good to be true.

"Yes. Club Hollywood. Check it out. I tell ya, you won't regret it. Well, I gotta run, you guys have fun here in Milan."

"Yeah, hey thanks," we all yell after her.

"Great, now, what do we have that we didn't have a minute ago?" I ask the knights of the round table, who stare back at me blankly. "A PLAN. We now have a plan, a place to go where the locals go, the hip locals, the people in the know. We'll be in with the in-crowd, homeboys."

"Problem is," reasons Simon, "we may be a few billion lira shy of a minimum down payment on any serious partying or reasonable facsimile thereof."

Tim, who was constantly getting wired money from Mom and Dad back home, perks up. He just might be horny enough, and supermodel enticed enough, to bankroll this little safari into the inner-sanctum of the ultra-leggy, supermodel jungle.

"I only have francs left," he sadly informs. "I'm going to go exchange them. If I can find a post office, a tobacco shop, a drug dealer, anything, a twenty-four hour bank, there's got to be a place where I can get some money."

He darts out the door as if he had found the pizza and fritter mother lode. "Good luck!" Simon yells after him. "Well, that's quite likely the last we'll see of Tim. Here, McGruff, here's 22,000 lira, get us another round of draft."

We sit and chat about nothing much, more time passes, it's after 11:00 p.m. now, and we've finished off another round waiting for Tim. We're giving the eye to some local girls when their boyfriends aren't looking. All of a sudden, we hear a fracas of some sort going on right outside the bar's front door. Moments later, Tim storms in, returns to his chair at the table, sits down, swearing all the time under his breath, and slams a pack of cigarettes down on the table.

"Let me guess, you've just decided to take up smoking and you're mad as hell about it," I joked.

"These guys at the front door, they said they could get me the liras, I gave them forty francs, was it fifty francs, oh, I don't even know!"

"What guys at the door?" asks Simon.

"The Pakistani towelheads from hell, those damn... merchants."

Marcy, whom we'd thought had left ages ago, suddenly reappeared, and began filling in the holes in Tim's story like an off-camera narrator, like Rod Serling at the beginning of *The Twilight Zone*. "They're Moroccan, actually."

"What?" we ask in unison.

"Moroccan. They're Moroccan."

"More rockin' than what? They ripped me off!" exclaims Tim.

"Moroccan, from Morocco. Idiot!" Even Simon was losing his patience with Tim.

Marcy explains, "These guys are street hustlers. They set up here every night around this time, selling cigarettes, gum, candy, and if you know the right signals and code words, cheap street heroin, switchblades, and handguns. They saw your friend coming. He tried to get them to exchange money. They said yes, and then, instead of the liras, they handed him a pack of Marlboros. When he complained, they simply said that's the deal they mutually agreed upon, and when the management came out to see what the fuss was about, they stuck to their story. They've moved on by now, that was their big score this hour."

That having been cleared up, Marcy again disappears into the woodwork, almost as if she is some sort of information fairy that just pops up when we have an unanswerable question.

"Well, Tim. Give me a cigarette!" demands Z.

"Yeah, I fancy one of those, too," says Simon. "Let's see, I'm just trying to work out the exchange rate in me head, well, then, this is about one of your American dollars for every cigarette. That's some pretty mean bargaining, I'd have to say!"

"Fuckin' Pakistani jackass!" swears Tim.

"No, he was more rockin'," chides Z.

FOLLOWING TIM'S CIGARETTE FIASCO, we're now strapped for cash more than ever, so we make the brisk evening walk across increasingly chilly Milanese streets to save on cab fare to Club Hollywood. We show up right around midnight, and we're buzzed with anticipation and more than a little tap beer. Simon and I walk up to the doorman, bypassing the queue, showing off business cards, and spewing several lines of bullshit. "Ah, yes, rock 'n' roll band on tour from America, looking for a place to blow off steam, Nikki Sixx recommended we come here, said ask for Mumble Harumph..."

It actually worked, and we're soon down four endless flights of stairs into the dank underworld of Club Hollywood. It's a dimly lit, lengthy, thin room stretching out from the entrance at the bottom of the stairs. A fat, Italian rapper is working through some shout-outs while his wiry sidekick spins the wheels of steel. We try to look nonchalant—not at all an easy feat as we are by-and-away the most shabbily dressed people we can immediately see—and we casually walk to the bar and order a round of beer.

Four cans—not bottles, for God's sake—of Heineken wholly deplete our supply of cash. We acknowledge this fact and walk toward the dance floor. We all stop, and silently share the same thought, no question about it.

My God! This is beyond the realm of comprehension. This is a veritable garden of earthly delights, a swarming beehive of Cosmopolitan magazine covers, all dressed in the wildest, très chic styles from Milan and Gay Paree. Surely we'd been run over by a bus outside, and we're now being deposited in Heaven.

There's a roped-off section for VIPs. We were let in for free. Therefore, we're VIPs. We assemble at a table behind the rope. No one talks for a few minutes. We just look into the sea of dancers, who are about eighty percent women, ninety-nine percent of whom are postcard magazine-cover beautiful.

Z leans over like he's gonna bum a smoke. "Can you believe this?!" he asks. "You'd never see this in L.A. Not anywhere."

"Nope. Not Beverly Hills, not Hollywood..." We look at each other.

"Not even the Rainbow!" we say to each other, chuckling. Another few minutes pass, and we just sit quietly, almost reverently, just watchin' the girls dance. The ladies all dance in this sort of detached manner, just kinda wafting about as if they're unaware of anyone else on the dance floor, even though they're packed in like sardines.

"We're about out of beer," says Tim. "Are we just going to sit here?" It's obvious we're all feeling too shy to dive into the sea.

"I have Traveler's Cheques," Z announces severely. "Maybe I could cash them in here, somehow."

"Go to that bloke at the front door that let us in. See if he can help you," offers Simon. "You're Sicilian, let him have it with some Italian bullshit."

About fifteen minutes pass and Z returns. "Wow, that was weird. The guy at the door says to me, 'Sure, we can probably cash those in for you. But you gotta see Guido, only he can do it.' So I wait around a few minutes, wonderin' what's goin' on. I go back up to the guy, and he tells me to just wait. Waiting, waiting. Then some other guy comes up and taps me on the shoulder and says, 'Come see Guido now.' So I followed him into this little office, and there's Guido, with the spats, the expensive overcoat with the white scarf tucked under the lapels, the slicked-back wavy white hair. It was wild. Guido just grumbles, mutters something, and sticks out his hand. I give him the checks and he goes over to the desk, then I notice these two thug-looking guys sitting over on a couch against the wall, just sittin' there watching me. So Guido opens the desk and pulls out the loot. I'm not sure, but I think I saw a Magnum in the drawer when he got out the money. Anyway, he gave me the money. Want a beer? Only the best for Guido's friends!"

"Yeah. Get me a beer, Z," responds Simon. "Just set it on the table. I've got the urge to go dancing."

Donna Summer couldn't have declared a more definitive rallying call. Tim stays behind while the remaining trio assaults the dance floor with a series of poorly executed hip-thrusts and bad-mannered pouts, occasionally tossing our hair. Strike the pose! Do Ya Wanna Funk with Me? We slither through the tangled web of Milan's petite and elite, splitting off solo here, only to regroup and catwalk side-by-side a few bars later. No one is really dancing with anyone else, it's all mixed groups of threes and fours, with other people dancing solo, hoping to assimilate into a group. None of us seem to be assimilating. After twenty minutes of this frivolity we tire and head back to the beers.

Nestled in the bosom of the VIP area, we drink expensive canned beer. "They don't seem to care about us," observes Z. "I thought that dame said we were going to be attacked."

"You're right," I say. "I've never felt so invisible. Do I look like Claude Rains?"

Back into the fray go the three, ready for more hijinks on the high seas of hip-hop. Simon has made contact with a pair of girls, perhaps sisters, thus forming a group, a trio in this case. A few minutes later someone touches my shoulder gently. I look back and see a mountain of teased black hair and a crooked smile. I smile back, it's the polite thing to do, and the next thing I know this creature of the night is grinding its pelvis into my leg. Freak out, Le Freak! Didn't they do that in *Saturday Night Fever*? I look directly at my newfound playmate and almost pop out of my shoes. Good lord, my mom's bridge partners are more fine! This woman is scary. I just start dancing in the other direction but she follows, grinning, a few steps behind. She still has a nice figure (given her incalculable descent into antiquity), and there's something oddly appealing about that John Waters wet dream hairdo, but that face, it's strictly

B-movie ocean monster, Black Lagoon a-Go-Go. I turn again but somehow she's in front of me, dancing. I fake to the right but she blocks, grabbing my arm. She says something in Italian, so I just reply, "I don't know."

"Oh, English. Buy me a drink, coke and whiskey. Okay, English?"

"No way. I'm down to my last four thousand lira. That's only enough for a cigarette or two."

She departs as quickly as she arrived. Back at the table Z is talking to a guy with tight jeans, perfect underwear ad hair, and no shirt, holding an acoustic guitar. He gets up and walks to the bar as I approach the table.

"That guy's a model," Z announces.

"You're kidding."

"Yeah. He plays guitar at this restaurant, too. He just came from there, wherever it is. He said last week Poison came in here. He said they walked in, grabbed two or three girls each, and split, like they were getting snacks at a drive-thru. Can you believe that?"

"Maybe we just ain't wearin' the right cologne. You dig me, Abraham?"

"Huh?"

DREAM SEQUENCE

THE STROBE LIGHT FLICKERS in a steady stream of black and white film noir contrast. A photo studio slowly comes into focus. Wearing trashed Levi's and a $200 Pierre Cardin white cotton shirt open to the waist, I stumble to the storage shelf and grab my favorite

Nikon. My assistant, Gil, who looks remarkably like Ratboy, comes into the spacious loft area carrying lighting umbrellas and electric cable. Everything is still stark and black and white.

"Claudette is here. Shall I show her in?"

"Yeah, yes, of course."

Claudette. I'm scheduled to do a fashion layout with Claudette, the hottest model in all Milan. Cosmo, Vogue, Glamour...been on the cover of all of them dozens of times. The public wants more and more shots of Claudette.

"I'm going to be happy for the rest of my life. When my brand new baby is my brand new wife, Claudette..."

Roy Orbison had written that for the Everlys. He in fact did make Claudette his wife. They rode their Harleys together into oblivion, only Claudette never came back. She rode hers into full-on Leader of the Pack destruction and doom. They say Roy was never the same again, and I don't doubt it, being the veteran of a few reasonably severe broken hearts myself, you never come back quite the same. But then again, they say a lot of things. Who knows?

Claudette—the one on hand at the moment—enters the room. She's all blue-steel cold and Nico icy, an Edie Sedgwick cream dream updated to the last decade of the present/final century. I know her eyes are brown, but they glare at me black, like a vampire. Her skin is like that too, almost translucent. Her hair, dark brown, one length, and parted in the middle, is surprisingly simple and unfashionable. In fact, nothing about her seems that amazing, but when you put the whole thing together and assess the big picture, she is an undeniable goddess of sensual beauty, a creature to be worshipped and desired. She does not extend her hand to greet me. She does not smile or blink.

"Shall we?" she intones in a voice so low and monotone it causes me to reassess my black and white world.

"Sure."

I flick on the lights and grab the Nikon.

"Over here, against the scrim."

She walks over in front of the white backdrop, stands, and looks at me. "What do you want me to do?"

"Just be you, that's all. Let the film capture it." I start clicking away. Gil comes into the scene and begins double-checking some cable, bringing out two glasses and a bottle of champagne in the meantime. He has his gig down, my main man.

"Thanks, Gil. Uh, you can go for the night. I'm all set. Lock up on your way out."

"You got it, McGruff."

Why did he call me McGruff? What does that mean?

"Alright, sell it to me. Sell those clothes to me. You to me!" I encourage, as my shutter keeps click-click-clicking away on Claudette's five-foot-eleven frame. Hands on hips with maximum pout, she is working it, and begins to come alive.

"That's good, real good, yeah, yeah, yeah, give me more baby, more. Attitude! Yeah, that's it, go all the way with it!"

It isn't long before she's on the floor, writhing like a snake in the midday sun, alternately smiling and pouting. She expounds unbridled raw sensuality. I straddle her, camera still snapping like an Uzi. I look down and purr encouragement. She seems to get increasingly hot and bothered by my encouragement, squirming and now working orgasmic moaning into her repertoire. She's extrapolating beyond the realms of fashion photography into a world where she and I exist purely and simply to be beautiful and, it follows, to make passionate love.

I set the camera down and lay my full weight on top of her, as her arms and legs ensnare me. There's no use for words as clothes begins to fly from our bodies, to be strewn about as casualties of love. I kiss her, a long, endless kiss, it seems to go on for hours, but it couldn't have, could it? When I once again open my eyes, the world is in color, a brash, harsh, videocam six o'clock news color. I look down and Claudette had transmogrified into something otherworldly.

The dream snaps, as my dreams have a tendency to do, and I realize it is a dream. Unfortunately, I am incapable of waking up. She turns into the girl that called me "English" at the club, an old withered bag with teased hair and evil eyes looking to separate me from my lira. Her eyes begin bulging out, and her whole head begins pulsating and growing in size. Her skin begins to crack and separate, blood spurts from the cracks, followed by a greenish-white puss-like ooze which seems to emanate from every pore on her face. The human skin dissolves, and a scaly, blue-green monster head with sharp teeth and bloody, slathering mouth makes itself known. The amphibian sea monster rises from the floor—teased black hair intact, and begins stalking me, fin-hands outstretched, as if trying to strangle me. Shit, why can't I wake up?! Damn, if I die in my dream, then I'll die for real. Bummer! Then I'll never know about the real girls of Italy, the ones that are supposed to drag us around by the hair in full cave woman conquest. I'll simply be a footnote in some Italian coroner's report. "Died in his sleep, not sure why. Had a hard-on the size of a Venice canal boat." Real great. What a way to go.

Music comes up around me—in mono—a Hans J. Salter monster movie tirade of screeching horns and thundering tympani. The chase is on as I hurl cameras, umbrellas, light rigs, anything to slow the beast down. I quickly turn to run out the door, but the door just leads to a hall that is endless. I run and run. I can move quickly and the monster moves at a Frankensteinian crawl, but every time I turn to check the progress of my escape, the creature is a few yards behind me. I turn again to look ahead and run smack dab dead into a wall.

I wake up with a start, all sweaty with morning wood.

END DREAM SEQUENCE

●

FOLLOWING OUR SEVERE EGO bashing at the hands of
Milan's beautiful, we land in Florence the next day to
set up in a huge venue, Auditorium Flog. We had met
up with Giovanni earlier in the day at our hotel. He is to
be our guide through our first day or two in Italy, much
like Kike was in Spain and Geordie was in France. The
first thing Giovanni does is hop in the van and direct us
to another hotel, a small, family run operation with—get
this—electric toilets.

European toilets had been a point of fascination for
all concerned, especially Jeff. He was particularly fond
of the Dutch toilets, which had a raised section in the
porcelain to catch shit before it drops into the water.
This way, you could get a good look and an equally good
whiff of your stool before you disposed of it. Dahl loved
this for some reason, and promised more pronounced
"shit shelves" in Germany. But here, in this little
hotel, was a technological variation on the world-class
commode that hadn't caught on. Your waste went from
the top of the bowl into a lower, small, square holding
tank. An electric motor would then shred it. Maybe with
all the pasta and whatnot, they figured their shit was just
a little tougher and could use a good grinding before
being pumped into some of Italy's finer sewers.

At any rate, the lady concierge at this delightful
hotel gives me a rundown in very rough English, "Don't
put anything in there besides what's supposed to go in

there—no paper, tampons, rubbers, financial documents, M-80s, nothin'." Okay, Okay, it's cool.

My room is super small, but it's all mine, and the television works. They have a channel with nothing but models on it twenty-four hours a day. Outside my door is a magazine rack with some interesting Italian mags. I steal one that's the Italian version of *Cosmopolitan*; I know that since Gina's Italian she'll probably get a kick out of it. There are a few other fashion mags, most with a liberal sprinkling of female nudity, more so than in their American counterparts. I take advantage of the visual stimulation and my momentary privacy and have a quick jack—ah, tension relieved.

Arriving at the Flog, we notice the Ramones headlined here a week ago, the Violent Femmes were coming up. It seemed like a cool place. They have a great spread for us, and Tim literally dives in as if it were a pool. We eat like animals for a solid twenty minutes. Then, we pull in our amps and drums. Two guys are setting up a massive P.A., and it is obvious it's going to take a while. The three Factsheeters depart for a walk in the oncoming drizzle.

As we walk, Rat complains about the tour—the conditions, the funding, the crowds, the music, the bossman, the usual. Z agrees, but is more easygoing; I don't think he cares that much, he's glad to be in Europe more than anything. I try to point out the good side of things— the travel, the sights, the occasionally great audience, the eh, eh...oh well, let's just try to enjoy Florence.

This city is, in fact, one of the few important European cities that missed out on the big World War II party. Most everything stands as it has for six or seven hundred years. A beautiful monastery is right behind the Flog, and we walk around it, checking out the amazing woodcarvings on the doors, the fantastic tile walkways, the stained glass. The light drizzle refuses to turn into rain. Ahead in the distance, I hear a sound, like gentle guitar chords. "Do you hear that?"

"Yeah, let's check it out," answers Rat.

We walk across a courtyard, through a playground, to what seems to be some sort of youth center. As we approach, we discover it's a band practicing. The music becomes more familiar, and we all laugh as we recognize it.

"It's fucking 'Hotel California.'"

"That's hysterical, too much!"

Back at the hall, soundcheck is about to commence. Dahl is strapping on his Les Paul Junior as he steps on to the stage. He plays a monstrous E chord as he hollers into the mic. "Shiiiittt!" he screams, and it booms through the P.A. along with the sound of static. "Man, I just got shocked bad!"

I take my bass, and being careful to hold on only to the wood, touch the metal tuning machine heads to my microphone. ZZIIIITT! You can see a small arc of electricity arc between the tuning heads and the mic, right where my face will be in a few hours. "It's not grounded. You have to ground the P.A.," I address the two PA guys.

They look at each other, then at the gear, then at the incomprehensibly confusing tangled web of wires and cables they have plugged together to make this thing, eh, work. They talk in Italian, and then, in rough English, confess they don't know what they're doing.

"You guys didn't electrocute the Ramones, did you?"

No answer. They flick a few switches, but no luck.

"What if we can't fix it?" they ask us.

"Then we can't play!" responds the ever-surprising Dahl, who usually takes every hardship with a smile. My boy don't like gettin' shocked, though.

Simon comes in with an elaborate power strip junction box, equipped to deal with a variety of plug and grounding variations. Finally, the English wizard sorts it out, and we can now check without fear of musician meltdown.

Following the check, Giovanni takes us to a simple little Italian café. There, we order genuine Italian pizza, tortellini, spaghetti—"the works, babe." Every bite is an orgasm, an explosion of taste bud ecstasy that's totally new, even to a second-generation Italian like Z. Though we try to resist, gorging like pigs seems imperative, even though it will make our performance sluggish at best.

Giovanni, a good natured, dark, and naturally attractive young guy, has repeatedly said that tonight's show is going to be packed. We go back to club with a fair bit of anticipation. So far Italy had been pretty cool, and tonight might just be a blowout.

We still are way early. There are mats all over the floor, laid out for people to come and sit and watch old movies that are shown before the band plays. There's a fortune teller setting up by two marvelously sexy coat check girls, word comes down the pike that the fortune teller doesn't like us and that we should avoid her. I pay no heed, and instead concern myself with assembling a few of these mats into a makeshift mattress for a quick nap. Z and Rat follow suit while Dahl goes to the dressing room. Simon and Tim take the stage and perform their version of Elvis: The Tone Deaf Years. Factsheet applauds and eggs them on as Simon delivers a suitably snarling vocal à la The King.

"Treat mah lock a foooooo, threat mah mean 'n' crooooo, bu-u-u-t LOVE ME!"

They play a movie of an Italian silent movie comedian. His name was Fernando or something, and a few people wander in and appreciatively giggle. They stare at the geeks on the floor, but all and all don't pay too much attention to us. Eventually, we're told by someone of dubious authority that we have to get up off the floor, so we head into the dressing room, where a weirdo is bugging Dahl with a million irrelevant questions. The Master is polite, but visibly uncomfortable.

This was unusual for Jeff, as he seemed most at home—lately anyways—in the social climate consisting of himself and his fans, but not with this guy. For some reason, this gentleman's overbearing manner, wild hand gestures, fantastically far-fetched stories concerning his success as a musician in his own right, and the certain indefinable something in his manner that suggested he could fly off the handle into a violent rage without any warning, seemed to make Dahl uneasy. Yet, there Jeff sat, arms folded, politely listening to the guy. Meanwhile, tuning was checked, beers were gulped, blank stares were exchanged. Pre-show boredoms.

Finally, an hour and a half later, we begin. I have one of those nights musicians dread. The mind is with it but the fingers just don't care. Maybe all that tortellini is clogging up my transmitters. We're playing to about 700 youthful Italians, an unusually even mix of boys and girls and our largest crowd so far. Come to find out, they don't know or much care who the hell we are. We are the "rock band" for the evening—they are not familiar with our name or our music. There was no preview of tonight's show in the local paper. We are merely what happens after the films and before the all-night disco. We could be anybody.

About a third of them are starting to get into us a bit, but a third are patiently waiting for us to finish, and the other third are visibly annoyed. Over to my right, in front of Ratboy, some guy is laying on stage, sandwiched in between two floor monitors, completely asleep. We are blaring at over one hundred decibels, but he sleeps through it just fine.

The second we finish playing, the club staff immediately begins transforming the venue. While we move amps, they set up a serving table on stage with a huge, festive cake and countless bottles of champagne. The audience crowds grabs small plates of cake and plastic champagne glasses filled with bubbly. A feisty, energetic red head appears seemingly out of nowhere, grabs me by the arm, and pulls me to the cake table. A few people recognize me as the guy in the band they never heard of that just played and hand me cake and champagne. I notice Ratboy getting the same treatment. He looks over at me from across the table and flashes his little Rat smile.

"Just like Dahl said. They grabbed me and said 'c'mere.'" We both laughed, spitting out small crumbs of cake.

Soon, the floor erupts with dancing, and the mix pits Creedence Clearwater against Donna Summer against Moby against sweet Gene Vincent. Factsheet hit the floor, where, instead of having to dance together like losers, we are surrounded by friendly, young, pretty girls, all smiles and gently waving arms. I do the hustle up next to m'man, Z.

"This is more like it. Champagne, cake, babes, dancing, anonymity, this is great."

"I know. I can't believe it. It's too good to be true."

Sure enough, no sooner had he said this that Simon burst the bubble of momentary enjoyment. "C'mon. We're goin'."

He turned and walked away.

"Fuck him," I yelled at Z. "We don't have to go. We've played our show. We did our job. It's Miller time." We dance on to three more songs before the Grim Reaper of Fun returns with his cloak and sickle. "I said, 'C'mon. We're going." Again, he turns and walks away.

"What's up with him? We don't have to go just because he said so," Rat insists.

We go off to the dressing room to cut the other three loose. Simon looks at us as we walk in. "Ok, great. You're ready. Let's go."

"We want to stay," states Rat, flatly. "We'll help you load the van, and then meet you back at the hotel later."

"You can't do that," barks Dahl in a voice so gruff and hoarse it was astonishing he finished the set. He punctuated his sentence with a frightening, heavy cough, the kind that reverberates deep down by the diaphragm with an almost echo-like effect. As if it were too difficult to continue speaking, he merely gives the cue, "Simon..."

"Right. The hotel locks up at night, and we only have one key between the six of us. We all have to return together."

"Well, we'll just come later and knock to get in," I offer.

"No, there's no night watchman. Our rooms are upstairs, so you'll wake the whole bottom floor."

"We'll take the van back to the hotel and drop you off and come back," smiles Rat, who probably remembered as he said it that this tact had failed before.

"You're not taking the van," says Simon.

"Period," hacked Jeff.

"Look," I say, "let us go back with you guys, lock you up tight, and come back here in a cab, is that alright?"

"No, we're all going together, ALRIGHT?" Simon said, at the end of his rope.

"This is bullshit, Jeff," said Ratboy, quietly but firmly. "You tell us over and over what fun it's going to be in Italy. We finally get here, and you want to lock us up like Cinderellas."

"Yeah, we play the show, we play your music and make you sound great, then we can't even party a bit," says Z, who shakes his head, picks up his stick bag, and heads outside, presumably toward the van.

"I'm sick of you guys and your stupid rock star attitudes. This isn't about that. It's about music. It happens to be about *my* music. This is *my* tour. You're here because of *me*. And I'm about to completely lose my voice..."

Indeed, he sounded like a radio being tuned out.

"...I can't argue about this anymore. If I lose my voice, we're all fucked."

"I can sing," I interject, not sure if I was trying to lighten things up or agitate them even further. "Tim can sing, for that matter."

At that, Simon just starts loading the van. We all silently pitched in, not even looking at Simon or Jeff. Simon is in the van, arranging drums toward the back. I hand him a tom case. When it's just the two of us, I say, "Dude, are you doing this just to get on Jeff's good side? This line of attack isn't like you. You of all sex starved people."

"That's not even funny, McGruff. Fuck you! I'm fucking knackered. I'm beat. You try driving all day, and dealing with the money, and hurrying you lot along. It gets to you. Jeff's the boss. I'm exhausted, and that's the way it is."

"But you overslept an hour today, we got you up, and we only had a three hour drive. The most difficult thing you've done all day was that Elvis impersonation."

"Damn you, I'm beat, and I'm sick to death of YOU. Get the fuck out of my face, get your gear packed, and let's fucking go!"

As I walk back to grab my bass, Z catches my arm.

"We have an auxiliary plan," he informs. "We're gonna go back to the hotel, go up to our rooms—me and Rat are together and you're solo—and come back down after they've gone in. Giovanni has a key and he's going to get us back here and make sure we don't get lost. It's all about Giovanni."

The ride back to the hotel is another silent one, accented with the basso profundo coughing of our leader. We park across the street from the hotel, grab our guitars, and go inside. It is exactly 2:00 a.m. as we reconvene in the street.

"How much is a cab?"

"It's two o'clock. Is it worth going?"

"Are you sure it's still going on?"

Giovanni assures us it doesn't end until 4:00 a.m., or later, and suggests we should just walk and save the money. We could do it in twenty minutes.

"It took us fifteen to drive it!" I point out.

"Yes, true, but I know a shortcut," Giovanni assures.

We walk quickly, which also helps keep us warm, laughing and running now and again. We cross a bigger intersection and notice we're being tailed by some cops. Within a block, they pull up alongside and shine a flashlight at us. Giovanni runs up to the small, battered, laughable police car. He says something in Italian and they split.

"They don't like long hair, or people that look like they might be American, or people under fifty, pretty much," he said, in the giggling fashion that was his happy-go-lucky nature.

Forty-five minutes later, we're huffing and puffing up the long driveway to the club. People are passing us by in groups. Giovanni inquires where everyone is going and is informed that the club is closing down.

"What happened to four o'clock?" The answer came in shrugs. Everything just seemed to burn out—no more champagne, no more Gene Vincent, no zing for living.

We go back on in, and some kids that liked the band see how disappointed we are and buy us a round of beers. We strike up conversation, and when we get asked to leave so the club can lock up some twenty minutes later, they give us a ride home. One of them knows Giovanni, I guess, and when they drop us back, they shout out plans to meet after work tomorrow. Rat points out how friendly, boisterous, and ultimately loud they are. We like them a lot, and bid our friends goodbye. I curl up in my room with some television, all the while keeping a watchful eye on that psychedelic toilet.

OUR SECOND AND LAST Italian date is a rescheduled, last minute engagement, where we're to play at a water park of all things, right on the Adriatic Sea. Keep in mind, this is the third week in February, not exactly prime beach weather. The resort is officially closed, but they do have regular Saturday Night dances there, and we're opening.

After we check-in, and the usual panic ensues about us getting to soundcheck hours before it's truly necessary, Rat and I decide to see the ocean. We walk through the nearly abandoned, Saturday afternoon streets of this old-fashioned resort toward the gentle rolling waves of the sea. A few scattered locals play and run along the beach, a big black dog swims out after a stick. It's a scene reminiscent of our childhoods. We collect seashells, and find some pretty cool ones. It is very relaxing, a whole hour off, and we drink in this quiet ocean's beauty and savor the moment—okay, off to soundcheck.

Walking back to our hotel, a group of elementary school kids circle us on their bikes, giggling and pointing.

"God," says Rat, "think about it. Even little kids think we are losers. They just laugh at us. They know."

Perhaps longhaired guys with velveteen caps, black leather jackets, and tight jeans didn't walk by everyday. Or maybe it was just obvious we were losers, even to eight-year-olds.

THE CLUB, CALLED THE Rock Planet, is right on the grounds of the water park. The room itself is situated between a huge, three-dimensional planet that serves as a marquee. A giant concrete whale stands guard over the algae-infested, temporarily abandoned water rides.

The club was nice, but it was colder than the tomb at Montargis. It had plush, half-moon booths for the patrons. I find a suitable one and curl up and crash out for an hour or so. The booth was made from purple velvet, the same color as my cap. So much that when I got up from my nap, the hat camouflaged with the cloth and I ended up leaving it behind. At a major loss, I mean, no one likes losing their favorite hat. At the time, I remained unaware of my carelessness.

Giovanni stayed in Florence. Aldo was sent in his place, a man who looks like GG Allin. Is it omen or coincidence, I silently ponder, as he rides in the van with us, escorting us to a restaurant where our feast will even out-do the previous evening. In fact, everything about tonight is an exaggeration of last night. The club is colder, the soundmen are more incompetent, the audience is younger, drunker, and more unconcerned about anything having to do with the band, and we spend even more time waiting around doing absolutely nothing.

Even though we'd mingled with the audience the previous evening, it was clearly not the beginning of a trend. We were back to the scenario so familiar in France and Holland. Now, we are perceived as so old by the crowd of fifteen-year-olds that we're not even within their social sphere. Following the show, Simon notices us quickly trying to get the gear in the van. The tables have effectively turned.

"Now, I like this, all these young flowers, waiting to be plucked," said the English one.

"I don't feel well. I've had a sore throat all day," Rat said, and it was true enough. "I just want to get back to the hotel."

"How 'bout you, McGruff. Bet you fancy a nibble."

"Simon, I could have fathered these children. Besides, they're not interested in us. We'd have better luck back in Milan, where the girls are at least old enough to drive."

"Oh, it's different when the shoe's on the other foot, isn't it?"

"Yeah, it is," Z counters, jumpin' right on in. "We won't make a stink if you wanna come back after we go home, or if you just want to stay here and let us go home. Do What Thou Wilt!"

As we load up the van, the Factsheet Three grumble about this and that, but mostly just marvel at how fucked up these kids are, tripping over each other, puking on each other, fondling each other in random bisexual combinations. A tall, skinny kid walks by. Z points him out to me.

"Hey, that punk's got yer hat!"

"That's impossible! How could he have my hat?"

"Sure looked like it. Where would a kid like that get a hat like that in a place like this?"

We look at each other, and I realize he's right. I'd blown it. I'd lost my favorite hat, and now some drunken, wet-nosed Italian scum was wearing it, free of charge. He didn't even have to go shopping for it. He probably just sat on it and discovered it. It made me seethe, but I could not see him anymore. The idea of running blindly into this veritable ticking time bomb of intoxicated youthful energy made me queasy.

I bitch about my hat all the way back to our seaside rendezvous, where Rat and I share a room. It's the first night I've seen him really sick, and if I'm not mistaken, the first night in ages I've been pegged to share with him. Is it an omen or a coincidence?

We settle in and—great luck—*The Rocky Horror Picture Show* is on, in English and uncut.

"Don't dream it, be it," Tim Curry gasps. It's like a postcard from home.

Italy had seemed like the place to go really wild and have the time of our lives, a time that either kills you or becomes family legend. But it didn't happen. Maybe another time, maybe under different circumstances. For now...

Ciao, Bella!

9
THEY KILL RABBITS, DON'T THEY?

(Prague)

FROM THE ADRIATIC SEA, Dahl takes the wheel and speeds us through an Austrian snowstorm. I navigate but finally fall asleep with the map crumbled in my lap, serving as a bib to catch my oozing drool. I haven't slept more than five hours since Lyon. I just can't keep from nodding out now. We wake at the German checkpoint. Serious border guards press their faces against the van's windows and survey our tiny travel chamber.

Everyone sort of wakes up at once. "What's happening, what's going on?"

"We're being rousted by the German federales, gentlemen," Dahl replies. "We gotta go talk turkey."

Two soldiers—I guess they were soldiers, they had khaki green uniforms and pistols on their belts—take us into a room. They speak German back and forth, and punctuate their foreign comments with excited laughter. This would usually follow a close observation of someone's hair or clothes, then, "Hahahaha."

They grow very serious all of a sudden, and stare Dahl down. "You, in there," they say, pointing to yet another room. They follow Dahl in and slam the door.

"What do you think they're doing in there?" Tim wonders.

"I don't know, but I'll tell you, these guys don't fuck around," Rat replies most earnestly.

"Mmm," Simon just nods his head.

"I used to cross these borders all of the time, coming in and out of Switzerland, going off to London, whatever," Rat recalls. "They would mess with you just for the hell of it, especially if you had funny hair or looked like a rocker or something like that. They assumed you had drugs. The German borders were among the worst. I remember they would always pull out the plastic gloves, and want to look up your asshole."

"Great. You don't see any plastic gloves lying anywhere, do you?" I ask.

"The trick is, you have to act like you want it. They'd get out the gloves, and I'd perk up, act like I was getting excited." Rat demonstrated, making the happy face that resembled a rat about to make a big cheese score. "I'd start to become overly cooperative. 'Oh, you want to look up my butt!? Shall I pull my pants down now??!!' I'd take my belt off, and they'd begin to back down. Pretty soon, they're hustling me along on my way as quickly as possible."

Dahl emerges from the room, slightly grinning. The Germans point to Z and simply say, "You. Come." Again the door slams.

"What happened?" everyone asks Dahl.

"Nothing. They just asked a few question and had me empty my pockets. Nothing to it."

"No plastic gloves, right?" I wanted to be sure.

"None for me, but you guys..." He looks mainly at Tim and I. "I don't know."

Everyone gets the same simple treatment as Dahl, and soon we're on our way. An hour later we're in Munich, to play once again with the Jon Spencer Blues Explosion. They're not around, so we endure another marathon soundcheck—geez, what's the point anymore? I've been cold all day, so I load up on coffee. Five cups, six cups, *How obnoxious is it possible to get?* I wonder, as the caffeine transforms me into hyper-jerkman. The human body is but a laboratory designed to withstand such investigation.

We think Spencer is headlining, but it turns out we are. With a critically acclaimed debut LP just out and years of NY art-noise-rock history behind him, Spencer is quietly miffed about his spot on the bill. Word is he views us as a nostalgia act, a group with a weak set, padded with covers. Hey, who's to argue? It's just showbiz, babe.

Spencer and his Blues Explosion show up as we finish our check, looking beat. They've been out just over ten days, but we look better off. We're going on five weeks. The band's other guitarist besides Spencer was Judah, a New Yawker. He sits down at my table and silently sips a cup of coffee.

"So, how's your tour coming along?"

"Eh, alright, I guess," he says. "Our road manager is insane. He's either crazy or he's just fuckin' stupid."

He's talking about Claude from Orlèans.

"The other night I was sleepin' in the van, and I woke up—the other guys were asleep. There's Claude, rollin' down the highway on the wrong side of the road, headlights comin' right at us. 'Hey, fuckface, look what the fuck yer doin'!' Moron, I tell ya. It's been going like that, yeah. It's been going a lot like that. We get lost in every city we go to, and most of them have been in France. The guy's supposed to be fuckin' French! He can't even set up our equipment right, and he's been doing it for a week. Look at him up there! Geez!"

Judah started chuckling at his predicament, and I joined in. I confessed we were lost most everywhere we went, too. Our tour had the luxury of hotels almost every night, while Spencer, like most American bands coming across the waters for the first time, were flopping where they could: fan's houses, club apartments, in the van, wherever. We'd only had to do that a couple of times so far, so by comparison, we were very lucky.

After a quick change at the hotel, we return to watch the Blues Explosion, who turn in an awesome, high-energy set of their skewed roots rock, while the crowd stands watching them, giving little back to the band. I felt a little bad for them. They were really playing well and getting limited enthusiasm from the nonchalant crowd. It reminded me of our Italian expedition.

The audience here tonight, despite their ambivalence to Spencer, is a rock crowd. They've come purposely to be rocked in one manner or another, unlike those Italians. And, to top it off, for the first time in a club for close to two weeks, there is artificial heat being pumped into the interior environment. We are not freezing.

Despite our exhaustion—I feel it's caught up with me recently more than anyone else—we play an extra-long set, to a pretty enthused crowd. Following the show, we chat with Spencer's guys in the dressing room, and gather up our shit to get a good night's sleep. I'm so damn tired I can barely walk properly.

"Hi! Where are you going?"

I turn—with difficulty—and look up to see a sexy girl with an Ilsa, She Wolf of the SS, blonde hairdo looking right at me. I try to make a nondescript exit to the van. She exhales a cloud of cigarette smoke in my direction.

"I guess I'm gonna go to my hotel and pass out."

She emits a forced laugh. "Well, why not come to a party with me? Me and my friends are going, it's going to be an all night orgy of alcohol."

She certainly has a commanding grasp of my native tongue. She tells me her name is Elke, and I attempt to explain my condition and situation to her. I try not to sound any more pathetic than I feel I need to.

"You see, I'm part of Factsheet. We wake up, we drive, we eat, play, and sleep, and that is all we do. It is the way."

"What a deadbeat. You're putting me on, right?"

"Not really, I mean, that's pretty much the story. We're in the army now. You know, even if I was Gene Simmons of KISS and needed to fill in a missing page in the legendary scrapbook, I think I'd have to take a rain check tonight. I've never been this tired before, ever. There's nothing I'd like better than to go to a party with you and get to know you a bit better, but tonight, I'll just be a liability. I'm sorry. You know, the Spencer guys might be up for a wingding."

"Yeah, maybe." Again, she stares me down, and begins chuckling. I look back, but lower my head out of embarrassment. She looks pretty damn good, and a night of drinking and who knows what with some German kitten with a whip would normally be just what the mad scientist ordered, but I just can't rally. I can hear Ratboy's signature slogan ringing in my ear: *We are such losers.* "You could have the time of your life tonight, but instead you're going to a hotel. Someone waiting for you there?"

"No one human."

"Well, baby, maybe some other time, then?"

Baby? Sure, maybe some other time I'll be back thru Munich, swing in and grab her, a delicious blonde Germanic ice-bitch—named Elke, no less—and we'll go out and tear this poor excuse for a city right to the goddamn ground. See ya 'round, baby.

As much as I might have desired her a few nights ago or a few nights in the future, tonight was for sleep. No dancing, no television, no topless game shows, no beer until the early hours, no passing the tequila, no hash, no cough syrup, no masturbation, no card games, no reading, no writing, no singing, no walking, no exploring, not even any dreaming. Tonight is for sweet blackness, the other side of consciousness. Goodbye, cruel world.

IT'S MONDAY. THE SKY is an endless haze of dull white, as the soft but unending snow flurries continue to come and block out the sun. The drive to Prague is pretty much like this the whole way. Everyone's rested and feeling kind of antsy as none of us have ever before been behind what once was the Iron Curtain. In the middle of what had been Czechoslovakia but was now Czechia, this was more alien to all of us than any place we'd been or would be going, and this included our Euro-natives Simon and Rat.

At the border, we endure another search, but it goes by quickly and painlessly. As we cross into Czechia, we're stuck on a two-lane road backed up for miles with freight trucks. It seems open trading on the European markets has brought in the business, but the roads haven't been updated to accommodate. Sitting stock still for twenty and thirty minutes at a time, Simon takes every opportunity to jam on the accelerator, skip ahead of trucks, and hope that no encroaching vehicles are trying to maneuver the other way. With all the curves in the road and the unappeased snowfall, this is hard to calculate. Still he passes wildly, grinning as if he dared the Devil himself to come and get him. Dahl, on the other hand, is not so eager to meet the Devil.

"Simon, goddamnit, slow down!" he hollers. "We'll get there soon enough, if you don't kill us. Just knock it off and drive right!"

The situation becomes almost mockingly parental, as Simon, the ornery kid, waits for his stern dad to nod off or loosen up the attention in some way, and as soon as he senses this, we are speeding merrily down the wrong side of the road. Dahl would then jerk awake, shake his head, and yell at Simon. This went on literally for close to four hours—that's how long we were backed up in this fucked-up traffic. Finally, it all thinned out and we were on our way.

One could almost hear Steppenwolf's "Born to be Wild" playing inside Simon's head, as he kicks the pedal to the metal and busts out onto the wide-open highway. Dahl bit his lip and decided not to say anything. The rest of us were anxious to get to Prague. We'd heard it was Europe's most romantic and beautiful city. Let Simon be Simon, the speed demon.

We zip around a curve when a puny little piece of shit car comes out from behind a bush and begins chasing us. A primitive, makeshift flashlight dangles from the car's roof, and blinks red behind us.

"I'm no expert, especially around here, but I believe we're being pulled over by the police," says Simon softly.

"You idiot! I knew this was going to happen. It's not coming out of band money!" Dahl yells, while the rest of us sit quietly, biting our lips and trying hard not to laugh out loud.

We pull over and the young Czech cop emerges from his Pinto-sized police car and sizes us up and down. He looks in the van and tries to figure out what type of criminals he's dealing with here. He barely speaks English, and mutters the word "you," points at us, then pantomimes playing the guitar. Yes. You called it, Sherlock. We're musicians.

Simon hops out of the van and begins negotiation. We can't really see what's going on, but he is talking to the youthful flatfoot for a while, and they are writing down figures on a piece of paper. Simon walks over to the passenger side of the van and sticks his head through the window.

"Well, it's not too bad. I can pay him right here and now. I think he'll take Deutsche Marks, which we have some of. We should be out of here in no time, lads."

The cop walks up behind Simon while he is talking to us through the passenger side window, taps him on the shoulder, and points to the interior dashboard area of the Renault. They walk away to talk some more, and we can see in the rearview Simon nodding, scratching his chin and saying, "Yeah, sure." Simon approaches the passenger window again.

"He says he'll take one of our cassette tapes and call it even. I guess the police can negotiate on the scene here, sort of skipping the standard judicial process."

"Count your blessings," I say.

"What should I give him?" Simon wonders.

The backseat is instantly in agreement. "Nirvana!" We chime in unison. "Give him the damn Nirvana tape so we don't ever have to hear it again."

"I like Nirvana!" defends Simon.

"We want you to give him Nirvana," confirms Rat.

"It's your penance, O guilty one," laughs Z.

"Oh, fuckin' hell, alright." He grabs the cassette and offers it to the Czechian Broderick Crawford. Simon quickly returns.

"He won't take it. Says he hates Nirvana. Give me the box, I'll let him pick."

We were all secretly hoping he'll take the second most played tape of our little jaunt, the severely beat to death Doors compilation we've been listening to since day one. The winner? A new collection by Melissa Etheridge of all things that Simon had brought along. I don't think we ever listened to it, and it had some real cool stuff by The Cramps on the other side. No accounting for taste, nope, not anywhere in the whole wide world.

WE ARRIVE LATER IN the day at Bunkr, the club we're suppose to play tomorrow. On one side, the club adjoins a coffee/beer bar that coughs out a cloud of hash smoke when the door swings open, and on the other, the fledging local underground rock radio station. Behind all of this were some adjoining offices, and above, the Bunkr's bunkers, which we're to call home for the next two nights. A girl that works for the club, trying her best to be a good hostess, takes us upstairs and shows us our accommodations.

The courtyard is frozen solid and is slippery. A half-decayed staircase goes up the far wall to the second floor balcony. From there, a double door leads into the "club apartments." They're anything but lavish, honeys:

two rooms, five ancient cots with moth-chewed, filthy mattresses. Dahl and Tim claim the room with two cots, figuring it to be the ambassador suite of the two. The Factsheet room is pretty shoddy. I nab what looks like the most comfortable cot in what is rapidly dissolving into an every-dog-for-himself situation. Rat nabs another luxury liner, leaving Z and Simon to double up. The wooden floors haven't been swept since the Seven Weeks' War of 1866, and the windows have no curtains.

The girl smiles somewhat sheepishly as she distributes blankets to us all. It feels a little like the last night before being shipped to The Front. She seems a little embarrassed, and I feel kind of sorry for her. We probably seem ungrateful—after all, we are ungrateful—but the fact is she is doing her best with what she has at hand. That's just the way it is.

It's not that we are in a poor area, though. The curtainless windows look across and up at lavish apartments. As I relax on my cot in the waning sunlight, I gaze up to watch a native Prague gentlemen log some miles on his exercise bike and stare back down at me as he thinks to himself: *More weirdoes sleeping in that hellhole over there.*

"You guys will not believe this," laughs Tim, entering the room. We follow him through our apartment's front double doors out to the balcony. He points ominously down to the end of the outside hall. "That's our bathroom, go check it out."

We approach slowly, cautiously. The door to the small outhouse has been unceremoniously ripped asunder and tossed to the side, covered in snowflakes. The toilet bowl has no seat and, as we get closer and look in, we see that it's filled with frozen turds. Apparently it doesn't flush, this is just a place for stool storage. Terrific. Two days, eh? Alternate means of defecation will have to be worked out.

The bathtub is inside, but it has dirt, garbage, and food wrappers caked on it, with rock hard towels freeze dried in place around its perimeter. The mirror above the sink is gone, expect for a sliver of glass that jags its way randomly through the center. Okay, we know they are trying, but this is kind of a drag.

After we nap for a few hours, we adjourn downstairs to the hash bar, where we meet up with the promoter for tomorrow night's show, Rene. Smoking a big spliff and drinking expensive bottled beer, he asks if we're happy with our accommodations. We anticipated this, and primed Simon up for our desired negotiations.

"Well, tell you the truth, Rene, not really," says Simon, acting as spokesman. "I know it's the best you've got, and the budget is stretched as far as it can go, but I've got some uncomfortable musicians on my hands. Those cots are reminiscent of the county jails back where this lot comes from. We can't even shit properly."

Rene looks uneasy, and he notices Jeff isn't with us.

"What does Jeff say?" He leans in closer to Simon and discreetly inquires, "Is he angry?"

"He was for a bit, but I bedded him down with a handful of Valium, so he'll be alright. This lot here, though, I can't just dope them up and pull the wool over their eyes. They know which way the wind blows, see what I mean?"

"Yes, well, what can I do? How can I correct the conditions, given my restrictions here?"

Simon precedes to secure for us passage to the Bunkr for the evening (our night off) which features—guess what?—dancing. Techno, rave, disco, rap, goth, funk, rock 'n' roll, you request it, we'll shake ass to it. No mean feat in and of itself, our man's real coup was securing more or less free drinks for the entire evening, free at least as long as Rene was able to financially keep up with us.

Fairly lubed and oiled by the time we hit the Bunkr rock 'n' disco (open till 6:00 a.m.), we scan the vicinity to see what's up with the locals. A mixed crowd, to be sure: kids, couples, dopers, hustlers, dancers, vixens. Toward the stage, youthful exuberance abounds on the dance floor; further back, the chain-linked DJ booth is flanked by legions of dead-eyed zombies awaiting instructions from some unseen master as to their next mindless mission. Past that, into the dimness, are the bathrooms. Outside of them, impassioned couples openly fondle each other, slinging all manner of meat like short-order cooks. After surveying the carnage, we return mid-club to the bar to place our orders with our host.

"Gin and tonic, beer, whiskey, vodka, any red wine?"

Rene wrinkles his brow and digs deep into his trouser pockets. "I'm not the Banque of Prague, you know? I can't just endlessly buy drinks for all five of you!"

With very serious looks, we silently encircle our balking benefactor as Simon again takes the reins. "Rene, it's show business. You give a little, you take a little. We've brought this band, by popular demand, all the way from the United States. We've got to keep them happy, you and I. Now, I've done my part, you can ask them. I've gotten them here safely, kept them fed and clean and happy. I can't let them down now! That's why I need your help tonight."

"Oh, you're unbelievable. Get these drunkards whatever they want," Rene shouts at the bartender. "Next I suppose you'll want me to set them up with local girls!?"

"Can you?" Simon asks without a blink.

At the far end of the dance floor was the stage we'd be giving the maximum rock 'n' roll treatment to tomorrow night.

"Shall we give it a test drive?" Z asks, winking.

"Yeah, sure," I answer. "Let's do it for the kids."

The two of us get on the stage and begin dancing as if we were on *American Bandstand* or in a cage at the Whisky A Go Go. There really is nothing like being drunk in a place you know you'll never be recognized or seen in again to loosen up the old inhibitions. While Z and I gyrate shamelessly, the DJ shouts, with a heavy Slavic accent, "Lonely, lonely time" during Zeppelin's "Rock & Roll," and lets loose a heartfelt "Fuck You!" during Ice-T and Bodycount's infamous "Cop Killer." He was reverently silent during "Smoke on the Water."

After these songs, I get tired and look to see what Rat is up to. Z stays onstage, dancing by himself with this detached, dazed grin on his face. He dances for over an hour more. What a guy. God knows I love him.

Rat is drinking beer and Simon vodka. They both watch Tim, who has attracted a young girl. Simon informs me that Rene procured her for him. I guess our man Rene is good to go, true to his word, a man for all seasons, hurrah.

This girl gets up on a pillar in the center of the room and undulates like a North Hollywood stripper for Tim, who pulls up a chair and gazes, as if in a trance, up at her pulsating hips and gyrating thighs.

"Things are going to get weird. I just know it," says Rat. "Care for another beer, McGruff?"

Z is back from dancehall duty and has struck up a conversation with some French girls, while Simon chats up some Dutch treats, who perhaps remind him of his Melanie back home. I dance here and there with various girls, and then by myself, just like Billy Idol. I'm talking with some English girls, and a young guy from Germany, who plans on coming to the show tomorrow. Then it dawns on me: except for Rene, I've talked to no one that is from Czechia. Everyone is here from someplace else. I guess in that respect, it's a bit like Los Angeles. And, like L.A., no one seems like they're going to stay here for too awfully long, just passin' through, you know, man?

This scene is fun enough, but around 3:00 a.m., I begin to get bored. Tim has disappeared, Simon looks to pass out soon enough, Rat and Z are talking with some other French girls. I nod to my comrades and head toward the exit. When I look to my right, I see a girl, seated. She stands out from the tourist-infested crowd of vagrants as vibrantly as fireworks in a crystal shop.

Dressed in a lacey, tight, long black dress, and a black, middle-parted hairdo that is positively sinister, she sits alone on a bench to the far side of the bar. She looks miserable, yet beautiful—youthful, yet weighed down with the sorrows of the ages. I can't resist.

"Hi, I'm Bruce. Would you like some company?"

She barely looks up, doesn't really acknowledge me, and shrugs.

"Well, would you like to dance?"

Again, no smile, no measurable reaction at all. "Not to this music, this awful music this horrible DJ has been playing."

"It might not be the best, but I've been dancing to it."

"Yes, I know," she deadpans, nodding toward the stage, indicating she's been here long enough to witness me making a fool of myself alongside my man Z. This makes me laugh out loud. I say no more to her. Instead I size up the situation and make a beeline for the DJ booth.

"Hey, I've got a request!" I say to the soul-shoutin' tune spinner.

"What would you like?"

"Play the most depressing thing you got!"

I'd pegged my little Morticia as a full-fledged goth. A gothic rocker: a black-clad, Egyptian mascara wearing, lunchbox carrying death rocker, goose-stepping to the iron-hearted sobs of cold wavers such as Sisters of Mercy, Bauhaus, Siouxsie and the Banshees, The Mission, and The Cure. Of course the DJ would have something along those lines, but I had no idea he'd go right to crux of the biscuit with the Goth Rock national anthem: Joy Division's "Love Will Tear us Apart."

As the poppy-yet-haunting synthesizer lines waft from the speakers, this dark teen queen gets up and does the goth dance; an arms-flailing-in-Egyptian-abandon, eyes-closed spiritual purge that in many ways resembles the LSD-induced soul shake of the undying Grateful Dead fan. But this came from a different spot within the brain, I suppose. As she twirls and divines her place in the cosmos, I sort of mildly bop around in front of her, content to watch the show she's putting on.

The DJ sloppily segues into "Papa's Got A Brand New Bag," and her trance breaks, but so does the wall around her. I learn her name in Tanya, and invite her to the bar for a drink.

"What's a nice goth rocker like you doing in a place like this?" She either doesn't get the joke, or more likely, just doesn't think it's at all funny.

"I'm here from Yugoslavia, where I grew up. I've spent a lot of time in Germany, too. I don't like it there, but I really hate it here. I have to live here with my parents for right now until I can get enough money and go back with the group, back to the forest where I want to live."

"What group is that? Are you in a band?"

"No, I'm not in a band." She has a way of saying "band" that makes it sound positively vile. "I was in a group, you might say cult. I was in a group of Satanists, Satanic worshippers. I'm a Satanist."

"Oh, really? I take it you don't practice your Satanism at home with mom and dad, while you're away from the group."

"No. I believe, I read, I plan, I wait. But I can't take part in ceremonies away from the group."

"What sort of ceremonies? Do you run around in robes and drink goat blood?"

"You think you are funny, don't you? This is serious to me."

She was most assuredly an extremely serious girl. I apologized for making light of her religion, and tried to get the conversation rolling smoothly again. I wanted to extract information from her, as I didn't anticipate having a social drink with a teenage Eastern European Satanist anytime in the near future, and didn't want to botch the opportunity.

As I sat directly in front of her, I could see she was a genuine, natural beauty, with huge dark brown eyes and the whitest, smoothest face, almost like china. The very slightest frown lines were beginning to creep in around her mouth. Oddly, they only appeared when she fought against a smile. Her hair, swept away in all directions from her face, was as black as it was possible for hair to be, and natural to boot. She would have been the envy of every gothic princess in Hollywood.

"Have you ever read any of Anton LeVey's stuff?" I asked, hoping to loosen things up a bit.

"No. Never heard of him."

"You've never heard of Anton LeVey? He's the head of the Satanic Church in the States. He's quite an interesting character, an ex-carnival barker/police photographer/burlesque showman turned Satanic high priest. He supposedly brought Hollywood-types such as Jayne Mansfield and Sammy Davis Jr. into his camp, and, well, look what happened to them. She lost her head! LeVey's books are actually pretty informative and eye opening. They have a lot to do with observing people and knowing how to use their weaknesses to your advantage, among many other things."

"Are you a Satanist?" she asks.

"I've played in some pretty deep punk-metal bands, but no, I'm not a Satanist. Too much negative PR."

"Why do you know so much about it?"

"I don't really know much at all. Just a few tidbits I grabbed here and there. Hey, when in Hell, do as the Hellions."

The topic shifts to Charles Manson, another mythic figure of California lore that she had no knowledge of. I question what kind of Satanist is ignorant of both Anton and Chuck, but I keep these queries to myself. The DJ spins "First and Last and Always" by The Sisters of Mercy, at which point dancing takes precedence over philosophical deliberation.

Drenched in sweat, we grab a seat and resume the conversation. "So, you're a teenage Satanist. What makes you a Satanist?"

"It's very complicated. I lived with a cult, you might call coven, and worshiped the dark ways. Lived very strict lives. Sometimes is was, eh, exhilarating, sometimes it was boring."

"Get to the good stuff. What about the ceremonies? Did you dress up in robes and drink the blood of your gym teacher while listening to Judas Priest? Give me the scoop."

This time she almost busts a smile, and reacts calmly to my ridiculous question. "People always want to know the grisly stuff. People refuse to let Satanists worship in peace, when the equally Paganistic Catholic religion is allowed to flourish."

"Hey, you'll get no argument from me there. But, you're avoiding the question. I mean, let's be frank, how far did you go—virgins, infants?"

"We would sacrifice rabbits at a certain ceremonial spot we had in the forest. That's really about all."

Rabbits? What the fuck kind of Satanists were these? Had they never heard Mötley Crüe or Christian Death? Oh well, to each his own. At least I didn't have to worry about her ripping my heart out, at least not literally. We drink and talk until, what, five in the morning?

"What are you doing tomorrow?" Tanya asks me.

"Probably exploring Prague with a reasonably severe hangover."

"Do you know where you're going?"

The answer to that was standard, no matter where in the world I was, "No!"

"I'll show you the city. Where are you staying?"

"About fifty yards the other side of that wall," I answered, nodding toward home.

"What time do you want to go?"

"Is twelve noon too early?"

"No, I will see you at twelve noon."

She was so grave sounding that I knew she would turn up. Great, I have a lovely, mysterious, haunted little vampyre to show me through the city of Kafka and romance. It all sounded so abstract I turned into a cockroach on the spot.

At this point, I'm really loopy, giddy from my encounter with Tanya, and drunker'n shit from my pillage of Rene. The rest of the guys are in the same boat, more or less. Tim's disappeared, possibly with that show-off dancing hussy, but most likely upstairs to bed alone. Simon can barely walk and can no longer form words at all. Rat can't stop laughing, but is nonetheless more coherent than Z, who is jibber-jabbering away in a language that belongs somewhere other than earth. I gather up the four of us, and we stumble out of Bunkr through the snow to our upstairs bungalows, laughing, tripping over our own feet, and feeling not an ounce of pain. Aw, alcohol, the greatest medicine in the world. How I pity the idiots who gave up drinking and frittered away their free time in unpleasant group meetings talking about their former drunken glories. Geez, what a tragedy, they could be out saucin' it up. This crosses my mind in a quick blink as we sluggishly flounder our way through the courtyard, guffawing loudly about nothing at all, dragging a rubbery-legged and slobbering Simon along with us as best we can. Up the stairs—no. Not the stairs! I fall down laughing in the snow right then and there—we ain't gonna make it up the friggin' stairs. Shit, they won't even hold us, they'll crumble right off the bleedin' wall.

We teeter up, dragging Simon behind us, while all the time Z continues to chatter in tongues. "Bibble-dee-bobble-dee-blech-und-zee-mufa-bibble-dee-blech" followed by uncontrollable laughter from all four of us. Somehow, countering any reasonable bets, we make it to the front door, which, of course, Dahl has locked, just in case some hooligans might try to break in during his slumber and remove from us our priceless instruments. At any rate, entry seems impossible, but, somehow, against all odds, I seem to be the most coherent of the bunch.

"Alright, who's got the key to the door of our luxurious bachelor pad?"

"Bibbledeebobbledee boo boo boo!"

"McGruff, don't you have it?" asked Rat, quite possibly bucking for the most in control and the least-needy-of-sobriety-meetings-when-we-get-back-to-the-States award.

"No, I don't think so." As I search my pocket, I let go of my supporting grip on Simon, and he crashes to the floor of the balcony. "Shit, that was rather loud. No,

I think Simon must have the key. Why don't you just reach in his front pants pocket and get it?"

"Goobledee Boobledee."

"How do I know it's there?" asked Rat. "And, if I reach in the pocket and it's not there, who knows what I'll find? You get it off him, McGruff."

"Nah, no way. We should just stand here and kick him until he wakes up."

So we did. "Hey, stupid fucker, where's the key, you limey lush?"

"Blee bleye blow blum. I smell the cum of an English bum."

"You sad grimleys, you sick lot," mumbles Simon, talking just slightly more cohesively than our man Z. Still collapsed in a heap on the balcony, he tosses out the key from the much-feared front pocket. We unlock the door and crash into the stuffy, over-heated crash pad, laughing and tripping over whatever was in our way. It must have sounded like a heard of cattle coming to stampede the sandman. From the inner sanctum of Dahl's presidential suite, came the comforting salutations we'd expected.

"SHUT THE FUCK UP RIGHT NOW. I MEAN IT!"

Much like pre-pubescent kids whose slumber party has just been broken up by a disgruntled parent, we try to regain composure, but mostly we just tone the rude laughing down to a sly snickering, punctuated by our stumbling boots traipsing across the unfamiliar floor in the dark looking for our rooms and our beds. We openly laugh and make rude jokes, and rebuttals seem to arise from the other side of the wall. In a matter of minutes, we all fade into unconsciousness in our bunker.

THE MORNING SUN PENETRATES the curtainless windows like a prison break. The sirens in hot pursuit came from within, caused by tinnitus, brought about by years of exposure to live rock music. It never really goes away, but sometimes you can forget about it and it can become more or less undetectable. This morning, however, the ringing was being run through the hangover-driven stereo amplifiers located right behind my sinuses. With temporary blindness and a piercing, nerve-splitting brain noise being my first two sensations, I woke up, and realized I had what felt like a dirt clod in my mouth and that I need to pee.

As I walked out of our room, I figured I'd try not to wake anyone—heaven forbid, it's too early for the extreme volume that accompanies a severe reprisal from the Master—and walk to the outdoor can and piss on the frozen turds, hoping that the site of the profane Butterfingers doesn't make me nauseous in my awakening queasiness. I notice Simon is busy in the apartment's indoor bathroom. I walk back to the balcony porch door and see a plastic sandwich bag (or something) whiz past me from a window.

"Oh, sorry there, McGruff! I didn't see you. Didn't nick you, did I?"

"No, what was that?"

"Ah, it was me morning shit. I shat into that little bag and lobbed it down there onto the courtyard. Being well below the temperature at which shit freezes—as we've seen and duly noted—I figured it was the most sane and logical way at hand to dispose of the unwanted stuff given our present lodgings."

"I see your point."

"Wonder if they'll be bringing around some kind of breakfast. Hungry?"

"Actually, no. For some reason the ol' appetite hasn't kicked in yet this morning."

The other citizens of our micro-world begin to rise from their creaking cots. No one talks much; mostly the silence is broken by painful grumbles and the punctuation of phlegm-spewing coughs.

Dahl enters and inquires about last night's misadventures. In recounting the bleary incidents of sin and degradation, it comes out that all five of the Bunkr night crawlers have arranged for female escorts to come meet us at our rock star digs and show us around Europe's number one most-hyped city of passion, Prague.

"How do you guys even know how to do it?" wondered Dahl in regards to our procurement of feminine companionship. "I've been married for almost twenty years, I wouldn't even know what to say," Dahl remarks offhandedly.

"Sure thing, bub," I challenge, nodding and winking. "That's what you tell all the babes, that tale of innocence and stolen youth is sure to ignite the nymphomaniac within even the most devout Catholic schoolgirl."

Even though Dahl had encouraged the arrangement that brought him off-the-typical-tour path to Prague, he opts to stay in, or at least not to come along with us. We descend the stairs of doom, and Tanya enters the opposite end of the courtyard. With her ankle-length black frock coat, wind-blown jet-black hair, pure white skin, dark eyes, and clandestine demeanor, she looks like a specter coming through the snowy courtyard to mingle with the other side.

"I thought you guys were meeting some people, too," I mention quietly as we walked toward Tanya.

"I'm sure they'll be here," confirms the Rat.

"Hello," says Tanya flatly.

She asks what we want to do. As we wait for the other girls, everyone stalls, perpetuating meaningless small talk.

"Well, I'm taking off. I wanna get some pizza," I announce. "I need to soak up the leftover booze in my stomach."

Tanya and I leave the courtyard and head down the cobblestone sidewalk while the other four huddle to discuss plans. She silently leads me to pizza. As we turn a corner toward a busier street, I notice the four following us, finally catching up.

"We might as well come along with you then, yeah?" Simon says. "I mean, she's from here, and she'll know a good place."

It would be a perfect afternoon, just me, Nosferatu's daughter, and four guys I can't help but loving, especially since we've been in such close quarters every day for the past thirty-three straight days.

"McGruff doesn't mind. Do ya, McGruff?" asks Z.

We seem to go up and down a lot of outdoor escalators through numerous train and bus stations, but we stay on foot at all times. After about twenty minutes of walking, I note aloud that pizza is rare in Prague and you really have to cover some territory to track any down.

"You want good pizza or lousy pizza?" asked Tanya, with an icier-than-usual chill factor in her inflection.

"Pizza. How bad can it be?"

"I'm taking you to a good place."

We soldier on and finally arrive at a small, nondescript pizza house serving an average pie. We eat slowly, talk little, and I sense that everyone is battling a bit of nausea as we eat and try to return to normal. The place has a bathroom with electric lights and working plumbing, and a visit each seems to right everyone's wrong. Tanya—now the full-fledged tour guide of the Jeff Dahl Band—asks us repeatedly what we want to do, but we have no ideas.

"I take you some place good."

Prague is an amazing city, with centuries-old architecture surviving in excellent condition. It's snowing lightly, and we are all walking along pretty quietly, taking in all the breathtaking sights—the river, the bridges, the churches, the shops, the market squares. Despite the fall of communism, you can still see the archetypical Soviet worker, in his gray factory jumpsuit, off to work toting a black lunch pale. Tanya takes us to the historical Old Jewish Cemetery of Prague. Dating back to the 1400s, the tombstones are literally inches apart from each other. People must've just been piled up five deep. The whole thing is about the size of a basketball court, but there must be at least six hundred markers. Once again, Euro-Blur 1993 winds through the land of the dead.

"Oh, I know this place. It's where they filmed that INXS video," says Simon.

"Yes, that's true," confirms Tanya. The rest of us shrug and assume they know what they're talking about. Next to the graveyard is a historical museum, which we take in. It's filled with artifacts from the Jewish concentration camp that occupied this site during World War II, most notably a number of very depressing paintings that were painted by the camp's prisoners. The black and white coal paintings spoke volumes on hopelessness and utter dismay. I took some photos of them. (Months later, while laying out a photo album, I juxtaposed the photos of these paintings opposite photos of the band in our Prague anti-apartment, and the effect was quite eerie, sort of prisoners of war meet prisoners of rock.)

We move on to the main town square, and at a sidewalk market, I spend a few minutes debating whether or not to buy one of those giant, fuzzy Russian hats. Tanya stands patiently behind me, letting me take my time. I discover that everyone else wandered off, and we decide whether or not to go looking for them. It begins to snow harder, so we continue on. She walks

me by the huge green opera house where they filmed
exteriors for *Amadeus*, and on to some record stores and
coffee houses. We walk past the famous, breathtaking
astronomical clock tower in the center of town square.
I look over at Tanya and again realize how strikingly
beautiful she is, albeit in her own particular fashion.

"Hey, lemme take your picture!" I request, forever
the tourist.

"No."

"No? Don't tell me you don't photograph. Do you
show up in mirrors? Come on."

"No. I never allow my picture to be taken."

"Oh, come on. Who will know? I'll be off to another
country by tomorrow. You're one of the coolest people
I've met, maybe the coolest I will meet. Stand with that
tower in the background."

"No!"

She says "no," but nonetheless turns for the photo
when she realizes I'm going to take it anyway. She even
cracks an ever-so-slight smile.

After I buy some hard-to-find CDs, she tosses me in
a cab, explains to the driver where I need to end up, and
heads the other direction back to her parent's house.
She says she'll be at the show, but I feel I've seen the last
of this dark princess.

LATER THAT AFTERNOON, DAHL and I do a radio interview
at the Bunkr station, which is surprisingly well stocked

with cool indie discs, much more so than most U.S. college stations. Rene comes by before our show and offers to treat us to dinner. Dahl and Simon quickly decline.

"I would like to get out of here and get some food, actually," Rat chimes in. Z and I second the idea. This, for unknown reasons, causes immense tension among the Euro-Blur Six, but as was the norm, the reason for this wasn't explained. The Factsheet look at each other and shrug. Fuck it. Let's eat.

Rene tells us where he wants to go and asks if we can go in the van. The bosses say no. We take a cab and Rene insists on paying for it.

The place he's chosen seems to be the full-on rock hangout of Prague. The wooden polls and walls are adorned with posters advertising recent local shows featuring the likes of L7, Faith No More, and Nick Cave. Guys and girls that look like they play in or hang around bands fill the booths. The place is a-fog with hash and tobacco smoke, and the hearty food hits the proverbial. Everyone checks us out: *Who are these foreign rock geezers?* A few people seem to know, and others just come up and start talking to us. Most of their English is pretty good, and everyone is very friendly. It seems being an American isn't as much of a crime here. Maybe it's just that we're among the international brethren of rock 'n' roll lovers.

MEANWHILE, BACK AT THE ranch, the rock show was about to begin. Backstage beer was at a disappointing low. Simon, who's had fuck-all to do today, is put to work as everyone rudely spews their rider demands: "Juice, chocolate, more beer, can we get some hard liquor for a goddamn change?"

We turn in a pretty decent performance that is met with disarming apathy—mostly people just stand there and look at us. Encores aren't really forthcoming, but Dahl wants to play them anyway. By now, they are so routine that, as soon as we get to the dressing room, he just says, "Regular three," which indicates we are to play the same three-song encore we've been playing every night for two weeks straight. The same set we've played every night since we began in Groningen.

Simon sits in the corner of the room looking surprisingly happy. It turns out he scored a fifth of vodka for us but has already polished it off by himself. We get ready to kick his ass but Dahl drags us back onstage.

Following a faithful rendering of the regular three, I pack up my bass onstage when I hear someone calling my name. I turn and there's Carol, a nightclub booking agent I know from Hollywood.

"Carol? What are you doing here?"

"I live here now. I'm going to be booking concerts here. I've been here a few months and I love it. I saw in the paper Jeff Dahl was playing and I remembered you'd been in the band, so I came down on the chance you might still be, and here you are."

Tanya had failed to show up, but it appeared I would
have some company for the evening anyway. Carol is a
pretty but unassuming girl, mid-twenties, five-foot-four
with straight blonde hair center-parted. She's quiet but
confident. I've always felt at ease around her. After the
gear is stashed, she and I head to the bar, where Rene
reluctantly gives the okay signal to the bartender and
once again the free beers flow. After a single sip, Carol
grabs my hand and drags me to the dance floor, where
some Pearl Jam has people movin 'n' groovin'.

"Bruce, you should move to Prague," she says to me
with genuine enthusiasm.

"What would I do here?"

"You could write for the daily paper, or produce
records, or just market things, or import cool stuff from
America. My brother is the one who turned me on to
this, he came over a few years ago and made a killing as
a stockbroker."

"I do like it here. It's beautiful. But I don't know, I'd
have to sell all my shit, learn a new language. I'm far too
lazy for that kind of commitment."

"Bullshit, you're one of the hardest workers I
know..."

And so it went, as we argued and debated the
endless possibilities of my relocation to the City of
New Fortunes, the carrot dangling from the end of the
hypothetical international stick. All the while, we never
miss a beat on the dance floor, and the more we drink,
the hotter the room gets, the more she wants to shake

it, baby. Z and Rat aren't far behind, dancing with a variety of girls and absorbing an assortment of alcohol. A rerun of the previous night's mindless debauchery seems inevitable. Z stops dancing long enough to make out with some French brunette right in the middle of the dance floor.

Frenchy departs moments later, and Z taps me on the shoulder. "These Dutch chicks have bags full of coke. You want some?"

"No, I'll pass. You don't know where it's been, so to speak. Besides, coke always makes me wanna crap, and given that the coffee shop's closed up, and I don't wanna squat in the snow, you know what I'm sayin'?"

"I hear ya. Just thought I'd ask. How 'bout these Dutch girls, eh? How 'bout my man McGruff and li'l Carol?"

Z was abnormally chatty and outgoing. It was safe to assume he ingested some coke already. He began singing a Chuck Berry song, which I didn't think that he even knew. "Whoa, Carol, don't ever take your heart away. Well, I got ta learn ta dance, if it takes me night 'n' day."

"That's real good, man. Just don't bust into a duck walk right here, okay?"

I return to the floor with Carol, where we shake it to some Consolidated, on the industrial dance tip. She is tireless. I try not to look like a total wuss and keep up with her as best I can. I look over, Z is making out with another girl, one of the Dutch clan. I exchange a glance with Ratboy, and he starts cracking up. Simon approaches the two of us, saying something below the level of audibility, given the music's volume—his slurred speech doesn't help, either. We have no idea what he said, but given our anger at him for bogarting the vodka, we instruct him to fuck off at the top of our voices.

Time stretches out, as it had the previous night. There seems to be no clear-cut closing time, so people just party full speed all night long. Now, completely in cocaine-fueled mode, Z holds courts with the Dutch trio, talking a mile a minute. Rat and I confer on this situation while on the dance floor, nonchalantly sliding over by one another to exchange opinions and laugh.

"Z is totally hysterical," laughs the Rat. "He goes from dance machine to debate team captain to Mr. Display of Public Affection. Amazing!"

We just get more and more into the dancing. In a scene that's straight out of *Saturday Night Fever*, Rat (now dancing with a barmaid), Carol, and I actually clear the dance floor with an enthusiastic display of inspired moves, twirls, kicks, and ritualistic four-way choreography. The song that inspires this ascension to new heights is somewhat unexpected, and one of my very favorites by The Velvet Underground, "She's My Best Friend."

> If you want to see me
> Sorry but I'm not around
> If you want to be me
> Turn around, I'm by the window where the light is

The remaining crowd stops dancing and gather around us in a circle. As we wind down at song's end, they applaud us. What a rush, I swear it was out of some cornball movie, the only thing missing was Ann-Margaret and Elvis. The ovation far exceeded anything we received earlier for playing music.

As the night begins to unwind, I evaluate my situation and decide it's time to move uptown with Carol. If I'm to relocate to Prague, I need a better feel for the town's domiciles.

"So, eh, Carol. Ya wanna see something really scary?"

"What did you have in mind?"

"Our apartment, upstairs. What must they think of musicians to toss us in such rag-tag accommodations? I'd be embarrassed if it weren't so damn comical."

"Didn't you say Jeff was asleep up there?"

"Well, yes, yes that's true. I guess I'm just trying to get you to take a little pity on me, as I'm trying to off-load out of here and get myself some more upscale digs, you see what I mean?"

"Uh huh."

"Yeah, don't get the wrong idea. I mean, you and me, we've been friends for a number of years. I was just thinking, maybe we could catch a cab to your place, and I could hang with you tonight. You know, I won't be in the way. I just want to take a bath and raid your refrigerator. Besides, it's getting very late, and a young American girl such as yourself shouldn't be out unescorted at this ungodly hour. Who knows what kind of weirdoes are out there?"

"Well, Bruce..."

"McGruff, check out Z!" interrupted Rat. Z was now surrounded by five girls, he had a two bottles of beer in one hand and what looked like a shot glass of gin in the other, the hand with the shot glass was holding a cigarette, and there was also a cigarette dangling from his chattering lips, which were still going nonstop. I laugh, but quickly return to my attention to Carol.

"I think I'm just gonna go," she says, deflating my bubble. "I've got a busy day tomorrow, and you've got to get going. I think we should just call it a night."

Ah well, nothing ventured, nothing gained, we'll always have Prague. I'm sure she doesn't believe that all I'm really after is the contents of her fridge and the comfort of warm bathwater, and why should she? I'm not sure I believe it myself.

Months later, back in Los Angeles, I'd get a transatlantic call from Carol. She told me she'd booked a reunited-yet-again Deep Purple into Prague. It was a bit of a chore, because guitarist, Ritchie Blackmore (my all time guitar hero), had to be treated as a separate entity from the rest of the band—separate car, hotel, meals, transportation to and from the airport, all apart from the rest of Deep Purple. During the conversation, she lets slip that after our night at the Bunkr, she got hassled by some dirty old man in an Aqualung overcoat. He harassed her until she finally was able to hail a cab.

THE FOLLOWING MORNING WE arise very slowly and with great difficulty. We have to dig the van out of the snow, and it's very hard to get everyone to help. Basically everyone just wants to look at the van and hope that it unearths itself, and then wait while all the equipment magically loads itself in. Fighting the cold and our increasingly omnipresent hangovers, we somehow manage to get these chores done, grumbling all the while. Once my stuff is onboard, I lose patience with everyone's slowness and grouchiness, and take off for the local market, to stock up on road supplies. I make a startling discovery there.

For the first time since leaving Los Angeles, I have found a mother lode of my favorite beverage, the revered Royal Crown Cola. The pride of the South, which Jolt tried to imitate. RC is the tastiest, most energizing concoction of caffeine and sugar known to man. Not only do they have it, they have it in sixteen-ounce bottles, practically unheard of even in the States. Now get this: these bottles are going for the equivalent of about thirty cents apiece. Granted, I'm not a rich man on this Euro-Blur excursion, but at thirty cents a pop, I can afford to buy the store out.

I walk out with two shopping bags full of RC and trudge through the snow back to the van, where I load my newfound treasure.

"What the fuck are you going to do with all that soda?" chides Tim.

"I'm gonna drink it, buddy boy."

"All that? No way."

"Well, that's *my* problem, then. At any rate—and I want to make this clear to all concerned—these are *my*

RCs. Not nobody else's. So if ya want an RC, well, you'll just have to hope someplace else along the way carries them."

Four hours later down the road from Prague, my RCs take on new meaning. Suddenly, everyone wants one.

"C'mon, McGruff. You can't drink them all yourself."

"Sure I can. There's a lot of this tour yet to go. No problem."

"C'mon, we'll buy them off you."

"Well, fellas, the going rate, right now, is a dollar or the equivalent thereof in any reasonable foreign currency per bottle of Royal Crown."

"A buck!"

"Take it, leave it, or drink whatever other shit is loose in the back of the van."

Begrudgingly, the dollars began to appear. This went on for many days, as my RCs turned into a prosperous cottage industry for me. There are many ways to make money on the road. You just have to have a nose for supply and demand.

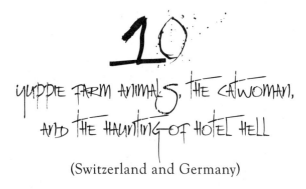

10

YUPPIE FARM ANIMALS, THE CATWOMAN, AND THE HAUNTING OF HOTEL HELL

(Switzerland and Germany)

CRASHING HARD FROM A sugar/caffeine near-coma, we roll into Stuttgart, Germany, birthplace of the Master, Jeff Dahl. We've got a lot of dates coming up in Deutschland, but tonight is just a stop on the way to Switzerland, land of the Ratboy. Perhaps because we're shooting through such ancestral territories, or perhaps because we're as exhausted as we've yet been on this tour, or maybe just because we've not touched bathwater for several days and can no longer bear each others' bodily odors, the drive seems unusually solemn, even for the Jeff Dahl Factsheet Plus Two.

In Germany, things seem more like the States, with well-equipped motor lodges and hotels everywhere. We check into a pretty stylin' place, and get a wide variety of rooms. Dahl and Tim get separate ones—more and more they seem to be detached from the pack and from each other—and I room with Simon in a fairly average hotel double. I'd loaned Z my shaving lotion back in Prague, and went knocking on his door at the end of the hall one floor up to see if he still had it.

"Go away!" It was Z's voice from behind the door.

"It's me. It's not Tim. Open up!"

"Who's with you, anyone?" This time it was Rat that I heard.

"No. No one's with me. I'm all alone. Let me in, for Crissakes!"

"Simon's not with you, is he?"

"You're beginning to piss me off, and I was in a pretty good mood. Open up!"

The door cracked open, with two beady little Rat eyes peeping out. Slowly the hotel room door opens to reveal the largest, most plush, most bodacious bachelor pad of an urban apartment I've ever seen outside of uptown Manhattan. Z and Rat begin giggling.

"This can't be real," I gasp, with my mouth open.

"Can you believe it?" laughs Rat, waving his arms around to show off what is, at least temporarily, his.

"How can this even be part of the same hotel?" I wonder. "It must be some kind of mistake, like the bridal suite, or the manager's hideaway, or a porthole to a parallel dimension or something."

"We just unlocked the door and here it was, big as life," says Rat, stumbling around in his pajamas, hitting off a bottle of vanilla liquor he'd lifted from the booze-atorium we'd discovered below the Basque Country Club. "We can't have Tim finding out, wanting to take a bath or something. We can't have him around, ruining everything. And Simon will want to stay and watch television. You're okay. I mean, you didn't want to stay that long anyway, did you?" Rat is giddy and beside himself

"McGruff," intones Z, getting ready to switch gears on the conversation. "I called work. We may not have jobs when we get back."

Nothing like dropping a nuclear bomb. Of course, history was rife with musicians going off to tour and returning to have the carpet pulled out from under them, but not us, not big shots at the little label, kings of Indieland. Surely we would return to day jobs.

"Why, what's the problem?"

"I think they're having major difficulties getting orders filled and dealing with the export business while I'm gone. I just think the whole operation's floundering too much, and by the time we get back, well, it may be too late."

"You mean to tell me that the whole thing's going belly up because of your absence? You're a fucking drummer, you can't have that much authority at the day job. I thought you just talked on the phone and exported a few CDs here and there."

"That's typical of you, to think I'm nothing. Look, shit is going down, and if they can't pull it together, I'm just sayin', well, we might be looking for work. We may have to go to the T-shirt printers or something."

"Right, T-shirt printing. Dude, I gave up printing a long time ago."

"Bullshit!" Z said, looking me square in the eye. "You're still printing."

Somewhat depressed and unnerved, I go back to my room, not really telling Simon about my conversation with Z. I try to reach the office to see how accurate Z's reports of encroaching doom are, but I can't get through. I decide to take a shower and wash out my long johns. After they're washed, I wrap them around the rod that served as a support bar of sorts for getting in and out of the shower. This had proven a good method for quickly wringing out the garments, at which point they could be placed on the radiator on which they'd completely dry by morning. As much as I'd chided Dahl for his Woolite, I too had developed my own methodology for completing the task of cleaning clothes on the go. As I twist the thermal underwear, squeezing out every drop, the bar breaks free from the wall, and as it snaps, the long johns act as a spring and my feet go out from under me on the wet floor. My right knee crashes hard into the corner of the shower stall, and shit seems to be flying everywhere. Simon, who was sorting through all manners of foreign money, comes running in.

"Are you alright?"

Embarrassed and sprawled rather unglamorously on the floor, I try to figure the answer. "Yeah, I guess. Damn, I fucked up!"

I stand up, and my knee sends a series of sharp pain signals up my spinal cord. "OOOWWW!"

"You didn't break anything, did you?" he says, genuinely concerned.

"Not since I cracked that rib. No, it just hurts." I limp like a loser over to my bed. While avoiding colds and pink eye and laryngitis and the like, I've managed to sustain the most bruises and bumps and contusions, which, truth be known, is somewhat typical of me. I've always been a klutz. I lie down on the bed in a modicum of discomfort, drink a room temperature beer, write in my journal, and watch a boring soccer game.

THE FOLLOWING MORNING I feel even more depressed. I'm in a reasonable amount of pain, and now I'm worried about my job. Simon heads out the door with his bags and tells me to hurry up. Instead, I get out my calling card and attempt to reach out and touch someone, my darling Gina back home in Hollywood. It should be about closing time the night before back at home. Again, I can't seem to get through. I pack my shit and walk out the door, but I look back at the phone and decide to give it one more try. I glance out the window and see that the van is almost packed and ready. To hell with them, they can wait for me for once. Again I begin the complex procedure of dialing across the waters.

Four rings. Five rings. "Hello?"

"Gina, it's me. What's happening?"

"Oh, not much. Well, a lot really." She starts to laugh, and as seems to be the norm, she sounds drunk, buzzed, or both. "I just got back from the Grammys. I got to go to the Grammys after party! Billy from Faith No More got me in. It was pretty cool. It was really cool. HYUP. Shit, I can't stop hiccupping. You know how I get. I met Stuttering John there. He was real nice."

Her words began to blur together to me. I look out the window again and see everyone impatiently waiting. Meanwhile, Gina's words fade as I focus more on the image of her all dressed up, partying with real rock stars, and living it up in the show biz capital of the world, while I'm limping around Stuttgart considering my employment opportunities.

"Oh, good news," she cut in, practically interrupting herself. "My boss has been talking to Ray, and he really likes Tim's tape."

My ears perk up. Ray is a partner of mine who I've worked with on dozens of musical endeavors, and is probably the best recording engineer I know. He came by the house for the Euro-Blur bon voyage dinner and had dropped off tape of his friend Tim, an almost rock star from a nearly famous band that was trying to make another stab at success with some cool, classic rock type material. I almost forgot about it, since I left for Europe immediately and hadn't heard his music since.

"Yeah, they're gonna launch this custom label with Tim. Ray's gonna produce it and you're the bass player. As soon as you get back it should be getting started. Looks like it'll be a good budget, so no more money worries. Isn't that great!?"

"Yeah, yeah, damn, that is great. Is it pretty for sure?"

"It seems like it. HYUP. Sorry. Wow, you wouldn't have believed the food spread at this party..."

And so it went. I missed her. I realized she was having the time of her life, but she still seemed to keep me in mind, and brought me good news as was fit to deliver. But now I had to go, onto Switzerland. Euro-Blur waits for no one man. The momentary good news had revived my spirits, and with a determined stride I marched out to the van. I told everyone about my upcoming LP project, and they all nodded at me. They were somewhat annoyed they had to wait for me, but I was the bearer of good fortune that applied only to myself. Things like this no longer mattered on the bloodied roads of Euro-Blur.

SOUNDCHECKS, FOR ME ANYWAY, could be eliminated by this point in our journey. Either the guy at the board knows how to get a good sound or he doesn't, and no amount of knob twiddling, endless pounding on the floor tom, or "testing one two one two" is going to make a difference. Yet here we are, enduring a particular lengthy one with an unusually unsympathetic sound geezer. With his polo-style shirt and thinning, slicked-back black hair, he suddenly approaches me.

"Do you mind?" he asks, pointing at my amp. I wasn't quite sure what he meant, but it is a rented amp, so I just shrug. He steps onstage and begins adjusting the tone equalizer on the amp. In my near twenty years playing live as a goddamn pro, no one has ever crossed the proscenium to alter my sound before. But then again, this is the first time I've ever played in Switzerland. He makes the bass sound incredibly mid-range-y and trebly, there's almost no bass left in it.

He re-adjusts the overall sound to boost the kick drum, de-emphasize the guitars, and puts the vocals way out front. Dahl begins to wig out.

"Look," he says, slightly raising his voice and obviously having a difficult time remaining composed, "we are not a disco band. We are a rock 'n' roll band. You are fucking up our sound!"

"No, it sounds good now. I know!"

"Turn up the guitars, man," says Ratboy.

"Guitars are just right," our tinned-ear saboteur responds.

We try another song. The bass is EQ-ed to virtually make it the lead instrument. Finding this amusing, I take off on a solo in the middle of the song. Dahl doesn't see the humor, tosses down his Les Paul, and sulks off to the dressing room.

"Tell you what," says Simon, trying to rescue the situation. "I'll go to the van and get one of Jeff's CDs and he can hear what it's supposed to sound like."

Good idea. Simon comes back with the disc and tosses it in the club CD player. As if to confirm our worst fears, the soundman violently clasps his hands to his ears and shouts, "But this sounds as bad as the band does onstage!"

"Yes, right, it does!" I shout. "That's the sound! Buzzsaw guitars, screaming vocals, and a subdued rhythm section. That's also what the punters will be paying to hear tonight. That's what you've got to get coming out of this P.A. system!"

"Oh, I can't do it." He throws up his hands, grabs his coat, and leaves the building. We all stand onstage, mouths open. We've just collectively never seen anything like it. A much younger guy who'd let us into the club is standing around watching all of this with his hands in his pockets.

"Well," he says, slowly at first, as if to carefully monitor his own speech. "I guess I'll do sound." Right, you bloody do it, mate. You don't need a degree in engineering. You don't need four semesters at the Juilliard School of Music. Just turn it up and let it rock! Even with our novice friend at the flight panel, the show goes fine.

Afterward, Rat visits with his sister and some friends who'd come to the show. We eat deli platter food and drink lukewarm beer, and while it's nice to see Rat so happy and in the bosom of his family, I'm personally feeling bored, which is an almost constant state of affairs, it would seem. If not bored, then frustrated, or homesick, or antsy, or lonely, or restless, or...or...GO ON, SAY IT!!

Horny. Yes indeed, baby. Horny as a marching band playing John Phillip Sousa at full tilt. Yet, girls weren't really coming to our shows. They most certainly weren't coming to our dressing room, and they couldn't even get past the desk clerk at the hotels we stayed at. Still, the fact remained. I'm horny as a cactus garden at high noon.

After the show, we return to our Swiss Family Robinson quaint Little Old Lady Who Lives In a Jackboot hotel in beautiful downtown Bern. It's a small but gorgeous city, with giant Dali-esque clock towers and snow-banked rivers and postcard perfect pastoral scenes just across the road. But tonight, the town has taken a rather ugly turn, as some sort of beer-drinking, costume-wearing, citywide celebration is in effect. None of us, or anyone we talk to, knows what the purpose of this festival is, or what they are ceremoniously applauding en masse. A change of season is hinted at, a blessing for the new crop, a tip of the mug to improved hops, fertility in the land and the women, who the fuck knows? But it seems to have roots in centuries that pre-date our silly and trivial American customs, so who are we to dare judge these crazy bastards. One thing that we have learned is that this grotesque masquerade (which features a lot of the attendees wearing ersatz animal heads for whatever reason) is mainly peopled by neighboring German yuppies, not the more low-key local Swiss contingency. Germans, even more than musicians, like to consume mass quantities of beer. Sitting in the hotel bar and watching this abstract parade of mythological creatures drinking their grogs and brandishing their credit cards is beyond surreal.

Simon is with some scraggly looking teenage Riot Grrrl from the club, a bass player no less. Given the ever increasing *I surrender* vibration of our throw-in-the-towel companions, everyone else from our party has gone directly to bed. I decide to carry on, since I can't even remember the last time I saw middle-aged women in Lederhosen wearing paper-mache pig heads. We retire to the hotel bar amidst all manner of inebriated middle-class farm animals.

We're reasonably unnoticed among the melee, and the three of us—Simon, Riot Grrrl, and your humble narrator—carry on small talk about music, basses, travel, and other unimportant bullshit. The still-nameless-to-me girl excuses herself for a pee.

"She wants my dick inside her," announces Simon without blinking.

"You've got to be joking. She's just a kid!"

"Oh, I don't know. She said she was sixteen, that's old enough."

I suppose the gap between my unparalleled antiquity and a sixteen-year-old was in fact many times greater than that between a twenty-two-year-old and a sixteen-year-old. Still, it didn't feel right, and I said so.

"Simon, she's just a nice kid. Why do you have to abuse her?"

"Because she wants it, you twat. Now fuck off!"

I hobble up to my room with my aches and pains and my brain going full speed, not in the slightest bit tired. Z is snoring like a lawnmower. Tomorrow, I'd hear about how this teen bassist ripped Simon's pants down the second I left them alone. Tonight, I would only hear the sound of Z's sinuses.

●●

A BIG FRIDAY NIGHT and we're entering Ravensburg, Germany, a town no one knows anything about and no one has an opinion on—no one except for Jeff Dahl, who's played here before.

"I played the U-Boat, man. That place was fucked. There were Nazi skinheads starting fights, people spitting at the stage, people sitting on the edge of the stage shooting up. It was just totally fucked!"

This trip we would play the Jugendhaus or Youth Center. It's three stories of teenage hideaway, a sanctuary from adult supervision. Inside, there are dorms with bunk beds, kitchens, recreation rooms with foosball and pool, rehearsal rooms for the local death metal bands, and a small concert room. The place is punk—that is, run down as all hell yet somehow functional.

After a joke of a soundcheck, we kill time by watching a television that really doesn't work and observing Simon and Tim play foosball with the local teenage girls.

"Look at that little smile he pastes on for these girls," I cynically remark.

"And look at Tim," smirks Ratboy. "He's trying to be Shaun Cassidy or something, a fallen teen idol."

Our two flirtatious dashing heroes shoot us looks that can only be interpreted as *fuck off and die.* I tire of this and seek out dinner.

We gather in the kitchen, a rather filthy place inhabited by some unkempt young women who are, for better or worse, cooking for us. They begin to dish up plates of rice and some kind of white meat. It's spongy, and, except for the curry sauce that seems to be included to the point of overkill, almost tasteless.

"Um, what are we eating?" I ask.

Without batting an eye, the master chef—a thin, disheveled young lass with stringy dark hair dangling in the food—responds: "It's like chicken."

Like chicken. Well, that certainly narrows it down. What, pheasant, pigeon, bug-eyed vulture, mutated squirrel, sacrificial Satanic rabbit? You tell me.

Forget eating, I venture into the concert room where a two-man industrial band is playing pure noise for noise purists, with strobe lights blinking and a smoke machine clogging the already stifling air. The music is remarkably hideous, yet, following my hallucination-inducing meal and considering the snowy cold outside, I'm compelled to endure it. The mostly male crowd stares at these two weirdoes with hypnotic fascination. Oh, it's too much to bear, I decide to go outside, have a cigarette, and freeze to death, when, much to my surprise, I see an unfamiliar sight on my way out.

It's a woman, a mature woman grown beyond the teenage years, wearing an actual tight, short, black dress. In fact, I'd dare say it's the kind of dress that women who enjoy the company of men are prone to wear. From my distance I could see that her brown hair was pulled back into a serious bun, and that she was almost my height and in possession of a firm, taut body, outlined fabulously by the black minidress. I throw caution to the wind and approach.

Standing right beside her, I extract a ciggy from my pack and fire it up. She looks over, and I hold out the pack offering her to join me in a lung cancer ritual. She accepts and smiles. It's far too loud to talk at the moment.

The band subsides for an instant, she turns to me, and remarks: "This music is horrible. What causes people to do this to other people?" Given her accent, she is obviously a local, yet her English shows that she pegged me right.

"I can't explain it," I reply.

We exchange names. Hers is Sabine. She seems to like me, and even attempts to hijack me. "I don't think I can take any more of this. I suppose I'm going to go. Would you come for a drink with me? I know an alright place nearby where you can get a real drink."

"There's nothing I'd like more. Unfortunately, I'm next up to torture people's eardrums."

"Do you play with Jeff Dahl?" I explain that I in fact do, and she tells me she saw him previously at the U-Boat and thought he was great. Okay, she decides to stick around.

Meeting girls has become an escape valve as much as anything. Can they facilitate freedom, afford easy passage through the corridors of the unknown? In other words...

"Do you have a car?" The answer is affirmative. I tell her we can get that drink after the show.

Ah, the show. Whatever is in the water, the air, or just the good old Ravensburg chromosomes seems to ensure that every event in this isolated township must border on dada, on surrealism, and verge on anarchy. Very drunk, extremely weird, wild-eyed guys, who spend the duration of the show making lurid, verbal sexual advances toward the band, surround the claustrophobic stage. This is funny for about a minute. For the following hour and twenty-nine minutes, it's a drag.

"I waaannnt yeeewww!" slurred the apparent ringleader loudly. Then he reaches toward my crotch, drooling. Ratboy laughs uncontrollably until he becomes the next target. "Yeeewww are God! I love yer tight leeetle ahss in those paantts!"

Now Dahl laughs at us, the subjects of such unbridled homosexual desire, until he becomes heralded. "No, Noooooo! YEE-EE-WW-WW ARE GOO-OOO-AAAA-WW-WW-DDD!!! You with the big pubic head! Love me! LOVE ME!"

This went on nonstop until the end of the set, at which point we launched into the most dadaist, exploratory, abstract, free-jazz, Ornette Coleman, epileptic fit extrapolation of the Stooges "Dirt" imaginable. This simplistic soul dirge had indeed become an emotional stress ventilator of sorts, and a dependable one. As if to take us away and guard us against the evils of the physical world, we are four repressed jazzbos, unleashed from the confines of pop song structure to float freely in chordless limbos, unshackled from the chains of rigid four-on-the-floor rock beats. Somehow, the crowd loved it, and the screaming boys followed us off to the stairs that led to our third-floor refuge. Sabine was there, too.

"Give me a minute to get rid of my bass, and I'll be back down." She barely curls her lips into smile.

WE GO FOR A drink at the infamous U-Boat, which is a small, rather typical bar filled with what passes for scenesters here in Ravensburg. I quite like it. Sabine, easing rather gracefully into her mid-thirties, is a cross between Vera Miles and Emma Peel with a somewhat work-weary countenance and strained, beady green eyes. I buy her a gin and tonic, a whiskey and coke for myself, and we perch at a booth opposite the bar of this cramped booze huddle. Sabine hunkers down and scowls.

"Eh, these people. They have nothing better to do, they all stare at us."

"Really? I didn't notice. I don't feel like I'm being stared at."

"I know a lot of them, and some were at the show. The town will be gossiping tomorrow, whispering as they are now about me, about me being out with you."

"You're kidding. You're probably overreacting—they don't even know who I am."

"Oh no. They think I'm out with some American musician, and that I think I'm a big shot or something like that. They make me craaazy!"

I ignore the rest of the U-Boat denizens, and listen semi-attentively as Sabine entrusts me with her life story, at least her recent life. She teaches German to Russian-Islamic Germans, that is, Germans and their descendants who fled to Russia following World War II. Folks who now, with the reunification of Germany, want to come on back home. She hates them.

"They are cretins—crude, uncivilized barbarians with no respect for anything or anyone, least of all women. To them, I'm an object to be ridiculed and abused. They are scum who deserve only a horrible, violent death."

The woman has a way with words. She also designs leather clothes and published a book of poetry, which piques my personal interest. She says she'll translate it for me, so I'll understand her better. Meanwhile, another round, more stories, and soon we disembark for my pathetic little hobble of a room.

The drive across Ravensburg from the bar to the hotel is like crossing a parking lot—the one time I snag a car and driver there's really nowhere to go. Nonetheless, Sabine manages to go the wrong way down a one-way street and we get stopped by a policeman in what has got to be the smallest fucking police car I have ever seen. It wouldn't even function as a golf cart in the States. The police cars are, seemingly, shrinking. First, the small cop car that accosted us in Florence, then the microscopic, ramshackle joke of a four-wheeled vehicle that pulled us over going into Prague, and now this.

She says, "I'll handle thees," so I let her, not being particularly anxious to exchange pleasantries with the local gendarme in the icy cold at 2:30 a.m.

BACK AT HOTEL HELL, we relax in my bed/sitting room and I put on some music my porta-stereo, a compilation tape featuring mellifluous sounds ranging from Siouxsie to Ciccone Youth to Moby Grape to (how appropriate) German chanteuse Dagmar Krause. The lights go dim and her long, full, wavy dark reddish-brown hair comes tumbling from its restrictive binding. Wordlessly, she begins to rub my shoulders and chest with the top of her head like a cat. Then, she paws me all over with her palms, again like a cat, with that same, soft but insistent left-right routine that cats drive you crazy with. This leads to a temple rub and back massage. Though I'm still awake (sort of), this all sends me off into a sort of quasi-dream state.

"You are not like most guys. No, you are not like most people. You have a good, positive energy," she purrs. There's a long pause as I silently enjoy the physical pampering. Then, she makes an unusual declaration. "I can touch your temple in such a way as to make your brain run backwards through scattered memories and dream fragments, like a video tape recorder."

"Do it."

My lover from college sits at the piano playing Chopin (which always gave her an orgasm) while the axle of the tour van separates outside Salt Lake, and my mom and I check out the alligator farm for my ninth birthday. The tape keeps rolling and I keep reeling. Who needs psychedelics when the electric spiritualized Catwoman is on the prowl? Practically in a full hypnotic trance at this point, I nonetheless muster the willpower and wherewithal to reach up and grab her eruption of hair and pull her face down so that our lips touch and tongues meet. Time passes in unusual ways, relative, I suppose. The clocks speeds up and slow down as they see fit, answering ancient rhythms that are primal, tribal, and mystic. Reality interrupts around 4:30 a.m. or thereabouts.

"I've got to teach those ignorant mongrels how to speak properly in a few hours. I must go, but I'll see you tomorrow."

She'll see me tomorrow? Hmmm, should I try to get hold of some catnip?

❧

"NO, NO, NO UNDERSTAND. You wait. Wait!"

The matronly woman of indeterminate age waddles off to locate her prepubescent daughter, who has a much better grasp on the English language. Here in the practically nonexistent mountain town of Ulm, English-speaking folks pass through infrequently. The daughter emerges from the small hotel's kitchen.

"Can I help you?"

"I hope so. I'd like to get a couple of glasses, for drinking liquids, you know. And I'd like to get some soap, and a towel, for bathing."

She disappears and re-emerges with a washrag-sized towel.

"No soap?"

"This is cheap hotel, sir."

Yes, well, no need to overstate the obvious. Earlier I'd actually had this poor girl come up to my room to get me some sheets for the bed.

The local market had these cheap little candles. I bought a bunch of them and took them back to my room. I close the blinds and survey this closet of a room. Dammit, I'm going to make it cool if it kills me. The bed isn't even a twin. It's barely a two by four with a lumpy pillow at one end. At the foot of the bed is a small hutch, which I decorate with my porta-stereo, candles, and drape my flashy, bejeweled, pastel tie-dyed neck scarf over the torn lamp shade. This is how Jimmy Page would do it, or Keith Richards. Yeah, turn even this pitiful hobble into a gypsy camp, a place of fun and romance. Who was I kidding? The room was so small there was barely enough room to squeeze between my bass case, resting against the wall, and the bed to get to the shower-sized bathroom. Pagey and Keef might be proud of the effort, but they'd be sad and shake their heads in dismay at the reality. "Po' fucka," they'd say. "Rock 'n' roll was never this fookin' dreary fer us!"

Following the gig—at another Jugendhaus, complete
with some stoned kid coming onstage to do a Johnny
Thunders impersonation and another guy wearing a
"Satanists Against Racial Prejudice" T-shirt—Sabine returns
with me to my closet of romance. She comes bearing gifts—
photos and copies of her writings—like a schoolgirl with a
crush. I'm a little touched. The back of the photo says:

> A moment
> In my life.
>
> You are
> My soul
> My security
> My danger
> Sabine

BABY, I'M JUST A shmuck on the road with a band, like a
million shmucks before me and a million comin' round
the pike. I ain't your soul, and I sure as hell ain't your
security. Your danger? You're the one who was tweakin'
my brain like a Panasonic ghetto blaster. Ease up.

I find it hard to settle in and get comfortable with a
strange girl in such confining space. Ah, well, nothing a
little John Lee Hooker cassette won't unravel.

"Ahhmm in the moood, the mood fo' luv!" intones
the blues master.

Turns out the Catwoman don't groove on the blues.
"Turn that off!" she veritably snaps. I calmly shoot her a

glance, but kill the sounds anyway. The resulting silence is deafening.

"Excuse me," I announce, adjourning to pee in the bathroom, a mere five inches away. I return to find a very serious looking Catwoman awaiting her prey pensively on the child-sized bed. Stripped down to her black bra and panties, and with a steel-eyed, piercing, X-ray vision burning from her lashes through my very soul, I feel naked already. She begins the cat routine again, and I feel suddenly extremely uncomfortable in her presence. Her bra comes off, and she is rubbing her butt against my crotch. I bend over her back and kiss her neck, feeling a sudden, bizarre, uncalled for desire to bite hard into her skin and draw blood. I resist, being ever the gentleman. The lights are out, the ludicrous candles are flickering away, now we're face to face, smoldering like the flame. It is an unusually tense moment, and to be sure, something just doesn't feel right.

"Are you ready?" she asks, demanding "Do it now!"

So much for foreplay. "Eh, you know what, I don't have a rubber." It was a lie. Simon put two in my leather jacket after coming to my room and seeing the budget love nest first hand. Be it guilt, paranoia, advanced shyness, sudden Catherine Deneuve-esque repulsion, I dunno, but I just didn't feel like delivering the final act, the home run, the rocket launch. I also had a weird feeling that we weren't alone. I suppose this violates the most sacred of all male laws: if ever a girl wants it, no matter how sickening an act it may look to be, the man must give it. No man may ever turn his back on ready 'n' willin' sex. It is the way. It is our duty to fuck whenever the opportunity presents itself. Anything too slow to get out of the way invariably has it coming.

"I have one!" She grabs her purse and flings useless artifacts from it, looking for the hermetically sealed second skin of safe and disinfected passion.

"Here, come here, just a minute first, let's relax for a second, alright?" I beseech, cradling the hyper-drive kitty in my arms.

"You know, something is different tonight from last time. You seem to have a negative energy, a black aura. You were so positive before. What went wrong?"

I don't answer, and this naked, desperate angel begins to cry next to me—or rather practically on top of me given my peasant-sized bed. Shit, I don't need this. So, her mystic meter reader says I'm coming up negative. Great.

I start kissing her, maybe it'll stop her crying and, what the hell, maybe I'll get in the mood. Yeah, that's the idea. What's wrong with me? Okay, she's a little worse for wear and tear, but she does look pretty good with her clothes off, and she's certainly anxious. A bit of preliminary grinding occurs when suddenly, surprisingly, the ashtray that was on the second shelf of the hutch flies off the shelf directly on top of us in bed, a distance of three feet. We both sit up.

"What was that?" asks Sabine loudly and nervously.

"It's an ashtray," I answer, picking it up and looking at it.

"It just flew into the bed!?"

"Yes, seems to be."

She glares at me, as if to demand an explanation.

"Maybe it's a manifestation of negative energy," I offer half-sarcastically. It's possible that in precoital grindage we jarred the ashtray from it's secure position, yet how do you explain it traveling the two and a half feet into the bed rather than just falling straight down? At this point, I don't wanna see what's going on anymore, so I somewhat nervously blow out the candles, put the ashtray back, and lay back down. Should I try to pick up where I left off? I wonder.

Then there's a thumping noise, right to the side of the bed. I turn on a little lamp and watch, incredulously, as my bass case bumps up and down all by itself and moves away from me along the wall toward the window. We both see this happening.

"What the fuck?" is the most intelligent thing I can muster.

"What's going on!?" she asks, obviously scared.

"I don't know. I'm not too versed on the paranormal. It seems we have visitors of some kind." The bass stops its dance and again there is calm. The light's still on, and we're still sitting up. We don't talk at all, and I'm unsure how much time passed. Finally, I click off the light and lie back down, sweating.

"Do you think this place is haunted?" she asks.

"Seems like a good bet." I considered my grade-Z accommodations for a moment. "Naw, you know what, it's probably just rats—big, hideous rats that can lift a fifteen-pound case and hurl ashtrays like Joe Namath. Yeah, that's all it is."

I feel extremely uneasy, feverish, dizzy, and the bed seems to swim as if at sea. I can feel her body, clammy and sweaty next to me. The bed itself holds two as easily as the back seat of the van holds four. We sleep off and on and don't speak to each other again until the morning.

SABINE JOINS THE ENTOURAGE for our typical budget breakfast of cheese, bread, butter, coffee, tea, milk, and juice. Small talk is exchanged, but mainly I can't get last night's poltergeist performance from my mind, and I can't help but see Sabine at the center of it. Her sad life, her desperate poetry, her sexual over-anxiousness, and her unwillingness to go away are on my now shattered nerves. She says she wants to follow us to the next stop, Stuttgart, where there is a famous modern art museum she could take us to. Rat and Z say how much they'd like that, despite me shooting them lethal glances. She'll follow the van in her car.

"Will you ride with me," she asks demurely. Damn, you'd think she'd be the last person who'd want my company.

"Eh, well, I can't really, see, there's some details regarding merchandising and the show that we have to discuss. It's really the only time we have alone to deal with our business."

Dahl overhears me and picks up on what I'm doing. "Oh, McGruff. Don't worry about it. We can handle it. Go on with her."

"Gee, thanks, Jeff, but I really think I should be in on it. In fact, we should get going now, shouldn't we, Simon?"

"Like to finish me tea, if you don't mind, lover. What's the rush?" It was obvious none of my bros had my back or intended on helping me out.

I ride in the van anyway. As we depart, I instruct Simon to attempt to lose her.

"Are you sure that's what you want? Who knows when you'll ever even see a girl again at one of the gigs on this tour."

"I'll chance it. Step on it, dammit!"

Everyone laughs at me as Simon gives his best James Bond chase scene effort to out-drive Sabine, but given we're in a van and she has a sports car, he fails. By 1:30 p.m., both vehicles pull into the hotel parking lot, back in Dahl's birthplace, Stuttgart.

HAVING BEEN TO THE Louvre, the modern art museum was a bit of a letdown. Much of it seemed like tomfoolery, pulling one over on the public, although sometimes that's the point. We all appreciated the Warhol exhibit, and that was perhaps the biggest shock of them all. Ratboy stood in front of a Jackson Pollack work, which consisted of three solid planes of color.

"Look at this," said the guitar-slinging art critic. "The paint isn't even spread smoothly. This guy couldn't paint a wall!"

As we wonder through the museum's rooms, Sabine clings to me like a bad habit (much to Z and Rat's delight) holding my hand and arm and so forth. Still, I enjoy the Otto Dix, Dali, and Ernst, and the coffee afterwards.

Back at the hotel, Simon has given me a single room again, though I specifically instructed him not to. Inside, I start to change my clothes while Sabine sits pensively on the bed.

"Look, you've got to understand, I've got a job to do here. I can't hang out with you all the time, I've got to go and play music. You've got to get back to your life."

"It's Sunday. I don't work today. I can just wait in the room until you come back, if I'm in the way."

Geez, there's just no easy way. Clearly I'm in a "be careful what you wish for" situation. "No, look, you just have to go. I have to get back to the groove I was in. I can't hang out. I want to be alone tonight. Don't take it personally, you're great, but I just have to get back to what I'm trying to concentrate on." Finally and firmly, I tell her, "You have to leave."

We kiss and once and for all she leaves. Is she upset? I don't know, she seems positively emotionless now. What a strange girl, so full of electric energy and cosmic debris. I wonder if it was feline power and psychic voodoo that was causing the Stephen King scene last night. Whatever, I surely didn't want to hurt her feelings, but I'm so glad she's gone. I flop down hard on my bed and issue a loud sigh of relief. Yeah, careful what you wish for. I pulled all those sly moves to entangle her in my web, only to find the real trick was getting her untangled. She always looked so sad. Well, who knows, maybe better luck tonight. It was just a game, now, a diversion tactic, something to ease the boredom. As the wise sage Lemmy once said, "The chase is better than the catch, you know it is!"

OUR GERMAN RECORD DISTRIBUTOR hooked up a support act called Mind Overboard for the rest of the German dates. We meet up with them and find that they are older geezers, and not so easily impressed by us. They are standoffish and quiet, only the drummer and the guitarist's girlfriend, who sells the T-shirts, speak decent English. They drive home every night and meet up with us the next day, never getting a hotel, no matter where we are playing. They are on a true no-budget outing—foodless, diesel-less, hotel-less, lifeless. They use our amps and eat our backstage food. The drummer has his neck in a brace, and looks like Pee-wee Herman. We never quite learn their names, but always refer to the drummer as Pee-wee. He doesn't seem to mind. They play hard, and get the crowd going very well—the fact that they speak German helps. As time wears on, the two groups become friendly and even supportive of each other, but this is a won trust, not a given, and as such, carries more weight and value.

Our German dates bottom-out by the time we get to Koln. As is common by this point in our journey, we can't find the club, and Simon, an honorary American dad driving the family cross-country on vacation, refuses to ask any locals for directions. After a good wasted hour, we arrive at the Underground, a truly bizarre combination of coffee shop, microbrewery, auto repair shop, and live music club. Some overtly unfriendly guy covered in grease shimmies his way out from under a Volkswagen bus and begrudgingly unlocks a room where we can stash our equipment. As in Prague, we have the first night off, and we are in accommodations provided by the club. Also, like Prague, there is one key for the six of us. We ask if, like Prague, there will be some wild shenanigans taking place on-site at the Underground, but Adolph Asshole merely informs us: "No. There's nothing for you here."

He's right. In fact, the accommodations, unlike the upstairs crash pad in Prague, are several kilometers away, beyond reasonable walking distance. Also, in Prague, we were sympathetic to the obviously kind and well-meaning people doing the best they could do given the budget they had. Köln was a large city in a wealthy country and the Underground was a big club. The "accommodations" in this case reflect the promoter's cheapness, which furthers the intended bastardization of musicians in general, an exploitative attitude implying that we'll be happy with just a bed and a toilet. Fuck 'em.

It's above a musical instrument shop, and the shop's proprietor shakes his head in pity as he lets us in. There's a room with a sink and a shower, neither of which work, a bunk bed, and another cramped room

with two bunks and a broken window. The radiator half
works (if you kick it), but it only stays on for an hour at
a time, so if you fall asleep while it's on it turns off and
lets the room temperature nosedive. The sheets lay in a
pile in the corner—washed? Who could say? The walls
are peeled and cracked, and above one bunk a previous
tenant has drawn on the wall, marking off the days spent
in groups of five, just like they do in prison movies.
There is garbage everywhere—food wrappers, beer cans,
empty packs of guitar strings, and cigarettes. It is beyond
depressing.

I cynically laugh about it all, my anger just barely
held in check. Z, Rat, and Tim, mope around grumbling
under their breath. Simon's all smiles, because his lovely
lass from home, Melanie, is in town and they're going to
be spending the night in a four-star motel across town.
How nice.

Dahl rebukes his band of babies. "It's not that bad.
You guys have never been on a punk tour." Them's
fighting words, bub, and both me and Rat respond.

"We've been on plenty of them, and you know it!" I
say, my voice tensing.

"The thing is," says Rat, quietly but firmly, "is that
you said we'd have hotels every night. We're supposed to
get a bare minimum of comfort since we're not getting
paid, per diems, or anything else. It's only what you said.
But whatever, I can deal with it."

Indeed, what choice would there be? The Factsheet
Three decide to get out on the town. It's unbearable here,

so off we go. We actually have some errands: we need to find an optician to clean Rat's screwed-up contact lens and to sell me more disposable ones. We cruise Koln for optics, beer, food, and guitar shops, anything to kill time yet save money. We're all essentially broke by this point. After dark, and after a decent Italian meal in a nondescript little restaurant not too far from Stalag Koln, we return.

"Didja bring me anything to eat? I haven't eaten all day," Dahl asks

"No, we weren't sure what you'd want," I reply. "Do you want to go get something while we stay here?"

"No. Fuck it."

"I'll go get you something if you like. I don't mind going back out."

"No, just forget it."

"You should eat if you're hungry."

"No."

"I know you're hungry. Is there a reason you don't want to go out and you don't want food brought to you?"

"No!"

Jeff of Arc, rock martyr. I didn't think it possible at this point, but he still is capable of becoming even more of a mystery to me. Silence again ensues as we all stare at the grotesque walls. Simon, chipper with the thought of being with his true love, stands up and prepares to exit this unfavorable scene for the honeymoon suite of some nearby hovel. I remember that he has a bottle of Southern Comfort, acquired for band consumption, safely tucked away in his bag.

"Gimme the Southern Comfort, since you're going off to have fun and we're stuck here."

"Oh, c'mon, I was going to drink it up with Melanie, have a few spots to increase the mood, you know."

"Forget it. It's a band bottle, and I intend on crawling inside of it and getting warm, cozy, and lost in its reassuring haze."

"Well, I don't see why you have any more right to it than I do."

"You can get a bottle of anything, anywhere. You have the van, money, freedom, a girl, a real hotel room. You got it all. I'm stuck here. Look, it's not really open to discussion. Give me the fucking bottle of Southern Comfort. NOW!!!"

"You fookin' cry baby." He throws the bottle at me.

"Goddamn, it's over half gone. You haven't even been sharing."

"Would you shut the fuck up about the booze?" shouts Dahl from the next room. Simon leaves and I commence to drink. Z and Rat have a little to keep warm, but mostly it's me, hitting straight off the bottle and enjoying that sweet, cough syrup rush that only the chosen elixir of Janis Joplin can administer. By 10:00 p.m., I'm drunk enough to fall asleep.

While I snore like a race car, Dahl paces the floor like a worried dad. Seems Tim has gone out on solo flight and has not returned. I wake up at 2:00 a.m., and Dahl is stumbling around.

"What are you doing, man?"

"Tim never came back, the idiot. I'm responsible for him!"

"Oh." Not being capable of mustering any concern for Tim, I go right back to sleep.

The next morning we learn that Tim was locked outside, and apparently we couldn't hear him pounding on the door from upstairs. As the worried father and prodigal son slumber, the remaining three go for breakfast. Ratboy just can't get over what he's going through.

"I'll never do this shit again. This is bullshit," he says offhandedly. "When my band goes on tour, it's going to be done right, with a proper budget and decent gigs, or forget it. None of this staying in Alcatraz Prison so I can play in a fucking auto garage the next night."

Koln is one gigantic mall, an endless indoor-outdoor shopping area. Given we have practically no money, we somehow manage to waste the whole day endlessly walking in and out of places we have no intention of buying anything in. Following a beer and pinball break, which is surprisingly refreshing without Simon along to slaughter us game after game, we return to the penitentiary by 4:00 p.m. I polish off more Southern Comfort, and once again I'm drunk, which I openly admit, and then it's off to yet another pointless waste of a soundcheck.

Usually when I drink, I get in a mellow, happy mood, but not tonight. Tonight, I'm in the mood to argue, fight, and/or carouse. I can feel myself ready to go off. At the club, the promoter tells us to move our van off the lot. Simon, who's in a terrific mood, sets off to comply, but I intervene. I set into the guy, raising my voice and saying it won't be moved because all of our luggage is in it, and it was clearly unsafe to leave it in the "club apartment." Later, the representative of our German distributor shows up, and tells Dahl we can't sell our CDs because they came from France and the U.S.—we must purchase them from him in Germany. Jeff agrees to this. It technically is none of my business, but I make it all mine anyway. I start an argument with the guy, saying we're supporting ourselves on the road with these friggin' CDs and what help has he been and how does he expect us to carry on and it's none of his affair and so on. Dahl vanishes, and I adjourn to the bar with this joker to resume discourse, joined by Z to aid in the debate. We're from the record company, after all, so to hell with what anyone else says, we're gonna call this shot. We argue for over an hour, and eventually Mr. Distributor gives in. I think just for the peace of not having to hear us anymore.

Blasting through the show faster and more furiously than normal, I look up and see Rich and Laura, friends of ours from a local Los Angeles band, The Tommyknockers. They are on a Euro Tour of their own, crisscrossing ours, and they're here to party, heckle, and kibitz with some homeboys. Laura, who I've never gotten along with, sneaks up behind a pole that is to the side of me onstage, and, once behind it, grabs me while I'm playing and gives me the hero's French kiss. She's perhaps not my type, but it feels pretty damn good. So good, in fact, that I manage to play the next song and a half without missing a note while making out with her. That's entertainment. I figure by this point, might as well give the punters a little something extra.

Meanwhile, a Swedish-style blonde beauty is soul mating with me as we head toward the encore. Perhaps Germany, not Italy, is the Promised Land. Then, a loud, erratic noise interrupts the proceeding as Rat's amp blows out. He plugs into Dahl's set up. Dahl takes center mic like a real lead singer while I go back to smooching with Laura, and Z throws drumsticks at me. We launch into yet another surfin'-on-the-astroplane rendition of "Dirt," made all the more warped by Dahl rolling on the floor and groaning during the more musically hypothetical moments.

Following the show, I give the blonde a personalized S.L. Duff pick—a look that says she will be mine—but she leaves with her boyfriend. How naïve of me.

"Laura, let's go outside and neck."

"Okay."

It's fun for about a minute, but it's cold outside, and we're only kissing out of abstract boredom. We don't even like each other and we both know it. We go into the bar where another touring band has shown up to blow off steam. Known—honestly—as the Scottish Sex Pistols, these wankers play the Pistols songbook lock, stock, and barrel, and are even a more punk rock Sha Na Na than we are. In keeping with their adopted image, they start a fight, talk in awful, phony Cockney accents and generally annoy everyone. As I continue to drink past the limit of any degree of sensibility, I notice Rat pouting in a chair by himself. I turn to my right and see a gorgeous brunette and point Rat out to her. She seems to think he's cute, a match made in heaven, perchance, but Rat doesn't want to be cheered. As much as I try to enjoy myself, there is always someone around who is unhappy. Ahhh, road life.

Back to spend our final night in the Koln Pen, I put on a tape of hard-rocking old school punk—Black Flag, Circle Jerks, Adolescents, Damned, the good stuff. From the other room, Dahl snaps a request for no more music. He's going straight to sleep, goddammit! Another party of one, I take my headphones and the dregs of the Comfort bottle to the upper bunk with me. I quickly pass out, and, as in France, wake up in a pool of my own piss, a suitable souvenir to leave for the next poor bastard. Maybe I'll skip drinking for a few nights.

THE NEXT MORNING WE have another band argument—as if you couldn't see that coming. I wake up understandably hungover and crabby, and complain about how shitty the food the Underground fed us was, how fucked up this dump is, and how, in general, the club treated us like tenth-rate losers. Dahl seems only concerned with making these cretins happy and not stepping on any toes so he'll be afforded the luxury of returning to play these holes for the fourth time. Then I launch into a new topic.

"You know, it woulda been nice to have been thanked for being the only bastard with enough balls to stand up to the promoter and the distributor when they both tried to railroad us."

"McGruff, you and Rat have been complaining nonstop," reckons Dahl. "You're making yourselves miserable. Fuck the situation with the distributor. We could easily just sell T-shirts the rest of the time here in Germany, no big deal."

"No big deal?! You just pocketed a couple hundred extra bucks because of me. And what about the van? You don't think that was important. I guarantee you, had we parked it on the street, we'd a been ripped off."

"There was nothing to worry about regarding the van," chirps Simon, the happy little bird. "He agreed to let me keep it where it was as soon as I asked him nicely."

"That's bullshit. You were running out with the keys and your tail between your legs as soon as you were told to."

"Nope." I see now that it's every dog for himself. Two weeks—slightly less than one fourth—of Euro-Blur left, and it's come to this.

"I'm sick of you guys and your bellyaching," Dahl says, starting to sound less rational and more emotional, as the military side wanes and the sensitive artist side rises. "I'm going to have to think long and hard about you guys going to Japan. I think I'm just going to get a band there."

Dahl leaves for the van. The Rat speaks. "I don't care if I go to Japan, I don't think I can deal with being in the presence of the Master much longer."

"Yeah, I don't care. Fuck this," added Z.

"Well, I fucking care. I haven't gone through all of this not to get a payday. We'll get paid in Japan, and besides, it's Japan. None of us have been there. Goddammit, it would be just like Dahl to have us do the dirty work and then reward someone else with the Japan trip."

"Forget it, McGruff," said Z, doing his best Jack Nicholson. "It's Chinatown."

❦

ONTO MÜNSTER, WHERE WE'RE treated much better, fed well, and generally kowtowed to in terms of sound and lights. The promoter here, Alfred, is a big, jovial, bearded redhead who aims to please. Largely obnoxious, drunken idiot guys, and a slew of young, cute girls attend the show. It reminds me of clubs in Orange County, California, where the ratio of knucklehead buffoon jarhead rejects and delectable sultry samples of femininity is roughly similar. The girls here gather at the front of the stage and dance, while the guys jump up onstage, yell into the mics, and then knock them over. This silly ritual continues throughout the whole show. As together as Alfred and the crew are, they didn't count on needing any security, which would have been pretty helpful.

After the show, a six-foot-tall dishwater blonde with big eyes and thin lips talks to Rat about their favorite

guitarists. Out of all these girls, she seems to be the only
one left who followed the show. Later, I'm carrying some
equipment out to the van when she walks up and starts
talking to me.

"I understand you like dancing."

"Besides playing the show, it's the only form of
exercise we've been able to organize on this little outing."
I pause for a second. "That's a stupid answer. I apologize.
Yes, I love dancing, where can we go tonight to trip the
light fantastic?"

"I was trying to think of someplace, but haven't
come up with anything gooot. Wednesday in Münster
is really not very gooot. Besides, you must have plenty of
GROUPIES to keep you busy."

Of course I laugh. "Groupies? We have no groupies.
There are no groupies on this tour. Just look around.
Desolation. This is how it is after every show."

Hadn't I explained this before, in France, in Belgium,
in fact wherever we tread? Like many before, she begins
giggling at our plight. "Really, no groupies?"

"Are you volunteering for the job?" asked Dahl as he
walked by.

She laughs with Jeff and then turns back to talk
quietly with me. "I'm going to go now, but I'll come see
you Friday. Alfred's going to go to your show and I'll
catch a ride with Heeem. I will see you then." She pulled
me close and kissed me. Hmm, sometimes cool things
are where you least expect them. Do I hear wedding
bells? I hoped she wouldn't turn out to be Catwoman II.

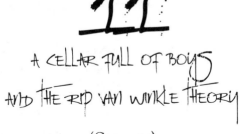

11.

A CELLAR FULL OF BOYS
AND THE RIP VAN WINKLE THEORY

(Germany)

G ERMANY HAS BECOME A haze of little towns you've
never heard of. Each day begins with a pretty short
drive, a hotel check-in, plenty of time to try and fill, a
soundcheck, hours of more time with nothing to do,
a show, back to the hotel, where, that's right, there's
nothing to do.

In a small, very pleasant town called Bochum,
the band is treated like kings with great food, a high-
fidelity soundcheck, and an A-1 hotel. I compliment
the promoter by saying, "A well-treated band is a happy
band!"

Dahl shoots a scowl at me and intones, "It just makes
for a fat and lazy band."

He was right about one thing: our tour regimen was
doing nothing for anyone's waistline. Simon and Dahl
seemed essentially unscathed—Simon due to his youth
and Dahl to his abstinence—but even the skinniest Rat
was packin' a tire, the ever-vain Z was getting slightly

frumpy, our very own Surf City Romeo, the mighty
Tim, was noticeably heading down the Orson Welles
highway, and I was doing my share to put the paunch
in raunch.

At the Bochum gig, the Master and Quasimodo—Dahl
and Simon—consent to allow Rat to do the unthinkable
and drive the van back to the hotel after soundcheck.
The three of us go back to my room to drink beer and
watch MTV—nothing special—but we were quite happy
to be out of the club environment and just kickin' it. Z
had also told me that our boss from the record company,
Peter, was going to be at the show tonight. He was in
town visiting our German distributor. I could grill him
face-to-face as to whether we'd be returning to gainful
employment or the soup line.

We return to the gig just slightly early. As we pull
the van into Zwischenfall's parking lot, Simon comes
running from the club waving his arms.

"Hurry, hurry. You're on right now! Dahl's right
pissed, he is."

As ever, Rat is calm. "Why are we on now? We're not
supposed to be on for another half hour."

"The support went on extra early, and now the
management is screaming for you to play!"

"That's not our fault," I point out, for if I've learned
one thing on this tour, it's to get that finger pointed
at someone other than yourself as quickly as possible.
"Besides, who ever heard of a band going onstage early?
How un-rock 'n' roll can you get?"

"It would figure that it's someone opening for us," chuckles Z.

We enter the club and all eyes are upon us. Some people start to clap 'cause they know the wait is almost over. Dahl is not among the cheering admirers. He's standing with Peter and the owner of our German label. "Nice of you to drop by," he says to us, and then to the label guys, "the big rock stars had to go to the hotel. That will never happen again."

After two minutes of flung open guitar cases and furiously untangled patch cords, we get on stage and start jammin'. I'm embarrassed after being called out like that, and kinda pissed, so it makes me wail that much harder. If nothing else, playing is good for getting a day's worth of pent-up anger out, at least partially.

After the show, Z, Pete, and I have a record honcho hoedown in the dressing room, kicking everyone else out and talking as long as we like. Besides getting reassured that there was no need to fear for my job and that the company was fine, it was nice to have Dahl waiting for us for a change, instead of vice versa as he did his endless fanzine interviews.

We walk out from the meeting. Pete shakes my hand and says he enjoyed our show, and takes off with his German comrade. Simon, meanwhile, walks around like a zombie, slowly moving things, not talking to anyone, looking completely dazed. Is he mad, burnt out, or just hating the fact that he's still cooped up with us and wishing he were dead? I decide to investigate outside by the van.

"What's up, man? You don't look right."

"I'm fine," he says in a monotone robot voice, almost as if he was putting me on.

"Is it something I said?" trying to inject that long-lost element of humor.

"It's nothing." He blinks quickly and his head suddenly twitches. "It's everything. It's you lot. You're a bunch of miserable bastards. I've never seen anything like it."

"Go on."

"Dahl's a Nazi commando, finally come home to rule in the homeland. Rat's a sourpuss, dragging around like he wants to die. Tim's a momma's boy with daddy's expense account. And you're a cynical prick that thinks his shit doesn't stink!"

"What about Z?" I ask, hating to feel that anyone's left out.

"Z's alright. He's the only one of the lot of you who just takes care of his business and gets his job done without a weird attitude. You all could learn a lot from Z."

As quickly as he shifts into hyperdrive, he slips back into his lugubrious death march. I decide not to pester him further, in case he might completely snap.

The following day we check into a pleasant family run hotel in a place called Osnabrück. There, Simon sits in his room staring at television static and listening to its white noise soundtrack full blast. It's evident that he's cracking.

I kill a lot of that day by hanging in the hotel bar, drinking straight bourbon, and eating these cakes that the owner, a big jolly geezer (originally from Hamburg, he tells me) has home baked. Yum! Simon now watches a game show on the lobby television—an improvement, I suppose, over static, though perhaps less New Age—and Tim yakks away about how he's leaving the tour.

"My dad is sending me a ticket. I'm going to fly to Rome, where we have an audience with the Pope."

I assume this is bullshit and don't even comment on it. Simon, still despondent, is seemingly incapable at this point of standard discourse. Later, while driving to the gig, Tim mentions it again.

"What, you were serious before? The Pope?" I query.

"Yeah, no shit. The Pope. My dad gives a lot of money to the church, so we're invited to hang out with the Pope. I think it'll be a trip."

"The Pope's gonna love you, man. I just know it," I laugh, and my laughing becomes more uncontrollable. Pretty soon everyone's cracking up. "The fucking Pope, that's beautiful. Too perfect. From Jeff Dahl to the Pope. You are truly blessed!"

THE OSNABRÜCK ONSLAUGHT IS perhaps the rowdiest and ugliest we would play on our outing, these kids being maybe even more out of control than the outlaws of the Basque in Spain. This Jugend Centrum is another multi-storied testimony to turning kids loose to run their own affairs like *Lord of the Flies*. There are a lot of zoned-out youth here, with some of the most bizarre hairstyles imaginable, asymmetric shavings, skewed pompadours, sideways Mohawks, and all kinds of damn things. A number of the kids are obnoxiously loud, swilling beer like sailors, and pointing and shouting, sitting near us while we eat and obviously laughing at us. Why? I don't know. We aren't particularly funny.

We seek the relative solace, or at least privacy, of the dressing room, where we'll be for another indeterminate length of time. It's Friday in Germany, which means naked girls on television. It keeps Dahl appeased, in fact, it's a bit of a task to eviscerate him from the couch and drag him onstage.

The wildly drunk and high audience is ready for war, heckling us, throwing garbage, falling down loaded, leaping onstage, knocking mics over, pushing musicians, throwing up. We stand our ground, staring the rabble down, shoving them offstage, spitting back, yelling at them. A buzz of warmth and understanding is in the air—somewhere, I'm sure, but most definitely not here.

Following the battle we call a set, I look down and the entire edge of the stage is lined with hypodermic syringes. A wacky teen party, Osnabrück style. Still agitated and on edge, I walk offstage and see our friends from Münster, promoter Alfred, and the six-foot blonde who said she'd be joining him. I invite them up to the dressing room. Alfred declines. She accepts. I realize I'd never learned her name, and find out it's Rheinheld. You gotta love these European names.

I offer her a soda and she gives me a Marlboro. We relax on the couch. For the first time on the entire tour, we are out of beer as the entire club has been drunk bone dry. There's absolutely not one drop of beer left. My guess is that all the heroin is gone, too.

Rheinheld looks good to me, with her straight hair parted to the side, tumbling across her face. She's a natural beauty, relying not at all on makeup or flashy clothes. She's soft spoken and pretty bright.

"You seemed so angry onstage, tonight," she observes. "So aggressive."

"I was having a little trouble communicating with my brothers and sisters in the crowd. I couldn't ignite the fire of love in the room."

She laughs and smiles, and notices the television, which now has advanced to softcore sex acts.

"Do you find this kind of entertainment erotic?" she asks with a knowing smile and more than a hint of sarcasm.

"Not really. It's like watching a film of someone eating a New York steak when you're really hungry. I prefer live theatre, I suppose."

We bullshit around for a while—for once, we're not being raced out of the club and into the van. Alfred appears and says he's ready to go.

"Okay, I'll be right down. Walk with me," she orders, turning to me. In control yet demure, six feet of Germanic dominance. I like this girl!

Halfway down the stairs she grabs me and pulls me to her. I look up slightly to gaze into her eyes.

"I'm sorry I didn't drive my own car. It was a bit eeefy. But I will see you again, if I can. Here's my number. Call with some places you will play in Holland. I will try to come see you, and stay with you."

Nothing more needed to be said, so we started kissing long and slow under the glaring, bright florescent white light in the stairway. Then she's gone as quickly as she came. Apparently, half the band walked by while we made out and we didn't notice the onlookers, but I would hear about it for the rest of the night. That's all right, I thought to myself. We'll always have Osnabrück.

MARBURG IS ONE OF the few German cities that has a lot of pre-WWII architecture left standing. We arrive early in the afternoon (surprise) and can't get in the club. The promoter, who we can't locate, has the keys to the house we're to stay at, so Tim goes off on his own (rehearsing his lines to the Pope, we presume) while Dahl hides out in the parked van. The rest of us hike way up this steep hill to a museum and a cathedral, and all of us seem to be in a mellow, good mood for a change. From the hill we can see for miles. We take it easy, taking pictures and smoking cigarettes.

The gig that night begins with a bald guy in a leather jacket (have you noticed this is becoming a recurrence) running up, smashing a beer bottle across the edge of the stage, and bursting into a wild spastic solo dance. Meanwhile, the local metal boys sit sullenly on the edge of the stage with their backs to us, looking out at the crowd. I reward this invasion of our space by going up behind them and jabbing my knees into their backs, leaning forward, then proceeding to rock, using them as a balance point. I have no idea how they will respond. I had assumed violently, but they actually seem to enjoy it. Maybe it's like some kind of therapeutic massage, I dunno. Whatever the case, they seem to like me now, and offer to take the band out for a drink after the show.

First we go to a bar, and when we ask for some rock 'n' roll on the tape machine, they play death metal, then we go to a disco, where the most bumpin' thing they're bustin' out is Sade and some tame acid jazz.

"Hey, man. Ya got anything that will cause booties to move, hips to shake, and muthafuggers to groove," I ask the uptight DJ.

"It's Saturday!"

"Yeah, let's get the party started!"

"We don't do that here on Saturday!"

"Look at your dance floor. You could drop a bomb in the middle of it and not hurt anyone!"

"Fuck off!"

We bust a move anyway, and as is our way, Rat, Z, and I just start dancing with each other, oblivious to anyone's opinion or attitude toward us. Our metal boy escorts just watch us, shaking their heads. *Are they straight or gay?* they seem to ask each other. Funny, that's precisely what we were wondering about them.

Within a few minutes we're surrounded by a gaggle of extremely homely girls who want to dance with us. Hey, homely girls need love, too. Meanwhile, I look over at Simon, who's been drinking a fair bit and is moments away from taking part in a fistfight.

"C'mon, then, you Kraut bastard! I'll spread your face across the floor."

"In your dreeeamz, you Engleesh faggot!"

"Alright, fellas, nothing's that important, let's all just try to have a good time, eh?" I intervene, stupidly stepping right in-between them.

"I'll punch your face off just to land a good one on him!" Simon threatens me.

"Simon, mellow out, or I'll sick these girls on you, and they look way tougher than all of us. Now, c'mon. Let's just walk away from this guy. Fuck him! C'mon, let's go get a beer."

"I appreciate what you're trying to do McGruff, but fuck you anyway." With that, he and Tim take their leave for the night. We continue to drink and dance and flirt with the girls, no matter how ugly they are. Z's making time with an adorable brunette, but she suddenly has to go. So close, so far. It's all becoming very familiar, isn't it? As if to keep the déjà vu intact, we return to the band house, and drunkenly awake the other three with our loud laughing and stumbling.

A GRIZZLED GEEZER STRAIGHT from a rough night sleeping in someone's doorway—probably the Chuck Bukowski of Marburg—joins us for breakfast at a café next door to our accommodations. Grumbling in any language is grumbling. He grabs a stack of napkins and starts writing notes to each of us in German. We look back at him blankly, wishing he would simply go away. Just one napkin left, but we all have our personalized notes already. He blows a big green gob of snot into it, throws in on the table, and lurches out of the café. Fortunately no shrapnel hit my muffin. I pop the last of my Excedrin supply and it's off to the van.

Dahl has an unusually chipper disposition this Sunday afternoon, as we head off to Frankfurt, a town I've actually heard of. "Yeah, we're staying at a really great place tonight. We're staying at the promoter's house. It's really great. We get the basement, with his record collection and excellent stereo, but best of all is his cat, Felix. Greatest cat in the world. And, wait till you have some of his coffee."

Z, Rat, and I look over at Dahl, but say nothing. I suppose the knowledge that we have a world-class fur ball and an award-winning cup of Joe just over the horizon has rendered us speechless.

We pull up to the club, aptly named Negativ, at precisely 3:00 p.m. A cold basement with grungy toilets and cracked mirrors, a slightly less cold upstairs with stools and a foosball table will be our world for the next ten hours. Outside, the entire city of Frankfurt is shut down. There ain't nothin' open. I walk for blocks just to find a pack of cigarettes, at least I kill a little over a half hour this way. I almost feel like going back for gum just to have something to do and chew up.

I spend an inordinate amount of time in the men's room toilet stall; for some reason now I have to defecate about every half hour. How could my body hold this much shit? At least the stall is covered with hilarious wall-to-wall graffiti to keep me amused, etched no doubt by countless traveling minstrels such as myself. My favorite ink-drawn caricature looks back at me dead on at eye level as I sit. It's a gnarly-looking horned devil skull, with these pleading, fearful, worried-looking eyes. Underneath is the inscription: "I can't stop shitting!" Apparently someone else found that this is what happens by the time you get to Frankfurt. Six weeks of bread and cheese are looking for an escape route.

Somehow I fall asleep upstairs in a chair while the soundman plays Alice In Chains at ear-splitting volume to an as yet unopened club. The other guys take turns thumbing through foreign newspapers and playing foosball. They spend a lot of time sitting in chairs looking off into space. Hours crawl past at a snail's pace.

After my eighth or ninth crap, I walk over to the bar, where Jurgen the promoter is cooking up some chicken and potatoes and generally doting after us. The club is now open for business. I get a beer and have a seat when, quite unexpectedly, in walks the same cute blonde who wanted me to go to a party in Munich, comin' in with some alterna-rock lookin' dude. I walk up to her to see if she remembers the sad rock loser.

"Of coourse I remembah. I knew you were playin', thaz why I caame!" Her name is Elke, I learn, and she works for Warner Brothers publishing, based in Munich. And, despite Frankfurt's Sunday kind of ghost town, she informs me she's in town for a big music business convention, and that our show should be packed tonight. The fellow she's with is just a friend, well, I think that's her opinion, he might have different thoughts. The three of us blab about nothing much for a while, and then, showtime.

Z now plays like a drum machine. He looks so bored and tired. His thing the last few days, with the exception of escape into the Marburg night, has been to sleep as much as humanly possible.

"See, if I sleep all the time we're not doing anything, which is more or less all the time, I can trim the days down to four or five total hours of consciousness. That way, the remaining two weeks of the tour will only seem like three or four days."

"You don't think there's any hope for us to have mad, hedonistic fun on this crazy continent?" I plead.

"McGruff, you've been here, right? You think everything is just gonna magically change in the eleventh hour? Forget it. Turn into Rip Van Winkle, like me."

Fuck that, there has to be hope. I plop down on the bar stool adjacent to the lovely Elke. I'm feeling a little dejected suddenly, but try not to show it. "Don't tell me you're too tired to come out with me tonight," she wants to know. "We could really have a time. I've got this!"

She reaches under her coat and into her blouse and whips out...a corporate credit card. "Back at my hotel, the bar's open till 4:00 a.m. John Entwistle has been staying there, getting drunk as can be every night, buying drinks like nobody's business. It doesn't matter anyway. I can charge as much alcohol to Warner Brothers as I want." She leans in closer. "I've got a great hotel room."

Let's see: a willing, bountiful blonde with a sky's-the-limit expense account hanging around the world's greatest bassist, Mr. John Entwistle. How can I screw this up?

"You got a car?" It had become a familiar question I present to the locals.

"No, dahling, but I can put a taxicab on the credit card."

In keeping with the rest of the day's non-activities, the aftershow dragged on interminably through time. Dahl was doing two lengthy interviews, Simon and Tim were having their billionth foosball championship, Jurgen was puttering around in the kitchen all in a tizzy, Z and Rat were lightly dozing on a couch, and the majority of the audience had moved on. Downstairs, by the decrepit, odorous bathrooms, Elke and I were passionately kissing. She confessed to me that she drinks too much and is probably an alcoholic, but who was I to cast aspersions in the lost city of Frankfurt. In a normal band, on a normal tour, I would have packed my equipment, placed it with the rest of the band's stuff, and hopped in a cab with my blonde Venus/Blue Angel, but this was—needless to say, I explained to her—the way of Factsheet as best I could, and she laughed and laughed, and after awhile, she came to actually believe the oblique tales of the sorry loser rockers were in fact true. "You seem so frussstrated."

Castrated was more like it. "Here's the deal: I can take off with you after the gear is loaded providing I can get everywhere I need to go independently of the rest of the band. Problem is, we're staying at this guy Jurgen's house. We're to follow him there. His address isn't even in the itinerary. I have no idea where it is, and I don't know my way around, obviously. So, I need to get back to Jürgen and Felix's—that's his cat, you see—house in the a.m. in order for us to get an early start for the next club so we can sit around there tomorrow all day and do nothing for a thousand hours in a row. I need to know exactly where his place is from your hotel or these guys will just leave me here." I reconsider my last statement. "Hang on, maybe I'm onto something."

"But Dahling, I don't know my way around Frankfurt. I'm a stranger here, also. Maybe thiz Jurgen vill help."

Being that she shares the German language with Jürgen and that she's an all around go-getter to boot, she has a five or six minute talk with Jürgen to sort out these pending logistics. Great, we should be on our way in moments now. Apparently preliminary negotiations don't go well.

"Well, I don't know. He gave me very confused directions. He says he doesn't really know how to get

back and forth. This he told me after he said he's
lived here all hiz life. The fact is he dozen vont you to
go with me."

"What does he care?"

"He vonts all the leedle rock boyzz unter hiz rooof.
Dahling, he's a faaahhg!"

Okay, Okay. So he's been swishing around all day
like Liberace on Vaseline, that's no reason to banter
about derogatory remarks. Looks like we're under the
care of the Brian Epstein of Frankfurt, who wants
nothing more than a Cellar Full of Boys. Great.

Elke hangs on my shoulder and leans over to kiss
my neck, laughing. She laughs a lot, the lovely sound
of gentle feminine amusement. It's hard to express how
happy I am that she has found humor in my continuing
situation. I look over and Simon, Z, and Rat just glare at
me. Her "friend" also seems to be doing a fair amount of
glaring. On the other side of me at the bar, two amazing,
exotic Arabian-looking girls in matching jumpsuits sit
down. They start singing Motown songs a cappella and
trying to get attention. Tim walks up and whispers to
me, "What's up with these girls? They look hot and
ready to go."

"Well, tell 'em you're a big American record producer,
and you'd like to engage them in a little late-night artist
development. You'll have a session going before you
know it." Sheesh, do I have to think of everything?

Amazingly, this advice works, and now Tim has a
double good, Doublemint dream date on his hands.

"We want to go to Mecca viss you, blon' boy."

"McGruff, what do they mean?" he asks.

"I think it's a religious thing. Just be cautious when they pull out those serrated sacrificial carving knives. Could get messy."

"Mecca is for dancing. It is in town." A club, in other words.

"There, you see, Tim. 'In town.' Better start working on your one-way ticket outa Jürgenville."

"What are you going to do, dahling," demands Elke sternly, who doesn't really care to exchange small talk with the Supremes of Tunisia.

"Well, I guess I'll go to the house, since the princess won't give us proper directions, and take a cab from there. Or maybe I can sweet-talk him into dropping me off at your hotel. I'm going to get there, don't you worry your pretty little face."

Simon, the band, Tim, and the Tunisian Supremes all pile into the van. The girls bounce up and down in the front seat, chanting, "Mecca! Mecca! Mecca!" Jürgen does know where that is, so he runs us by, presumably to off-load the girls as quickly as possible. Everyone encourages Tim to go with them, but he declines. He too has the Factsheet flu. "Noooo, I better nnnnot," he sheepishly whines.

I'm just as bad. I should get this queen's number, go to Elke's hotel, and just call them in the morning and tell them where I am. I could be exchanging bass secrets with John the Ox and rolling in satin sheets with a blue-eyed German temptress, but instead I'm racing toward potent coffee and a cat named Felix.

Jürgen lives far from the club in some suburb or something. Hell, we might have been driving in circles for all I know. Down in the basement, everyone is hanging out and Jürgen is showing off his extensive collection of Fela Kuti records.

"Hey, Jürgen. Let's go out. Whatdya say?"

He looks at me blankly.

"Yeah, you know, go get a drink. Just you and me, whatdya think? Well, whatdya know, I got the address to a great little bar right here in my pocket. See?"

He looks, and his eyes cross as his brow tenses. "That is a hotel."

"Yeah, well, it's got a bar, a damn fine one, I'm told. Open all night!"

"Not on Sunday."

"The hell you say! Especially on Sunday."

"Oh, I don't think so. You guys need your rest."

"Jurgen, I'm serious. Look at me, I'm rested. I've either been on a barstool or a toilet all day. I'm rested. Any more rest and I'm gonna bust."

"No, no." He begins looking around the room at everyone else.

"Just go and take a cab, McGruffwich," say Rat, as he takes off his pants, revealing his scanty briefs, which in turn greatly diverts Jurgen's attention.

"Right. Jurgen, how much is a cab gonna cost me to get to this hotel? Jurgen? Jurgen??"

"Oh, I don't know. A lot. Stay here."

Z starts giggling to himself. He looks at the record collection stashed in the corner. "Got any Benny Goodman?" he half-heartedly inquires.

I try for another twenty minutes to negotiate directions and a cash advance toward cab fare, but Jurgen is aloof, quietly waiting around for the next boy to disrobe. This is too much. I don't even have enough money to afford a few hours of freedom. No Elke, no expense account, no Boris the Spider. I finally have the perfect night lined up, exactly as I'd professed to Z was still possible, and I can't pull it off. I can't get a ride, or pocket money, or directions, or our host's address to return to should I escape, or a phone number to call back in the morning and tell them where to pick me up. These would all be normal things that guys would be willing to work out in the regular world. But in this parallel dimension, this backward world, I can't even get this together. It's better to regret something you have done than to regret something you haven't done—it's an age-old proverb of more than a little truth. I give up and go to bed fully clothed—no assistance getting a ride for me, no floorshow for our host.

The next morning begins with the usual grog, as guys in long underwear and day-old stubble arise to scratch their balls and seek out a cup of coffee. Jurgen's parents are up and about upstairs, stern looking upper-middle class folks who appear to be wondering just exactly where they went wrong in raising their only son.

Sashayin' around in a housecoat, fetching cappuccinos for the travelin' old-school punk rock minstrel show. Already losing his hair and gay to boot, Jurgen was a skeleton in this reserved family's closet. I nod to the barely-tolerant father as I pick up his phone and dial.

I ring up Elke's room to see what sort of shenanigans I missed. Why I decide to torture myself in this manner is unknown to even me. It was no surprise she was in the early stages of nursing a hangover, but reasonably chipper just the same. I explain the tribulations that caused my failure to attend the festivities. Yes, Entwistle was there, drinks flowed all night long, blah blah blah. "But if you were here, I'm sure we wouldn't have stayed on long with them. We'd have come up to my room, but I doubt we would have slept much."

I can't take it. I drop the phone. These were words of hope and desperation for me and my penis to hold on to for a while. Once again, the loser aspect of life on the Factsheet Euro-Blur Smell o' Death Extravaganza had made a joker out of me. Words to remember as we lamely limped to our next destination, wherever the hell it might be, as we began to wind up our little musical vacation. Down in the basement, Ratboy has the ever-present sounds of Mr. Tom Waits on the stereo.

> Well I've lost my equilibrium
> And my car keys and my pride
> The tattoo parlor's warm
> And so I huddle there inside
> The grinding of the buzz saw
> "What you want that thing to say?"

I says, "Just don't misspell her name
Buddy, she's the one that got away

HANOVER, AT LEAST THE area we are in, is a sleazy place. If you're looking for quick, meaningless homosexual encounters and an easy place to score street heroin, let me recommend Hanover for your upcoming holiday. We get a buyout at the club and decide to turn as much of a profit as possible. A buyout means that rather than feeding us, the promoter gives us money to go out and buy our dinner. To turn a profit, the cheapest food rendering the most change is the goal. Our whole party—except for Dahl (is it even necessary to point out his absence on such expeditions away from clubs and hotels anymore?)— walks several blocks to the nearby McDonalds. On the way, hordes of dazed-looking young men in leather accost us with all manner of propositions, from male prostitution, drug deals, to offers of quickies in a nearby alley. In the McDonalds, similar freaks intermingle with normal folks in search of leftover junk food tidbits and a modest variety of other quick hustles. This Mickey D's has an upstairs, where we settle in amidst florescent light and Ronald McDonald bright vinyl benches and tables. A guy stumbles up next to us and scrounges a goopy mound of melted ice cream directly off the adjacent table. Mmm mmm good. He falters back from the table, nearly losing his balance, rights himself, and then stares us down. While he fixes his unfocused gaze at us, we notice the crotch of his Levi's darken as he wets himself. That completed, he trips off just as quickly.

Z is more depressed than ever. He no longer desires to leave the hotels during the day, much like our leader. Ratboy and I have been spending the recent German days scouring the local record shops, scoring some noteworthy finds, but Z is too bored and dejected to tag along. After the Hanover performance, he disappears.

"You probably know Z the best, wouldn't you say?" Simon asks me when no one's paying attention.

"Yeah, me or Rat, that would be fair to say."

"He told me he was going back toward the red light district to score some heroin. What do ya reckon?"

The fact was that Z was no stranger to the breakfast of chump-ions. He had a problem before, especially during his rock 'n' roll slumming days in the seedier parts of Hollywood. But that was quite a while ago. Surely he wouldn't backslide now, here. I gave him the benefit of the doubt.

"Naw, he was just pullin' your leg. I'm sure he'll be right back." That's what I say, anyway, but in reality I am more than a little worried. After we load the van, he turns up and claims he just took a stroll through the red light district. Duly noted. He hops in the van, and we head to the hotel.

After some morning CD shopping in beautiful downtown Hanover, we make the short drive to Kassal, where Z and I share a room. Z makes a less-than-startling confession.

"The truth is, I did buy some heroin last night. Fifty marks, I got this much and an outfit." He rolls up his sleeve and begins the ritual. I guess I'm in no position to chastise him, as I had purchased a huge chunk of hashish, which I was rolling up with some tobacco as Z fixed.

"You wanna snort some?" he offered.

"No, that's okay. I'm fine with my hash. Are you sure that's a good idea for you? You remember how fucked up you got behind that shit before?"

"I don't care anymore. Fuck it." He pushes the plunger in, while my Bic ignites a hashish spliff. A moment later, Z is at the sink, vomiting. What a joy being a full-time junkie must be, daily puke fests being just a sidebar to the complete article. Z looks sick the rest of the day, colorless and vampiric. I'm pleasantly stoned as we walk through the one-street curiosity known as Kassal to get some air, but Z is almost greenish, deathly looking. But it ain't my place to play daddy, besides, Z is his own man, he'll do what he wants anyway, even if he knows full well that it's stupid.

The gig tonight is at Spot, and I think they mean that as in blemish. The outside walls of the venue are decorated/defaced with skinhead and Satanic graffiti. Make no mistake, the Devil walks among us has a lot of pals amongst the youth of Germany. Spot breaks three existing tour records all at once: It is the absolute coldest place we'll play, even worse than the meat locker in Montargis. We will remain longer on the premises than any other place we are to play, longer even than the Frankfort/Jürgen holding tank. And it will have the worst sound, even topping the incompetence of soundmen in places like Italy and Spain. Even our buddies, Mind Overboard, who theoretically are more used to this than we are, seem to be freezing to death and restless.

The pinball machines don't work, even Tim and Simon seem like they can take foosball anymore. Rat and Z play pool (poorly) in a dormant lounge beside the main concert room. Dahl is once again sniffing and sneezing, sitting in a corner looking miserable. We find a boom box and some tapes behind the bar, and crank up some unknown surf music. Z retrieves a Sinatra tape, and, in what is a teary, touching scene, Rat and I slow dance to "The Shadow of Your Smile." Something in 3/4 kicks in, and Rat attempts to teach me how to waltz, proving that proper European breeding has its cultural advantages.

We get another buy-out, but only the Factsheeters are interested in eating. Actually, we're more keen on thawing, so we walk a couple of blocks to an Indian restaurant with superb food, best since Italy. When you've been eating almost nothing but bread and cheese and McDonalds buy-outs, a really killer meal is all the more head spinning and hallucination inducing. We sit, eat, and grouse about what a fuckin' drag this whole thing has become, how the days and nights have begun to stretch out into eternity since we've been crawling through Deutschland.

Upon returning to Spot, Dahl informs us that he's instructed the DJ to play some Johnny Thunders records—two more songs to be exact—and then we're on. Beginning to feel the consequences of our elaborate curried cuisine, Rat and I inform the Master that we need to defecate prior to dishing out the rock.

The men's bathroom is as fucked up as everything else at Spot. There are five stalls, three of which appear to be unoccupied and locked from the inside, while a fourth is backed up and unusable, and the fifth occupied by somebody who isn't in much of a hurry. Finally, he exits, as Johnny Thunders' "Pirate Love" jams through the P.A. Rat goes up to bat. I wait. These things must be done delicately, ya know. Finally, as Thunders' "Goin' Steady" begins to rock the house, it's my turn. I'm dealing with the situation at hand when the song ends, and I hear Dahl's voice through the P.A.: "We'd like to start but our bass player's takin' a shit!" Jeff then plays his solo rendition of Thunders' "You Can't Put Your Arms Around a Memory." He could have just waited one more DJ song, but oh well, if he wants to play solo, that's cool with me.

I emerge from stall number five, get my bass, and walk onstage, smiling, as I think it's pretty funny in a way that the audience knows what I've been doing. Dahl is not sharing in my mirth. In fact, he's pretty pissed off. "Thanks a lot!" he snaps at me, as if I've ruined the whole show.

Rat looks at him, then at me, and just shakes his head. Dahl wants to be a little baby, so I decide to join him, and instead of doing our usual rock show, I just stand back by Z and stare stone-faced at the crowd. I pass on my vocal parts, too. Knowing full well there's fuck-all to do in this shit excuse for a place to live, when the show's over, I just wanna get the hell back to the hotel, smoke hash, and not be bothered by anyone.

"He's insane, you know that, don't you?" Z asks, once inside our little drug den.

"Who?"

"Dahl. That was the fucking stupidest thing I ever saw tonight. Who cares if we can't start the split second some Johnny Thunders record ends. Rock music shouldn't run on such a tight schedule. It's not the evening news."

"Yeah, you're right," I agreed, starting to get riled up. Z, after being high for quite awhile, decides to nod off. He makes strange weeping-singing noises in his sleep while I toss and turn, haunted by a sense of boredom mixed with a doom that I can't quite get a handle on. Tomorrow, we take Berlin.

THE DRIVE STARTS OFF on a bad note when I, referring to our leader, loudly ask Tim, "Where's Dickface?"

"He's up on top in the back," which meant that he indeed heard me reducing myself to such childish retaliation as name-calling. Meanwhile, Z is junk sick in the back seat. I'm sure he did the rest of his score this morning, as he spends a fair amount of time at our roadside stops throwing up. Z has only told me that he had the junk, but Rat figures it out easily enough.

We get to Berlin with extra time to see the sights for a full two hours. Dahl naturally stays in, Rat decides to make some calls, and Z has a sleep in hope of recovery. The remainders head off to the Berlin Wall, where we each buy a small piece of it for a couple of marks. We see Checkpoint Charlie, the Brandenburg Gates, and walk into East Germany. We see various remnants and reminders of the armies and generals who once raged as kings down these very streets. Two hours pass fast, and we'll never make it all the way back in time for soundcheck on foot, and not wanting to cause yet another uproar, we pool our dwindling German money and cab it back to Factsheet Central.

The club is called Trash, and it's the kind of well set up, yet much worn club that you expect to see in a major city. The staff is rude and unfriendly, but the audience is one of the best we've had, making it our first straight-up fun show in some time. The Mind Overboard guys come onstage and join us on such essential rockage as "Sonic Reducer" and two complete run-throughs of "Louie Louie." It's the last show with Overboard, which we'll miss in a way. They invite us out for drinks, but of course we don't go, not at this point, not in the Master's van, not as broke as we are.

No one, band or crew, is talking to Dahl. It can be real tough to be the boss, sometimes. The good news is, we can once and for all say auf Wiedersehen to Germany.

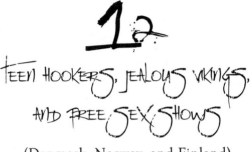

12

TEEN HOOKERS, JEALOUS VIKINGS, AND FREE SEX SHOWS

(Denmark, Norway, and Finland)

A SLIGHT LIFT IN anticipation level surrounds our little search party as we drive toward the ferryboat that will take us to Copenhagen, Denmark's legendary city of sin and, once upon a time, the international capital of pornography. A good town to pop in to for a quick sex change as well, I'm told. Simon's opted to take a longer drive, shorter ferry ride, but by the time we get to port we learn we missed the boat by five minutes. We sit in the van, watching the huge ferry depart for foreign shores. Simon gets out to see when the next boat leaves. As is the norm now, no one speaks during his absence. Dahl stares out the window, Tim is still struggling through my Burroughs novel, I'm reading Kerouac's tales of fun road travels, Z's getting aroused by Henry Miller, Ratboy grooves with Lightning Hopkins on his headphones. Please, no talking in the library, or should I say bookmobile.

"The next boat leaves in two and a half hours," Simon states flatly.

"Why don't we go back down the road to a restaurant, or someplace to get some breakfast?" asks Rat.

"Get some coffee, sounds good," says Z, trying to make the best of it.

"No," is all Simon says.

"Why not?" I want to know, my voice tensing slightly. "What are we supposed to do in this parking lot for two and a half hours?"

"You can do whatever you want. My job is to get you to the ferry, which I've done. Beyond that, I can't be bothered."

"You can't be bothered to get us here on time, either," says Dahl, seemingly siding with us for a change.

"I'm not driving anywhere, the van's not moving, and that's that. Why don't you lot walk back to that store and restaurant at the other end of the marina? The walk will do you good and kill time."

What is this, a hiking variation on Z's Rip Van Winkle theory? Everybody gets upset all at the same time.

"Simon! You jerk. Drive us where we want to go. You work for us, goddammit!! Let's go, let's go," everyone hollers all at once at the man previously referred to as God.

"No."

"You're an asshole, Simon. I can't even believe it," moans Rat.

We all call Simon various derogatory names as we exit the van, even Dahl, who has been riding in back to avoid the rest of us. For a moment, all musicians and even Tim are united against the common enemy, our road manager.

We hit a duty-free shop for the usual supply of Walkman batteries, cigarettes, toothpaste, and what not, and then Dahl has had enough socializing and heads back to the van. This fifteen-minute walk together was probably the most any of us have seen him in a relaxed setting outside of a hotel since Switzerland, where he actually strolled through the streets of Bern with Simon and myself. The rest of us head to some sort of truck stop-style restaurant for artery-clogging pork, coleslaw, and spuds. Conversation is peppered with the familiar anti-tour complaining, which has markedly switched from "fuck Dahl" to "fuck Simon." We sit and talk quietly, but all eyes are upon us. Guess they don't get many longhaired weirdoes in funny hats and leather jackets 'round here.

Two hours later, we finally get onboard the ferry, and I take a seat up on the middle deck by myself to watch the ocean roll by and have a smoke. Simon joins me and wants to talk about why he did what he did and why he's being the way he's being, but I wave him off and tell him I don't want to argue in public and I just want to be alone. Actually, alone is nice. The calming sea, the blissful nicotine, the reclining seats. I'm sure I'll see my five traveling companions in close quarters again before I know it, but for now I'm at peace.

I hear an outburst of hollering behind me, and turn to see it's Ratboy and Simon. Simon's tried to give Rat the same song and dance, and instead of declining as I did Rat dove in headfirst. I walk up to the top deck so I don't have to hear it.

I take heed of Z's Rip Van Winkle approach, and after a few brews on the ferry, I sleep for the remainder of the van ride to Copenhagen, wake up for soundcheck, and then off to the hotel, nary a word to anyone.

I've got a solo room in a nice hotel, the only disturbance being some sort of high school function with loads of seventeen-year-old kids drunk out of their minds running up and down the halls. After a shower, I settle in for some CNN on the telly, only to be interrupted by a knock at the door.

"Hey, what's up?" It's Tim, trying to be cheerful, attempting to get the most out of his last few Euro-Blur days before he off-loads to the Vatican.

"Nothing. I'm just watching the news."

"You wanna go do something? I figured if anyone would want to explore Copenhagen, it'd be you. Everyone else seems content just to sit around and be mad about everything."

"An astute observation. Well, let's synchronize. I figure we've got about an hour-fifteen before we have to head off for tonight's rock-a-thon. Yeah, let's see what the natives around here do for kicks."

Who'd have thought, the last two folks able to get along and not devote all their energies to griping about the tour would be me and Tim. Off we go, nonetheless, into the mysterious Copenhagen night. As a bonus, we have dinner buy-out money. Oh, the thrills of budget traveling.

After grabbing something quick and cheap to eat, we check our watches and see we've got just under an hour to get into trouble. Since we have no idea of where to go or what to do, we start off by going into the stripper bar directly across from the hotel. Before even negotiating for our admission, we're told to beat it because Tim's wearing Levi's and that don't meet the dress requirements for this fine establishment. While were dickering with the door guy, a red curtain opens and I get a quick peak at the revelry inside.

We exit, and I say to Tim: "Don't worry about it. I saw in there and it looked pretty dismal, just a bunch of old businessmen sitting around talking to overpriced hookers. Didn't seem like anything for us."

"Excuse me, gentlemen," calls a voice from behind us. It's some shifty looking guy in a cheap suit about five paces to our rear. "I couldn't help but hear what happened. I know a place I could take you where they have what you want."

"Oh yeah?" Tim inquires a little too eagerly.

"How do you know what we want?" I ask, assuming the role of voice of reason and caution.

"You want to see some girls put on a show, a good show, right? Not some place where they're just sitting around talking?"

"Well, yeah, and time is precious. What do you have in mind," I ask, seeing if his cards will come to the table.

"I'll take you there. It's just up here a few blocks."

"Great," enthuses Tim, again a little too eagerly.

"We're not exactly rolling in cash," I warn, giving him the signal early on that we're poor robbery targets.

"C'mon along then," he says, and we follow this guy, who mentions as we walk that he recently relocated here from Pakistan.

"You're low on money, then," he tries to confirm.

Again, the eager one steps up to bat with his foot in his mouth. "Oh, I've got enough money. No problem."

I grab Tim by the arm and pull him a few steps behind our tour guide. "Don't tell this joker shit like that," I whisper. "We don't know what his scam is. He may have some crony waiting around a corner to bonk us on the heads and make off with our wallets. This guy emerged from a strip club to lead us into the night. It's a tenuous situation at best. Keep your mouth shut and stay on your toes."

As it turns out, the guy is actually on the level. He takes us across a major boulevard and down a side street to an unmarked black door. We follow him in, and what do you know, a strip show is in progress, and there's no cover charge.

The scam unfolds quickly enough. This guy combs the neighborhood for confused, lonely, horny foreign guys (like us) to bring to this establishment, wherein they are to become separated from their cash upon arrival. The deal is, the show—what there is of it—*is*, in fact, free. The girls dance, and then come and sit down by you. They make a minimum of small talk before instigating negotiations for a more private form of entertainment. In front of us, an English businessman argues with what appears to be the madam on duty about his accrued credit card charges. A good hand job just ain't as cheap as it used to be.

The girls are young and pretty, but tainted with the look of desperation that comes with this form of low-level prostitution. An Asian princess sits down by me, and a few "Hey Sailors" later gets the picture that my buyout money doesn't quite get into her level of finance. A tall blonde, presumably the product of strict Danish breeding, is wiggling about onstage in her négligée—sheesh, they don't even reveal as much as German quiz shows—and following her sensual two-step, sits down next to me to try her luck with the traveling rocker. For all she knows, I could be in Pearl Jam and rolling with a huge expense account and per diems. Meanwhile, Tim tries to shake the Queen of Asia.

We order a couple of beers at fifty Krowns each, approximately ten bucks, and Blondie relaxes and sorta turns into a more or less normal girl. She realizes she hasn't hit pay dirt with me, and at the same time she's confident that I'm not gonna try and come on to her.

She's a student, paying her way through college shaking ass and appeasing traveling old guys. It's a job. "I won't be doing it forever, you know. I'm going to get a job in the advertising field."

We finish our beers, watch a few other ladies do their non-strips, and it's off for the show. Our Pakistani friend has obviously gone off in search of more recruits.

"Try to come back later," Blondie asks me, but I somehow can't imagine it, even as I look at her five-foot-nine chiseled, fading beauty. Shit, there's nothing wrong with her that a few hundred Krowns wouldn't correct.

That evening, our show is boring. The crowd is polite, though polite is really not high on the list of qualities that makes for an outstanding rock 'n' roll audience. As if to compensate, one extremely drunk moron keeps running up to the front of the stage and heckling us. He finally starts jumping on the stage and grabbing the mic, yelling incoherent bullshit over our semi-coherent music. He's bumping into us and being a real asshole, so I grab him and toss him off the stage. He turns and grabs at my face, yelling, "Get a haircut," at me. Now, I'm mad. I toss down my bass and get ready to meet my adversary head-on, when some bouncers grab him and throw him out. Good, better them than me!

FROM THE NATION'S CAPITAL to the country's most obscure little village, that's the way we do it, honey. Friday, March 12th, finds the traveling freak show in a pleasant little gingerbread village called Ålborg, complete with cobblestone streets and a windmill. We arrive at the club just after lunchtime. It's upstairs in a little bar you'd see in an old Frankenstein movie, where the villagers gather to decide what to do about the monster. It's run by volunteer music fans, community funded, but booked by private promoters. The only person on payroll is an accountant. It all seems to run along fine, but they are off the beaten path, not many bands make it up this way.

Antiseen had just played here, a band who will later join us in Finland.

Given that it's volunteer run, I try to get the girl at the bar to donate some coffee, tea, beer, bread, or anything to us since we've had nothing today—which, in fact, isn't exactly true, but sometimes you don't get ahead by strictly telling the truth. She feels a little sorry for us, and offers us whatever we'd like. Okay, make mine whiskey and coke.

I sit and have a drink while the rest of the entourage is buzzing around doing something. God knows what. Watching the girls who work here, I get a strong lesbian vibe from them. When I watch two walk into the back room and start making out, it seems like my hunch was accurate. In fact, all the volunteers are young women. There seem to be no men at all involved in this operation. We also work with our first and only soundwoman of the tour at this venue.

The mild, mellowing buzz the whiskey affords me softens the blow of tonight's living quarters. Across the courtyard, and out the back of the upstairs of the club, is a barren room with a well-worn mattress strewn on the floor. Sleeping bags and blankets lay in piles. Ominously, in the middle of the floor, is a third-world pinball machine that runs endlessly for free. None of us can make out the point of the game, but it is a free, loud, clanging, time waster, and we all spend hours on it.

"If we're going to make the ferry on time—and I know you guys want to—we have to be up and on our way by six in the morning tomorrow," Simon announces. This makes our flophouse somewhat more bearable. We'll only be on these moth-eaten mattresses a few hours. The club lets us use the phone. I have to presume they know we don't know a lot of people in Ålborg and that we're going to be calling the States. I call Gina at work, so I can hear her sober for a change, and she tells me how she's lost some weight and is looking hot. Girls really know how to work ya up when they want to. "I can't wait to see your body in all its glory," I tell her.

Christ, I'm thinking about her and it makes me step away from the desk where the phone is, stumbling dizzily. Gina is an odd one in oh so many ways, and thinking about her in any level of detail starts to make me feel conflicted. I miss her. I resent her. I idolize her. I disrespect her. I negate her. What's wrong with us? What's wrong with me?

♣

ON THE CRAMPED STAGE, the show goes well, and its more fun to play than it's been in quite a few days. The audience is reserved on the whole, but offset by a few decidedly carefree individuals who make it their business to get the party started, dancing and yanking on each other's privates, pulling rude and funny faces, and basically acting the collective fool. A short blonde, with that Marianne Faithfull haircut that drives me wild and a fluffy fur coat, comes and stands up front and grooves to our increasingly accelerating, pulsating and lascivious juvenile delinquent rock 'n' roll beat. Dahl and Z both shoot glances at me. They're thinking the same thing I am. This Ms. Faithfull could double for my ex-girlfriend who went on the road with us to San Francisco. Dahl snickers and goes back to paying attention to his vocals. Next to this appealing vision are two equally lovely girls making out with each other. Ålborg may be off the beaten track, but it is a liberal, do-what-thou-wilt kind of a place.

After the show is wrapped, I begin to map out my possibilities. This town is dinky, but just around the corner from the bar, and our digs, is a strip loaded with discos, bars, clubs, and nightlife. I'm not going to sit around our upstairs hideaway while everything is within walking distance. I walk up to the girl in the fur and get to the point.

"I want you to go with me dancing and drinking, right now! Well, yes or no!?"

She laughs, takes a look at her friend occupied in conversation elsewhere, and turns back toward me. "Sure, why not? I want to say hallo to ah few people here that ah know first."

"Great, I've got to hide my bass, and I'll be ready."

HER NAME IS HELENE, and she's French. Upon making quick introductions, I learn she's a few months older than me and even has a fifteen-year-old daughter. That doesn't make me feel any younger, but it's too late in the game to worry about my ego. Besides, she looks good and the years have obviously been kind to her. She takes Tim, Rat, and me to a rock club just down the street to kick out the dance floor jams. We all hit the floor in this manic party joint, even Tim. Rat has someone to talk French with, so he's happy. I walk up to the bar, and a teenage vamp is staring me down. She walks past me, and shoots her hand up between my thighs and gives my prick a quick yank. She turns to wink and walks on. Choices! Do I want the mature French Venus in Furs with the Nico-do, or the teenage slut I can just carry on my shoulders up to the filthy mattresses of wanton sin? I'll decide later. Right now I want to hip-shake my blues away.

Rat leans over as we move on the floor and points out the teen troublemaker, saying she asked him if I was up for grabs. This was before she grabbed me, I guess. They take things so literally around here. Helene walks up behind me, pulls me to the center of the dance floor, and we dance like swingin' Nashville teens to the oh-so-long-ago sounds of The Beatles' "I Saw Her Standing There." For a moment, we are lost in past glories, sounds of our individual, obviously very different youths, still maintaining a common ground of mutual love of the Fab Four.

Rat and Tim announce they're going to go back to the barracks. After all, it's early to rise tomorrow. With Jeff, Z, and Simon already bedded down back at Camp Ålborg, I had been awarded the responsibility of key-keeper, he who will have entrance to our hideaway and lord over the lock on the door. I must go let them in and lock it all up. It's just the way we do it.

I tell Helene I'll be back momentarily, and walk the block and a half to put my brethren to beddy-bye. As I lock them safely away, and walk down the worn staircase that leads back to the party-mad streets below, I'm overcome by a strange feeling. At first I don't recognize it, but it comes to me eventually. I'm alone. I have the key. I can come and go as I please without anyone else's company or consent. I'm free from my constricting compatriots to run wild with the raging wind. I don't need cab fare, the van keys, or permission to do anything. It feels kind of like what I imagine adulthood to be like. I am overwhelmed with simple, pure joy, skipping without caution down the steps, and bouncing out into the street. It's such an elementary, basic thing giving me such unparalleled pleasure. Always a lone wolf, an only child, and used to traveling alone on magazine and record company assignments, this prolonged boy scout adventure we called a tour had begun to feel like a prison sentence, and the promise of a few hours of sheer, unmonitored freedom gave me a rush of adrenaline.

Helene is as I left her, but rather than dance we nab a table and bond. She tells me she's married, which for some illogical reason makes me want to kiss her all the more, which I do.

"Where is this lucky guy you're married to?"

"Well, he eez around. He won't be in here, that's one of zee reasons I brought you here, heez been banned from this club. Too much fighting."

I try to envision some crazed street-fighting man stumbling in on us, hopped up on the local liquor, and itching to kick some Yankee butt. "Banned, eh? C'mere, I want to kiss ya some mo'."

"I shouldn't do this," she says softly but not convincingly.

"None of us should do anything we do. You'll learn that when you're my age."

"But I'm older than you."

"Oh yeah, well, tell you what, you get a couple of drinks, and I'll go get the DJ to play more songs we like."

As I make my way through the club, another teenage vixette grabs my ass. Is it the same girl? Jeez, I can't tell them apart. They're all blonde, pert, alive, and ready to step into the roll of Lolita. I know one thing for sure: I love this town. They like to kiss in this town, they like to grab and fondle, and no one seems to get too upset about who's doing what with whom. I wondered if this liberal attitude would be present in Helene's husband.

I return to the table, and, speak of the Devil, find that Helene's husband wears furs, too. He also looks like a Viking and is about eight feet tall. Many years younger than his wife, Helene's husband looks fit, strong, drunk, and angry. After some clumsy introductions, I figure it's about time for me to evaporate, so I start to fade into the woodwork, resurfacing to look for youthful dick-yankers. Meanwhile, two crazy looking geek guys in ties and glasses start doing some form of Lambadi with each other, rubbing their crotches together and dancing about in wild abandon. They leap on tables and all manner of beverage flies through the air. Helene's Viking prince approaches the melee with an eye on returning the situation to order, maybe just to keep in practice, and I use the diversion to sweep her out of there and walk me home.

We walk arm and arm through the cold, clear Danish night, and stop to smooch at the doorway at the bottom of the stairs to the Dahl/Factsheet hideaway. "I feel a connection with you, something special," she tells me. Is this true, or just something she concocts to ease the guilt she feels for ignoring matrimonial oaths? We promise to write, and off she goes. I check my watch. It's 4:30 a.m.

AN HOUR AND A half later it's rise and shine. I barely rise. I'm quite sure I ain't shinin'. Out in the courtyard, there are some breakfast rolls and juice. I nibble at something and try to open my eyes. Helene walks in, surprising me to say the least, and sits down next to Ratboy, continuing some conversation from the previous night in French. I feel uncomfortable—it's one thing to carry on with a girl in the door stoop, but not in front of the guys. She senses my discomfort, gives me a quick nod, and is off. I ask Rat nothing and he offers me no information. Dahl watches her leave and then turns to me.

"Man, I can't get over how much she looks like..."

"Yes, yes, be quiet now," I cut him off.

"Well, this is it," says Tim. "I'm out of here." He's catching a cab, to a bus, to a jet, to the Pope—a meeting of the minds from which we may never learn the outcome, never truly understand the ongoing international impact. Goodbyes are a bizarre blend of sincerity and superficiality, as Tim steps through the door and fades into the sunrise, spaghetti western style. Off-loaded once and for all and no longer a piece in our private little puzzle.

OFF TO ANOTHER FERRY, a terrible ride on a glorified fishing boat. I'm woozy and booze sick, sloshing about the deck in semi-hallucination. Finally, back on land, we hit top speed for the Swedish border.

The border guards take a serious look at us inside the van and order us to pull over next to their garage. They open the garage, and instruct us to pull in, closing the huge door behind us. "Out of the van."

"What's all this?" they ask, looking at our cased equipment and bags of luggage. We tell them, and they instruct us to unload everything for the drug dogs. Shit, how many drugs have been in and out of those bags in the last week alone, what with Z's heroin, our hashish, and who even knows what else? Does Dahl's French cough syrup count? I get real nervous, but try to conceal my unease. Given my general queasiness, though, I feel like I'm an open book.

While the garage is prepared for the drug hounds, the prisoners are led into interrogation rooms. Rat and Z take seats while the rest of us stand and wait, and a guard stands attentively observing us. Another guard walks in with—oh no—it's the PLASTIC GLOVES. Shit! There is no way I'm going to survive a stiff-fingered butt probe at this hour of the morning following the preceding night's binge and the subsequent ferry ride without coloring the walls with the contents of my digestive system.

The tension in the room is electrifying. We collectively clench like a fist. The box of plastic gloves ominously sits on a desk while guards and suspects nervously exchange glances. Ratboy sulks forward in his seat and moans, "Oh no."

He sits there shaking his head with worry. "What's the matter?" I ask him quietly.

"I can't remember." He seemed to be sure everyone was listening. "I can't remember when I showered last."

The room was absurdly hushed. Rat continued as if unaware of the growing concern around him. "Was it a week ago, ten days?"

The tough-looking guard with the Rutger Hauer chin swallows hard and picks up the gloves. He takes them out of the room while we display the pitiful contents of our pockets and are told we could go. We quickly pack up the van, and off we go. Rat's experience with crossing Euro borders has once again paid off. There's nothing like having a homeboy in the band. When I look in my overnight bag later, I find my things have been neatly repacked, and that they disassembled my stick deodorant, checked out my film containers, and dumped out my vitamins. All in a day's thorough work for the border patrol. "This one's safe to let through, comrade."

The drive to Oslo is long, slow, and dreary. It seems to pass as if just a foggy recollection, as something vaguely slept through—but from which no rest was obtained. The venue is a huge ballroom, capacity probably around 800. About thirty people turn out to see Jeff Dahl and the two local bands. It is unbelievably dismal. In a particularly fragile moment, I dedicate a song to my ex-wife, a tall, dark goddess of strong Norwegian stock. Meanwhile, five guys decide to start slam dancing, and their makeshift mosh pit drive the other twenty-five audience members away. We come offstage and, incredibly, Dahl asks us with a straight face, "Regular three?"

STOCKHOLM IS WHERE WE'LL take the ferry to Finland. It is an awesome looking city, and given that Simon gets lost looking for port, we see a lot of it. I nibble on a bag of potato chips that will be my complete diet for the day, riding shotgun, making sure Simon stays awake on yet another drive that begins at 6:30 a.m. Finland looks to be the Promised Land, a place where Dahl can actually sell records and where Hanoi Rocks-style raunch 'n' roll is godhead. Truth is, Denmark and Norway were just stepping stones to get to Finland. There was virtually no awareness of Dahlrock in these places, hence the dislocated, weird, under-attended shows.

At about 5:00 p.m., after ten straight hours on the road, we finally are driving up into the ferry. This one's huge, a seven decker complete with private rooms, casinos, restaurants, shops, a disco, an old-fashioned band of married men, and people of all nationalities passing in the corridors and on deck. Nonetheless, with all this to do and see, all five of us are sound asleep in our cabins by 6:00 p.m., letting the ocean rock us to sleep for the next twelve hours. After the long drives and the nearly sleepless nights, it's time for some catch-up.

I wake up at about 7:00 a.m. Finland time to hear a loud grinding, crunching, cracking sound on the other side of the cabin wall. Our cabin, down on deck two, is actually below sea level. I jolt awake but notice my cabin mates are either dead or nearly dead. Not wanting to wake anyone but not able to roll back asleep, I decide to go up on deck and investigate. Imagine, I'm on this gigantic ship, and here I am on deck completely alone, not another soul in sight. The blackest of nights, and as far as I can see down the length of the ship, there is no other sign of life. Hope someone's got a grip on the wheel. I look over the side, down to the icy waters below, and discover what the noise was. The ship is crashing through the ice, the frozen ocean. We are indeed in a cold part of the world, something Southern California boys like me don't see a great deal of. In the mist and fog, I snap pictures of the cracking ice while the rest of my comrades sleep warmly in their bunks. Crunnnch. It is even colder than one might imagine given the wind, the mist, and the frozen waters, but I'm mesmerized by the glorious solitude of it. Standing right on the furthermost front tip of this vessel, it almost seems I could leap off the edge and take flight.

OUR LOCAL PROMOTER, LENNY, meets us at the dock, and we follow his BMW to the luxury hotel we're to stay in. Right on the icy bay, with snow everywhere, it's a cold but beautiful sight from our stately rooms. We have to fill out semi-lengthy questionnaires at the check-in desk, inquiring as to our professions and purpose of visit. Rat fills in Occupation: "Rocker." Purpose of Stay: "I have to rock." A few hours to stumble around Helsinki are supervened by a 3:00 p.m. sound check.

The venue is gymnasium-sized, with a large private dressing area backstage and a cafeteria serving up hot chili and tea. We settle in there, play a little pool, and indulge in some chili. Checking out the locals convinces me that this must be where white people were invented. These are white people! Pure white skin—almost translucent—sky-blue eyes, and natural blonde, bright yellow hair. We have a ninety-minute sound check that leaves us sounding loud and proud.

Returning from the hotel for showtime, the place is really starting to fill up. It seems like an old seventies rock concert with four bands and a young crowd of boys and girls anxious to party. There is no beer for sale here. The only beer is in the musician's dressing room, which is beginning to fill with hangers-on for that very reason.

Rat walks in with two exquisite women: one a tall, flaxen blonde beauty calling herself Jennifer who seems particularly taken with our guitar slinger. They sit on a couch, talking quietly and sipping beer. An actual dressing room filled with cute girls—isn't this how it's supposed to be every night? Otherwise, why not just play in the symphony?

Dahl and Z walk in and Dahl announces: "We're reviving the Parisian glam rock act. Get that makeup on and spray that hair, boys." I guess he figured since we were in the land of Hanoi Rocks, we'd pay our own form of tribute.

I begin struggling with some eyeliner when Jennifer volunteers to assist. Leaning over me, exposing her firm breasts slightly as her silky hair tumbles in my face, I can see the appeal of being fussed over as a real star might. Enjoy it for the moment. It won't last long, to be sure.

"What did you say your name was?" I ask this beauty.

"Mina."

"I thought you said it was Jennifer."

"Oh, yaass." She giggles for a minute or so.

"Well, which is it?"

"They both are my name, depending on who yoooouuuu are."

"Whatever. Listen, don't be delicate with this stuff," I request, indicating the eye makeup. "Pile it on. I want to look scary, not pretty."

"You mean like Aleez Cooopah? I can do that, sit back, prettee boyee." More giggles. "There, what you tink of zat?" she asks as she points me toward a mirror.

"It's grotesque! Perfect, thanks."

I step onto the side of the stage to check out Antiseen, some country boys from the South, mixing Black Oak Arkansas good-time washboard rock with hyperdrive punk. After some super high-energy workouts, the group's heavyset singer, a gentleman named Jeff Clayton, takes his washboard and rubs it across his face like a cheese grater. Various scars (obtained by doing this routine in the past) open up and bleed easily, causing red curtains to pour from his forehead and cheeks.

"Hey, good set," I say to the bloody mess as he mops his face with a towel.

"Ah, hell, thanks. Thanks a lot. I can't wait to see y'all's set."

"So, how much more of your tour have you got left?"

"This is our third gig. We got forty more left."

"Do you open up your face at every show like that?"

"Well, not every show, pardner, but quite a few of them."

"Take care of yourself then. Do be careful, won't you?"

"Don't you worry about me. I'll be okay."

Wow, I can't believe how parental I just acted. He seemed to appreciate it in some strange way. Maybe he doesn't ever hear anyone express concern, just: "When are you gonna bleed all over the place again?" I like the guy, though, and don't mind letting him know it.

＊

OUR SHOW GOES WELL, and it ends this swing of our tour on a high note. Maybe it was the best show of the whole run. The crowd is a good three or four hundred strong, and way into what we are doing, causing the band to play at the pinnacle of our abilities. Too bad every night can't be this gratifying, but that wouldn't be real. The floor's filled with blindingly white people all shaking their hair in choreographed perfection. It will make for a lasting and strong memory, something I can take to my grave with minimum embarrassment.

The dressing room is packed with fans, taking photos and having us sign this and that. Rat continues to carry on with Jennifer/Mina, who leaves with him for the van. Yo, Rat, making his move in the eleventh hour, twelve o'clock high.

Back at our hotel, in the room we're sharing, Simon pours drinks and pops beers. Rat, Z, and the girl stop in to party with us before going down to their room. The television is on, we're all drinking and talking, then Rat and Z suddenly rise and excuse themselves. "We're going to go to sleep, I guess," says Rat. They leave and the girl stays behind.

"My name is really Christa," she says softly, sitting with her back arched on Simon's bed and her legs crossed seductively. Simon, where was Simon? I hear the toilet flush in the next room and that answers that.

"Don't be so shy, come a little closer."

"I thought you came here with Ratboy? I can't just step in on his find, that goes against the laws of the open road!"

"Laws?" She laughs, stands to face me, and puts her arms around my neck.

"Don't touch me. We musicians have honor amongst ourselves, like thieves."

I had no idea what I was talking about, and as good as this cream puff looked to me, it didn't feel right to be with her, not even close. I had to assess the situation. I've been slogging it out on this blind run of a tour for two straight months now, and much of the time it had been a competition with myself to land the perfect daydream, to interact with foreigners in a directly physical yet obliquely spiritual and overtly erotic manner. Could it be done? Did it make sense? Was it a goal worth pursuing in the first place, or was it just something I gravitated toward because of a heightened sense of boredom and a diminishing appraisal of self-worth?

It was all a lot to cross-register as I considered my options at the present moment. I've been avoiding sex by playing around on dance floors, and at the same time repeatedly trying to get an another-side-of-the-globe fix on the real love of my life, Gina, who was back at home, doing who knows what? But when it came right down to it, despite her good times, her hiccupping, her partying, and her occasional departures from this dimension, she seemed to be as faithful to me as could be hoped for.

In the meantime, these women that have been presented to me in a variety of forms and images, real and imagined—a veritable parade of earthly delights. Would my simple coupling with them have been rewarding in a slightly altered set of circumstances? Many even more cynical than myself might have looked back over their shoulders and sneered, "What are you waiting for? Your best days have already left you behind..."

There she sits, Jennifer/Mina/Christa, an animal waiting to pounce, no hunger except for blood in its purist extraction, eyeing me as if I was nothing more than a passing form of disposable satisfaction. Had I looked at any of my conquests—potential or theoretically realized—any differently? Is there any real reason I don't just throw her down on my bed and fuck her in half? She's as sexy as any girl I've ever seen, why not just go for it and worry about the right/wrong and otherwise of it later. Philosophy, who needs it?

"Wait here a minute. I'll be right back," I announce, and head down the hall to Casa de la Rat y Z.

"What's up, Rat? I thought you wanted to party and hang out with this girl?"

"No, that's okay," Rat monotones. "I can see Simon making moves on her, that little smile thing he does. It sickens me. I don't care. I'm gonna watch some television, drink some rum, and go to bed."

"You brought this girl back here. I don't want her in my room!"

"She's yours and Simon's now. Hurry back, or Simon will have already cornered her."

Damn, survival of the fittest, dog eat dog, cavemen-troglodytes, I think to myself as I stroll back to our room. Guess Rat called it right 'cause Simon's lying on top of this three-named Finnish tart kissing her frantically.

"Oh, McGruff, don't mind us." The girl pushes him aside and sits up on the bed. Now she wants to talk, but I just wanna watch television and remain uninvolved, while Simon clearly is not interested in either of those activities. She babbles on about music and whatever, I try to answer her as politely but as briefly as possible. Watching Simon's frustration is laughable for a moment. I decide to turn in, climb in to my bed, and pull the covers up tight. The lights go out, and the slurping sounds of sloppy kisses fill the room. A few minutes later, as my eyes adjust to the dark, I roll over on my side to see if I can at least get a free show.

Simon's mounted her by now, and begins pumping, slowly at first, but soon enough energetically. I wonder if he can see my eyes peepin' through my covers? This goes on for some time. Damn, Simon's got some pretty good staying power. Hey, why doesn't she get on top, Little Miss Don't Be Shy? Finally, after some significant moans and groans, Simon goes down on her ("She was a real blonde," I would hear later. "You were watchin', weren't ya, ya twat!"), and while he may be a good lay, he knows fuck all about cunnilingus. Kids.

Z AND RAT HOOK up with some old friend of Rat's and cruise the bars and shops of Helsinki on their day off. I opt to stay in and go for a swim in the hotel pool. Turns out the pool is private, you get a key at the front desk and go into this subterranean recreation area all by yourself, play pool, watch television, take a sauna, and swim naked. They probably monitor it for closed circuit entertainment in the beer bar. Nah, not everyone's as perverted as we are. The pool is really a giant metal tank, like you'd keep some barracudas in or something. It is not heated, which I am unaware of until I dive in headfirst. It is probably about forty-five degrees, unbearably cold. I swim a few laps to prove I can do it, and then run for a hot shower as my body begins to shrivel and prune. Back up in my room, Chaplin's *The Great Dictator* is on the tube. Somehow this seems appropriate. I later learn Z and Rat had hit the town in the afternoon while I pruned myself, saying they enjoyed this area of Helsinki more than any of our other stops. Oh well, I'll just have to pop back some day. Too bad I don't know any Finnish musicians I can collaborate with.

By 4:00 p.m. that afternoon, we are back on the ferry, our final destination being Holland. Simon and I grab some rather crappy buffet food. He turns in while I check out the budget Tony Orlando holding court in the deck five lounge. Down the hall some geezer is struggling with the finer points of "Georgia On My Mind" at the piano bar. This cruise casino ocean liner is everything you could imagine, and worse.

The next day is Tuesday, a completely unremarkable travel day, only notable in that it begins in Finnish waters, and two ferry rides later we begin our drive to Holland, passing through Denmark, Sweden, and Germany along the way. Five countries in one day, parting the seas and burnin' up the road, babe. Two months of Euro-Blur down, three shows to go.

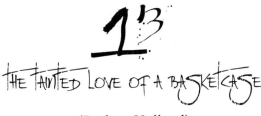

13
THE TAINTED LOVE OF A BASKETCASE

(Back in Holland)

A FTER THE FIVE-COUNTRIES-IN-ONE-DAY TRAVEL rally, we all sleep in late and awake in typical Dutch budget lodgings, familiar from our tour's naïve beginnings. Clean but simple, bathroom and shower down the hall, breakfast downstairs. Everyone's well rested, and given the two months plus change length of our mission, we're in pretty good shape.

Everyone is playin' it cool. There are only three shows left. The finish line is in sight, illuminated by the light at the end of the tunnel. Best now to avoid all possible confrontations and potential friction-creating situations. We're all one big dysfunctional family, trying to get through the holidays together without killing one another. The knife is only supposed to be used to carve the turkey.

⁘

Z, SIMON, AND I stroll around the town of Enschede, spending the day as relaxed tourists might, window shopping, sampling the local version of Mexican cuisine, trying the local beer. Watching the world go by from a tavern window, conversation is small talk strung together with unmapped realms of soothing silence. Simon interrupts the placidity.

"Why didn't Ratboy come along, then? I'm going to miss the Ratboy."

"Sure you are," I reply, trying to stir things up a bit. (What the hell? Please pass the carving knife.) "He's good for procuring the real blondes."

"Oh, come on," Simon shoots back. "That's not fair. He wasn't interested in that girl."

"He brought her back to the hotel for something."

"Well, he has to get on it, then, or else it's fair game."

"Anything for some pussy passing in the night, eh? Dude, you sold him down the river, for a girl! The trust of the road dogs was betrayed for the promise of wagging tail. For shame!"

"Bros, not hos," clarified Z, our man of few words.

"Oh, Rat doesn't think like that. He doesn't give a shit," exclaimed Simon, who nonetheless seemed to be considering the possibility of us being correct.

"Where is he then? Where is the littlest Rat? You sold him down the river for a two-bit Scandinavian one-nighter. Damn!"

Simon now seems truly dejected, fine by me. He has perhaps gone through the most changes as a result of the Master and Factsheet's mental abuse. From hero of the masses to slave driver to slave to Dudley Moore-like buffoon, his transition and repositioning has been exceptionally harsh. We have done nothing to make it easier for him to emerge on the other side. When we were first in Holland, what seems so long ago now, we openly proclaimed through the public address system that he was God! As such, one would suppose he had the farthest to fall. It's hard to be so completely dysfunctional so consistently, but we try.

Z and I saddle up for a friendly game of chess in the bar, which is perfect for letting time speed by and obtaining a heightened sense of relaxation. It is the chosen game of the Rip Van Winkle set. Simon is more restless than ever. "Don't play that, you bloody lot are so slow. It'll take all day!"

"Fine, let it," says Z.

"We don't have any pressing engagements with the Pope," I add.

"Bloody hell." He sits in the corner and sulks, until a local catches his attention and then he's fine again.

I beat Z at the first game, which I've never done before. We begin round two, while Z and I review some of the past two month's escapades. Worst gig: Montargis. Oslo a close second, though much warmer. Best gig: hmm, not quite so hands down. Toulouse? Madrid? Helsinki, perhaps?

"With shows like Madrid and Toulouse, isn't half of it the events that surrounded the show, the girls, the clubs, the dancing?" wonders Z.

"No. More than half," I estimate. "The tour is about the adventure. The exploration of the unknown."

"What about the music?"

"The music is the thread that tenuously binds the whole thing together. The music is the excuse for obtaining a passport."

"Hey, listen. It's nothing to me. I came along for the ride and made no pretense about it. I've never listened to Jeff Dahl records and really don't anticipate an upswing in that activity upon my return home. But, you seem to be saying, in a situation such as this, the music isn't as important as the time spent goofing off, chasing girls, getting drunk, looking for heroin, cruising red light districts, discovering local culinary delights..."

"Drinking and whoring!" I clarify for us both. "Say it. Revel in it! The music can't be as important. Our art—if that term applies—provides the reason, the excuse, and the commerce—if that term applies and that condition exists. But the adventures will ultimately provide the next collection of art, the new music, the new batch, the future inspiration. The adventures provide the memories. Presumably, we already know the music. Once that music makes its way to magnetic tape, it's already been lived, digested, rewritten, rethought, and it's as fresh as yesterday's papers. The artist is really the only one who knows this, the public will still perceive it as new, and hopefully, if everything works right, the hype will breath new life into it, interest will spark, and then the geezer in question can mount another tour and continue the charade another year. See, the important thing is to continue to live full speed with your eyes open so you continue to have something to write about."

"Checkmate."

❧

THE EVENING'S SHOW IS being opened by a fine young band called Five Man Vomit. I leave the main concert hall to retain what's left of my hearing, and walk past our new T-shirt salesman, Simon. He looks down.

"I love the road, but I have to admit, I can't wait to get home and see Melanie."

"I know, champ, I know." I pat him on the back and walk on.

As I walk past the bar, I notice sitting there is six feet of Germanic beauty going by the name of Rheinheld. "It's my favorite bass player," she says as I approach.

I had been wondering if one of my German dahlings would turn up before the big bird launched me back to Yankeeville. The tall, sleek, and demure Rheinheld had said she would while the card-wielding Elke offered up a maybe. Despite the prevailing mood of the group that dictated an attempt to return to normal (non-road) behavior, I was nonetheless happy to see her.

"C'mon upstairs," I invite. "It's a little more quiet. We have No Man Vomit up there."

"What?"

"Never mind."

I learn my lovely friend from Munster is twenty-eight and working on graduating from business classes in college. She has a two-year-old son named Nick, her reason for living. Daddy is a German rocker with a dope habit and little desire to be called "poppa." She carries the weight with seeming ease, although just past the "everything's alright" façade, the hardship and heartache is visible if one cares to look. She is soft yet strong, smooth but tough, chiseled with determination. We pile into the van after the show. Taller than any of the guys on the tour, Rheinheld pulls herself onboard and asks: "Is there room for a leetle German girl?" She does have style.

After off-loading to the hotel, Rheinheld, Simon, and I walk to a nearby bar for all-night drinking and dancing. Simon buys us a drink, we toast, and Rheiny pulls me off to the dance floor. It's terribly crowded with Dutch yuppie types, and the music isn't very good (when Soft Cell's version of the Ed Cobb masterpiece "Tainted Love" comes on, it's actually a relief), but there seems to be nothing else shakin' Thursday night in Enschede Rock City, so you learn to go with the flow.

Following almost every dance, Rheiny grabs me and pulls me close for kissing. Then she hugs and squeezes. Nice girl, but methinks she's been a little under par in the receiving-affection department, maybe about a quart low. I can relate, but honey, lemme come up for air.

Simon orders up another round. "You're doing alright," he says, nodding discreetly toward Rheiny. "Huh? Yeah, yes, right."

"Something wrong, McGruff? Too much of a good thing, perhaps?"

"I don't know. Hey, you ever see that movie, *The Man Who Knew Too Much?*

"No."

"Well, they killed him in the end."

"I see. I'll keep that in mind."

"Thanks for the drink."

Around four in the morning we leave. Simon seems all detached and spaced out again, like he's going to return to his static-watching robot state of mind. He insists on going off his own way, and walks the opposite direction of our hotel by himself.

"Iz he always like that?" asks Rheiny.

"No, only about a third of the time, I'd estimate."

We walk to her car parked nearby, and find it's been broken into during the night.

"I can't believe it. There was nothing in it. It looks like they took my jacket. Shit, I'll have to get a new window."

I felt sorry for her, but in a sick sort of way, the incident made me long for home. In L.A., cars are routinely broken into and nothing stolen, as if thieves just feel the need to keep their chops up.

✿

IT'S AROUND 4:30 IN the morning, and we're back at my hotel room, a single for the night, as it turns out. The radiator is cranked and one lamp glows in the corner. Rheiny, now stripped down to her black bra and panties, requests the use of my toothbrush. Of course, help yourself.

"My God, look at this thing! It looks like you've been repairing cars with it!"

"Well, it's been a long tour, you know."

"Believe it or not, they sell toothbrushes in Europe."

"Really? I thought they were strictly American commodities, like brooms, coherent directions, and Michael Bolton."

"Shut up, you." She put her arms around me, and we tumbled on down.

The night surrenders to dawn with relative ease, soft pillow talk, and good old-fashioned lovin' carrying us through until the morning.

"It's been a long time since someone's truly been kind and loving to me," she whispers.

"It's nothing, really. Much less than you deserve. You're without a doubt the coolest person I've met in Europe. By far."

"Yet, despite how much you seem to like me, I can tell from leetle sings that you do that your heart truly belongs to anozer. You have a girlfrien' waiting at home, don't you?"

It's my personal belief that women, while frequently cited as being feline in nature, have an equal amount of canine qualities. A woman can smell another woman on your clothes like a bloodhound, and can spot one lurking around in your heart like a wolf.

"Yes, you're correct. I'll be back at her side in a matter of days."

"I sense you actually feel gill-tee about what we do."

"You might say I'm an honorary Catholic. I guess I wish I'd gotten together with you way back in Münster instead of three days before departure. Time helps soften the guilt, eases ya back into the normality of your daily routine."

"I don't mean to make you feel bad," she says softly, with genuine understanding and caring.

Her eyes seem to glow, illuminated by the rising sun shining through the window. I pull myself on top of her

lengthy frame, and I'm literally swimmin' in wimmen.
I've decided to feel bad, guilty, and weighed down with
regret about all of this tomorrow. For right now, lemme
enjoy this tainted love.

•♦

RHEINHELD DEPARTS AFTER BREAKFAST, which is followed by the
usual interrogation from my travel mates, "Didja, didja?" A
gentleman never tells, at least not until he gets a publisher.

Why did I go through with it, a mere two gigs before
I'm back in the arms of my one true love? Vanity, that's
way up there, and proving to myself I could make the
relatively (in most normal cases) simple acquisition of
what the commoners and proletariats call groupie, which
I call sanctuary and respite. But at a quarter to midnight,
my timing, in life as in music, is not the greatest. Why
didn't we just go to the club, do a little dancing, have a
couple cocktails, hell, make out a little bit, and then call
it a morning? I just couldn't leave well enough alone.
Never the greatest liar, how will this serve when I return
home? Best not to dwell on this now. Best to push it
under the old denial throw rug.

We snake our way to Sneek (pronounced "snake"),
another nondescript Dutch town. I room once again
with Z, and we choose to veg out all day in the hotel
room and watch television. Bands crossing the greater
United States take television for granted. There's no
Twilight Zone on at 2:00 a.m. in Holland. There's no
porno channel on your hotel television in Switzerland.

You don't even have a television in Spain. Okay, the U.S. is too uptight for titty game shows, but believe me, you're better off with cable.

Sneek is even less socially advanced than Enschede. At least Enschede had a few other establishments besides the one we were playing at to go out to—the same claim could not be made in Sneek. Following the less-than-eventful gig, we returned to our comfy beds and our hung-on-the-wall television. Immediately getting dressed for bed (Z still with his nightshirt and cap), we happily gawk blankly at our beaming fourteen-inch color friend.

A knock at the door reveals a surprise guest: Jeff Dahl, his own bad self. "Hey, I nabbed this homegrown weed from a guy at the show last night. Want to smoke some?"

"Sure."

Dahl rolls a joint with Z's cigarette rolling papers, fires it up, sucks in a big hit, and passes it to Z.

"No thanks."

It comes my way. I take a huge toke, and pass it to Dahl. He takes another puff, as do I, and we sit back for a moment. Our television spews forth some dependable Friday night softcore, which seems to inspire Jeff to want to return to his private room.

"Thanks, Jeff," I holler after him. "Oh, hey, the rest of your joint!"

"Keep it, polish it off. You guys have a good night."

"You see?" I say to Z. "The Master is good deep down. Sometimes his leadership responsibilities get him a little mixed up, that's all."

"He sure likes to rush back to his own room once the naked girls hit the screen," notes Z with a sly smile.

"Let every man relieve his personal pressure as he best sees fit. Me, I'm gonna fire up this reefer and let some brain cells roam free. Sure you don't want any?"

I puff away on the handmade mind melter, drifting through various stages of consciousness. The day had been so dedicated to relaxation and nothingness that it wasn't difficult to wind all the way down and drift off to sleep. Soon, flashing visions of a race of Amazonian/Aryan princesses wielding bayonets, reptilian super models, and Ratboy in a toga fly about within the confines of my rapid eye movements.

DREAM SEQUENCE

THE SEA OF ATROCITIES part and there, on the throne of all knowledge, sits the Lord, whadiya know? The Lord's a skirt! She looks just like...just like...

Gina!

"You've been a bad boy, haven't you?" boomed the austere, angry voice, made all the more menacing with some added digital delay. "You couldn't wait THREE MORE DAYS. You've been a regular asshole, a typical...MALE." The word "male" echoed with Wall of Sound precision.

END DREAM SEQUENCE

I JERK AWAKE. DAMN, some strong-ass weed. I rise to take a piss in our microscopic adjoining bathroom, and notice

Z sleeping soundly. I look at myself in the mirror. Let's see, sunken, weary, bloodshot eyes, highlighted by huge black circles, patchy skin, pale complexion, dark roots in my hair a few inches long. Glamour isn't dead. Hey, wait a minute. I've forgotten how to piss. Ah, here we go. Damn it, now I can't stop. Okay, okay, there, everything's cool. Shit, was Dahl trying to get me high or poison me?

Returning to bed, I roll on my side and try to go back to sleep. Suddenly, the arm I'm laying on goes numb. I roll on my back and grab my right numb arm with my good left arm. Shaking it, I can't seem to get any feeling in it at all. I give up and lie on my back. Hang on, now I can't feel either arm. I have no arms! What the fuck?!?

A heightened awareness of impending paranoia overtakes me, as I sense my own doom and demise lurking just under the bed. My head is spinning, and I'm busting into a cold sweat. Shit, now I can't feel my legs. I'm limbless, a literal basket case. I have trouble catching my breath and I try to stand up. Though I can't feel my legs, they seem to work, and I go back to the bathroom and try to splash water on my face. My rubber arms don't want to respond at first, but after a few tries and much water everywhere I manage to complete the Herculean task.

I sit down on the toilet and try to compose myself. What the hell was in that stuff? Was it the marijuana itself, or is it the preceding two months of mishap and mayhem, fear and submission, swelling up inside of me to be purged once and for all? It's as if all of this poison is begging to be squeezed from the whitehead of my soul.

Could it be same said soul screaming to off-load the needless baggage I've accrued along our fitful journey? Is it the actual substance of death, that which has been like a hellhound on our trail since day one, rolled and squeezed into cigarette form? Or is it merely the most mind-ripping sweat leaf just in from Amsterdam, waiting to either imprison you or set you free, daddio?

I try to lie down again, and I still feel mighty weird. What's the worst that could happen? This could be the early signs of a heart attack, in which case I'll probably check out for good in this nothing hotel in this nowhere town. Most likely, though, I'll just have more fitful dreams and wake up recovered and ready to meet and greet our final Saturday night of rock 'n' roll glory head on.

　　　　　　　　　⁖

OUR HOTEL FOR MY final night in Europe is probably the fanciest and most modern of the tour. Huge lobby, luxurious rooms with fancy drapes and velvet bedspreads make us feel like traveling royalty. The only eyesore in evidence is our van, which hasn't been washed once during the tour. Dahl's theory is, if it looks filthy and trashed, no one will think there's anything valuable in it. I offered that all the accumulated scum provided a protective coating as well, a shield of gritty armor for our trusty friend.

I'm sharing with Z for the final time. He and Ratboy will return to Switzerland tomorrow. Rat has arranged for them to stay with his sister and get some R & R (rest and relaxation instead of rock and roll) for a few days before flying back to the States. I think in a way Z would rather just head back, see Rita, and cruise the streets of Hollywood in his big blue Cadillac. In fact, speaking of the lovely Rita, as we sit in our room, Z frantically tries to reach his bleached-blonde beauty back home.

"Bitch!" He slams the phone down.

"What's wrong?"

"Every fucking time I call, she's gone. *Please leave a message at the sound of the tone.* It's hard enough to even get through with these stupid phones."

"So she's out doing something. What do you expect?"

"She shouldn't be out having so much...FUN. I'm not!"

"Oh, come on. Let the girl kick up her heels a bit. You're so Italian. Besides, forget that, we have a few hours off, we're gonna take the train to Amsterdam."

As in Paris, our tour didn't quite stop in the big city. We were in an outlying burg called Haarlem, a cheery-enough place with nothing much to do. No point in spending the day doing the Haarlem Shuffle when Amsterdam was only twenty minutes away by train.

Simon, Z, and I take a cab to the train station. Simon literally beams with joy. He's going to meet his precious Melanie at the station in Amsterdam, symbolic confirmation to him that his ordeal with the likes of us is all but over. Soon he would be back home, spinning records in the local clubs, drinking strong Dutch beer, and romancing his sweetheart.

"I'm going to ask her to marry me, you know?" he had told me in a German hotel room.

"You, the king of road poontang? Gonna settle down and be Jimmy Stewart?"

"Yeah, sure. I've had enough of this. I'd like to get a job in the business, you know, managing a band or something like that, yeah, I'd fancy a bit of that. Do you think I'd be good at it?"

"I don't know. Would you like to be strapped to a desk and a phone twelve hours a day to earn fifteen percent of nothing? I don't know. I have a hard time imagining you settling down."

"You'll see."

❧

SIMON MEETS HIS TRUE love and the theoretical future Mrs. Easton at the station. Pointing me and Z in a direction, the two of them quickly go their own way. The train station in Amsterdam opens up directly to what seems like a whole new world. Offensive, contemporary storefronts and theaters collide with old-world architecture along the main boulevard, as if it has always been that way. Canals crisscross, and everywhere people buzz by, a mix of every nationality, some residents, some just passing through, some hustling, some taking snapshots. A lot of shady types approach us and offer up every type of drug imaginable.

"Want speed? You like skag? China white? I got the best. "Hashish, my American friend? Good trips. How about an ounce? You looking for some coke?"

We practically had to cut through these guys with machetes, they were so thick. "No, go away." With our hair and clothes giving us away as potential dope-gulping lowlifes, the dealers just kept on approaching us. Someone could actually make some money printing up *No, we don't want any drugs* T-shirts. We kept on passing these specialized street merchants by, more interested in taking in the glorious sights of this historical city and snapping photos like the other tourists.

It was a city built on sin, notorious for its hash bars, red light district, sex emporiums, and anything goes legal system. A playground of ill repute, Amsterdam was a revered stop on any self-respecting rock 'n' roll tour, a place where you could get high, get laid, and get away with it. You just needed a little pocket fuel.

Indeed, we were low on money. But we were also short on desire. It'd been over nine weeks of sustained disquiet and prolonged, cramped travel. We'd been in the back of the Renault for so much incalculable time that our legs were practically frozen in a permanent sitting position. Normal walking was actually uncomfortable. When free time was afforded us, and we were actually in a place where there might be some trouble to get into, we'd already spent so much time and energy swilling beer, scrounging for illicit substances, and sniffing around for stray night crawlers that now, at the end of it all, that sort of desperate thrill-seeking had lost its appeal. We were Mom and Pop America seeking not amorous thrills and mind-bending euphoria, but rather a good, long look at the town square and the graceful waters of the canals. We were through with debauchery and had surrendered to tourism.

With our cheesy little map of Amsterdam, procured at the train station, we look for something to do and how to get there. Deciding on the Van Gogh museum, we begin to make our way across town, choosing to walk instead of cabbing it. We want to see the sights and, honestly, we still need to save money. As has been typical throughout our sojourn, we get lost. Crossing a street with our eyes upwards looking for a street name we can locate on the map, we are practically mowed down by three elderly women speeding by on bicycles. I don't know if we'll ever get used to these manic Dutch bike riders.

"Bike lane! Look out!" they yell as they whisk by. Another guy on a bike notices our dilemma, rides up and shows us on our map how to get where we're going. A mere mile off target, we trek off for our destination once we're back on track.

It's a somber stroll indeed through the three floors of the Van Gogh museum. The place is arranged so that you walk past the Dutch master's works in chronological order—hence, you can visually observe his dissent into madness and dementia as you go. His paintings get more three-dimensional as they progress, with the paint piled on in spots so thick it extends from the canvas. As at the Louvre, we are humbled in the presence of true brilliance. We realize that we are just journeymen hacking away within the disposable world of pop music. Walking back toward the train, we stop for a beer at an outdoor café. A bit weary from our extended hike, the cool air, sunny day, and cold beer make for a relaxed moment, soon to be interrupted by a young street musician in tattered jeans.

"How 'bout it, lads, a gilder for your request?" he beckons.

"You're barking up the wrong tree, mate," I inform. "We can't afford cab fare. We're poor musicians, too."

"You can afford beer!" he sneers, turning to accost the next sucker.

A casual stroll back to the train relaxes us even more. We look around for Simon and Melanie, but there's no sign of them, so we hop the train back to Haarlem. Half-sleep on the train, a thought crosses my mind.

"Hey, Z. What's the name of our hotel?"

"Um, I dunno, beats me. Don't you know?"

"No. Maybe I have it written down. Let me look in my wallet."

Precious little money, a bar receipt, a guitar pick, Elke and Rheinheld's phone numbers, but nothing from our current digs. "Do you remember where it was from the train station?" I ask my friend.

"No, not really."

All this way, all this time on tour, so responsible, never missed a gig or a sound check, and now we're separated from the pack and we can't remember where the pack is. In the Haarlem station, I decide we should try and call the club and ask them if they know where the band is staying. Somehow, we recalled the name of the club.

"Let me see if I can get my calling card to work here," I say to Z when we learn that neither of us has any change acceptable to this payphone. First try, disconnected. Second try, no answer. Third try, operator doesn't understand English. Fourth try, operator does understand English, but doesn't accept my card. She gives me another number to call that will allow for ATT.

"What number do you want, sir?"

"The Patronaat, a nightclub in Haarlem."

"Here you go."

A message machine says a lot of Dutch stuff with the name Jeff Dahl recognizable amidst it all. Right club, at least. I repeat the procedure and ask the operator if there is an office number for the club. One ring. Two, three, and four.

"Hallo."

"Sprecken Zee Anglais?"

"English, yah, a little. Yes?"

"I need to know the name of the hotel where the Jeff Dahl Band is staying, please."

"Oh, I don't know. Please hold." Silence. "Are you a fan of Jeff? He'll be here soon enough for sound check."

"No, no. I'm in the band. I'm here in Haarlem, and I can't remember where the hell we're staying."

"You should have already checked in by now," said the voice on the other end of the line, trying to be helpful.

"I have checked in. Me and the drummer went to Amsterdam and we can't find the hotel. We don't remember what it was called."

"Amsterdam, oh yass. I understand. The hotel is the Zuid."

"Huh?"

"Zuid."

"You're a life saver. You got an address on this place?"

"Zuid. On Toekanweg. Any driver will know." Crises averted, and we return to Zuid barely on time for our last-ever sound check.

THIS NIGHT, OUR OPENING act is a Spanish all-girl rock group named—I'm not making this up—Chicas del Rock. They have mediocre songs but play and sing much better than average. And they're cute, too, which doesn't hurt. All of our entourage, a meager five with Tim gone and no local promoters traveling with us, enjoy them as we waste time around Patronaat.

Our show is, well, another show. We play just about every song we know, using most of the same spoken introductions, do most of the same cover songs, do the same pogo choreography in the Vibrators' "Baby Baby," pull the same silly faces, make the same rock poses, leave the planet on another improvisational flight through "Dirt," play "Living in Lisa's World" faster than ever before, lay on the floor under blankets of feedback, and say goodnight for the final time.

Remember Eric and Charles from France, who first visited us in Eeklo, Belgium? They ended up coming to five shows along the way between Holland, France, and Belgium. They have tonight traveled to Amsterdam for their fifth Jeff Dahl concert in two months. They seem like family now. It's always a pleasure when they come around. As fanatical as they are, they're pretty down to earth, normal guys that just happen to be rock 'n' roll nuts.

"You guys are the greatest. I wish there was something special we could do for you," I offer.

"Do you guys drink? There's some wine. None of us drink wine," says Jeff.

"Wait a minute. Let's do something really special," says Rat. "I'll be back in a second."

Rat gets the keys to the van and returns with the double-large pillow stolen from the Uden hotel that has served as cushion, pacifier, and friend since the beginning of our travels. "I want to give you something that has meant a lot to us. We've outgrown it now. You should have it. It is an eternal symbol of the Jeff Dahl tour..."

"Of the Euro-Blur experience," adds Z.

"Of Eeklo nights and Ravensburg days," I contribute.

Dahl shakes his head, convinced his band has the loosest screws of any musical ensemble around. Eric and Charles stare at their present with bemusement. It's not exactly something you'd take home and put on your mantle. They probably couldn't care less about this mangy pillow, but they accept it graciously in the spirit in which it was given.

Down the hall, Chicas del Rock celebrates the birthday of their bass player. They are all boisterous and outgoing, sexy in the way only Spanish women can be. Their dressing room is packed with them and their friends. We are warmly welcomed to join in the party. Tequila slammers with champagne are the drug of choice, and soon pain and woe are things of the past, just vague memories.

"Do you get a bit of a dyke vibe from these chicks?" Simon whispers to me.

"Maybe. Don't know. Don't care really. They're nice girls. Lesbians need love, too, you know."

"You have a point. I think I'm going to miss you a bit, McGruff."

"I'm gonna miss you, too, Scarecrow. Ah, hell, don't get all weepy on me now. You'll be in Los Angeles looking for a record company job before you know it. We'll hit Sunset Boulevard right between the eyes."

"You, Blondie. Have another slammer," the voluptuous singer beckons me. I oblige, and as was far from uncommon at this point of Euro-Blur, my world was becoming somewhat blurry. Turn off the light on your way out, love.

Someone told one of the girls I worked at a record company back in the States, and suddenly I am having phone numbers thrust at me and promises that fabulous tapes chock full of original hit tunes will be crossing my desk upon my return. In the meantime, please keep the tequila coming. By 2:00 a.m., the party is waning and we are loading the van for the final time.

I WAS ALMOST PACKED when the wake-up call sounded. I

gulp my tea and throw the last few items in my bag. Rat comes in the room.

"Well, McGruff. It's been gay, that's for sure. I guess I'll see you next time you're in New York."

"That you will, Mr. Ratboy. That you will. Take care of Z in Switzerland. It may not be that obvious, but he's primed and ready to topple over the edge."

"Oh, I know, I know," he laughed. Rat, the sensible one, the calm one, the even-keeled, the dour, the wry-humored. I'll most definitely miss him, his calming presence, his self-deflating jokes, his firm grip on reality, his grasp of the cosmic laugh that is the rock 'n' roll lifestyle.

"Okay, McGruff. Here we go." It was Dahl, rallying his dwindling troops one last time. I leap up on the still-slumbering Z's bed and jump up and down, with him in-between my feet.

"See ya back at home, Z. Try not to be too depressed stuck here in Europe one more week." He laughed. I left.

•

SIMON WAS ALREADY GONE, figuratively. Melanie was with us so he was already back at home in his mind. He gave me his address and a hug, waving goodbye as Dahl and I headed into the terminal to be shipped back home like so much damaged baggage.

14
AN OUTCAST IN LISA'S WORLD

(Epilogue—Los Angeles, New York, Tilburg, Phoenix)

> *"Well, I don't really think that the end can be assessed*
> *as of itself as being the end because what does the end*
> *feel like? It's like saying when you try to extrapolate*
> *the end of the universe, you say, if the universe is in-*
> *deed infinite, then how—what does that mean? How*
> *far is all the way, and then if it stops, what's stopping*
> *it, and what's behind what's stopping it? So, what's*
> *the end, you know, is my question to you."*
> —David St. Hubbins, *This is Spinal Tap*

> *"This is the end, beautiful friend."*
> —The Doors (Simon presumably still has the tape.)

I PATIENTLY WAIT FOR the drug dogs to sniff to their canine heart's content. They're frisky and friendly and want to play.

"Don't pet the dogs," barks a customs cop without the faintest trace of humor or humanity.

Gina looks amazing at the baggage claim in a black corset and tight, torn jeans. She is thinner, and her hair is darker than when I saw her last. I hug her and give her a long, luscious kiss. Dahl even tells her she looks great. Indeed, both our eyes are a little sore, I'm sure.

We give Jeff a ride to the terminal where he'll catch his flight to Arizona. I give him a hug, which seems to catch him a little off guard, though I don't know why. Loosen up, Jack. See you in a month for Japan! I guess those weren't our last sound checks and shows after all.

Finally alone, Gina and I get in her Oldsmobile to head from LAX to Hollywood. "I don't know how to tell you this, so I'm just going to tell you," she started. "I lost my job. I got laid off three days ago. The record label they were starting isn't going to happen, so they let me go. That means the record you were going to do with Tim and Ray is off, too. I thought I was doing so well. I fixed up the apartment, took off some weight, got some independence, built some confidence, and got tossed out on my ass again."

She fought hard to hold back the tears. "Don't worry, darling. Everything will be all right. I'm just so happy to be home with you." We went home and made long, passionate love.

BUT THINGS TRULY WERE not all right. During my absence, I'd counted on an investment (in which all of my life savings were tied up) to pan out and garner enough of a profit for us not to have to worry about financial setbacks such as a layoff. During the two months I was in Europe, however, the ten thousand plus dollars I had been advised to invest in a major pharmaceutical concern had evaporated. It's net worth now hovering around thirty bucks. I learned that diversification is key the hard way.

Gina tried for months to get a job. I went back to work at the indie record company and pumped out as much rock magazine piddle as I could, but things were tough. Money problems continually dragged us down. Gina did what she could to remain optimistic, but ultimately sank into a deep depression, from which she could not seem to recover.

We were watching television one night and an ad came on for some check-yourself-in-and-give-us-all-your-money institution.

"Do you find that you sleep all day? Do you have trouble motivating yourself? Do you cry for no perceivable reason?"

"Yes!" she yelled at the television. By Thanksgiving she moved back to Cincinnati, to live in her parents' basement, build up her finances somehow, and strike out somewhere else. We didn't technically break-up, but as she wasn't happy with herself, she truly wasn't happy with me. I was making less than half the money I was when we met, and that had to show me in a different light. Though we talked of starting over some other time, some other place. It never happened. After returning from Japan, I asked her to marry me, but she said no. I learned later that she thought my proposal was inspired by guilt, a guilt born of unfaithfulness on the road.

Still, lasting with her until November turned out to be better than average. Z and Rita broke up almost immediately upon his return. The nearly $1,000 phone bill accrued during Trans-Atlantic communication didn't help their matters, either. My Toyota van and I were hauling furniture out of their apartment about a month after we got back from Japan. Z later joined a group that was well-financed and toured England and America the following year. He claimed it was a completely different experience from Euro-Blur.

"Having a per diem and traveling in a big van where you can stretch out made so much of a difference. It's the only way to do it."

Rat and Lizzie were broken up around the end of summer. She toured the States with her band and he kept their apartment in the Village. He never talked about it much to me, and seemed to deal with it with the same quiet self-assurance he dealt with most things on the road. He toured Canada and the East Coast with his band, Pillbox, the following year. He kept his job at the record store and upon request sends me rare gems when they cross his counter. I always look him up and go out with him for a beer and a catch-up conversation whenever I'm doing time in New York. In an odd, unexpected twist, his cultural adaptability and ease at learning languages paid off for him years after these chapters closed. Rat married a Japanese woman, had some kids, moved to Japan, and eventually ended up being a Swiss ambassador to Japan.

Simon wrote me from Tilburg, Holland a few months later following the tour. Some excerpts: "Since I last saw you guys, I've become a manager, a lyricist, and single again. That last point should tell you that I'm no longer with Melanie. I decided to break it off mid-May. Things weren't going too good, and I also met another girl, Marjolein. She's real cute, but it's still just 'friends.' The manager part is a band called Merry-Go-Round. They asked me to do the job, so I've been trying to arrange them some support slots. So far I've had limited success, but I will succeed (even if they don't)."

"How's the other guys?" he wanted to know. "Is Z still with Rita? Is Ratboy still in NY? Are you still with Gina? Is Brenda still with Dylan?! Anyway, McGruff, I'm going to cut this letter short. I want to catch the post. So, until I hear from you again, take care and keep smiling."

He went on to say that he went back out on the road with Dutch homeboy, psyche-rockers The Soft Machine, who he'd toured with prior to us, and that he'd be going out in the summer with U.S. prep-metalists, Helmet. He was also writing lyrics with the keyboardist of The Soft Machine, but what came of that union I don't know. He said he'd be over to the States soon and would look me up, but I never heard from him again.

No one I know has any idea what ever happened to Tim. I saw him once at a music convention in Los Angeles, hanging out with a couple of similar-looking dudes (none of whom were the Pope), but I chose not to approach him. There just weren't quite enough good old times to revive between us.

Following our reunion for the Japan dates, questions arose at the record company involving the European tour advance and where all the money went. Was there really no profit? It turned out that the money we were all struggling so hard to recoup was to be recouped off of record sales, not from tour profits, so Z and I wanted to know where were the tour profits. Dahl was furious, as he felt we overstepped our bounds into his business. To a large degree, this was true, but the owner of the label (our boss) was more than slightly curious himself as a result of our questions—and probably enjoying the resulting drama which was ultimately no sweat off of his brow—and began faxing Dahl inquiries regarding these financial questions. Come the end of the day, despite past friendships and record company business, as far as the tour went, we were hired guns he didn't need to pay, nosey at that, and, like all musicians, ultimately expendable.

Dahl severed all communication with Rat, Z, and me. Occasionally faxes would come into the label addressed to one of us, strictly business, but none of us directly spoke with him ever again after Japan (which went smoothly, by the way, with Dahl exploring the city and joining in the nightlife with the rest of us). Money and business had broken up our relationship, not too differently than it had destroyed mine and Gina's.

Dahl's next album after Euro-Blur, Leather Frankenstein, contained one of the angriest, most vehement selections ever recorded, a sonic slice of hatred entitled "European Vacation." In it, Dahl puked forth his anger for Factsheet with lines like "Lame motherfucker with stars in your eyes, kiss my ass, you can fuck off and die / Piss and moan on the telephone, call your momma, she ain't home." His parting salutation via the song was, "You're so damn boring, you're so lame / Just get out of my face and stay out of my way." It wasn't Shakespeare, but it left little to the imagination. Working at the label, of course, Z and I heard it before it was released. Personally, I wasn't surprised, what with Dahl holed-up in endless hotel rooms writing about who-knew-what, I figured we were potential targets at some point. Z didn't seem to care, as he'd already come back from a successful tour with another band and was over it, so to speak. Rat heard the tune a few months later when it came into his shop, and he was less amused. Disturbed, he fired off a letter to Dahl, wanting to know just exactly what the problem was, and what was eating him so much. Dahl never responded. Ironically, Z and I found out after the fact that due to his financial situation, Rat had been given something of an advance to cover some bills before we left for Europe, whereas Z and I weren't. Z felt somewhat betrayed that Rat, an old roommate no less, had never spoke of this to him prior to or on the road. Again, none of our business. On the other hand, Z and I received two weeks vacation pay before we left the states, which provided something of a financial cushion the others didn't get, that is if you can cover nine weeks with two weeks pay, and ultimately it was probably more

than Dahl advanced Rat come the end of the day. Well,
maybe. The sad thing was that my friendship with Dahl—
we'd been close for years—was permanently damaged.
It had been initially solidified by music and genuine
camaraderie and ultimately, irrevocably ruined over
money and road bickering. Years later, I spoke with him
occasionally on the phone—I don't believe any of the
others did—but it was never, ever the same between us.
Eventually, after I left the left the label to produce and
publicize shows for a venue, Dahl and I became friends
again, and without question the geographical distance
between us helped the friendship mend.

JEFF DAHL RETURNED EVERY year to Europe and Japan
like clockwork, always with a different band, typically
complaining of drunken swine backing musicians who
missed their stupid girlfriends back home. Nonetheless,
while those around him watched their relationships
crumble, Dahl and his wife Sylvia stayed together, much
as they had for twenty years.

Me, I eventually got back on my feet, got back in
the studio, got back on the road, and continued down
the indie rock path of obscurity. I returned for more
punk rock touring in the old country with a newer
band, under even harsher circumstances. But by then, I
was a seasoned pro on the Euro Tour circuit, not much
could get under my skin. As far as touring goes, be it
low budget, no budget, or an expedition on the fringes

of reality, it's the adventure that's important, that and the subsequent music that it inspires you to make. Let the big rock stars have their touring buses, arena shows, plush backstages peopled with silicone goddesses, and drug-wielding hangers-on. Let them have their hard working crews that afford them every comfort and keep them from ever having to lift a finger. Punk rock and it's various offshoots live slightly more off to the left of the main highway, and it is in these out of the way environs and on the desolate side roads that it will continue to thrive. Or maybe not. I could be completely full of crap. Tour bus, minivan, or motorcycle with an acoustic guitar strapped to it, it doesn't matter. The important thing is to just get on board and ride.

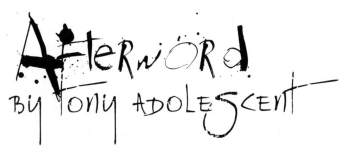

Afterword
By Tony Adolescent

Sleep No More, Forever

R EADING BRUCE'S BOOK WAS a blast. There were things I probably didn't need to know, but I read them anyway. I am nosy like that. There were insights about people I know and love that I may disagree with. I am disagreeable like that. Bruce and I made noise together for many years, and our friendship outlasted many of the pitfalls that rock and roll egos usually lay to waste.

See, I know most of the people in this story on one level or another because the people in the main narrative all lived in Los Angeles, at least for a spell, and that spell was when this narrative took place. Some of them are my friends, and all of them are people I respect. It wasn't easy to read some of this. I wanted to yell at them, "Don't say that! Don't do that!" Some of their actions could have been game changing finales.

Ratboy. Bruce. Z-Man. Dahl. They were all part of an exciting rock and roll scene that essentially went ignored by the bulk of America, but fortunately not by the rest of the world. There were parts of the world where people actually cared about rock and roll. The trick then, as it is now, lay in finding those boroughs of light in the darkness. The time chronicled here was the beginning of an age of some of the greatest rock and roll bands to grace the planet. It was dirty, sweaty, and fun rock and roll infused with all of the pitfalls of punk rock. One of many golden ages, this one was the beginning of the age dominated by bands like The Humpers, The Dragons, Clawhammer, and, of course, by Jeff Dahl. Unlike other great eras of rock, however, this one was largely ignored by the larger audiences, too.

Jeff is a great singer/songwriter, and I saw him play many times, going back to the time he was in Vox Pop. I was lucky enough to see many great bands before I was sixteen years old, including the Germs, The Weirdos, The Zeros, X, Middle Class, D.O.A., Red Kross, Black Flag, and Agent Orange. It was a fertile time. By the time the eighties were drawing to and end, and the nineties were upon us, the scene that had once flourished was but a microcosm of what it had been, and the bands had taken refuge in small bars and parties throughout Los Angeles, Orange, and San Diego counties. It was kept alive by dedicated musicians and fans.

Touring any band is rife with unwritten rules, and is absolutely dominated by survival. Many bands disintegrated as a result of touring. So did relationships—romantic and otherwise. They dissolved into a bitter pill that was impossible to swallow. Touring was a difficult, debt infested disaster at every turn. The trick was, and is, keeping as far out of the red as possible in case that money was needed for a bailout of some sort.

This tour diary is truly about a different time. The Berlin Wall had only been down a short time. This was a era without cell phones, without computers, and without GPS for navigation. In Europe, there was no single currency, and to pay out a per diem in one country would prove utterly useless in another. Record labels were clueless on how to help. Though eager to send their bands out, they generally lacked the knowledge necessary to navigate through promoters, clubs, and hanger-ons to actually provide the support needed. It was a different time.

For someone handling the managerial aspects of touring, this meant maximizing output while minimizing costs. Failure to do so meant bankrupting the tour, possibly being stranded yourself, leaving a lot of other people stranded, sinking your recorded output into a debt so severe that you'd never recoup the advances you probably used on the tour in the first place, and never getting your music back. This is what record labels were founded on, and it was not a pretty picture.

The manager, or in this case, the leader of the band, has a great deal on the line. This is not a shared responsibility. If the tour does not recoup, the band leader has to absorb the debt. Unlike a manager who can cut, bait and run like hell, in another direction, the band leader is bound to the record label through a financial obligation that almost exclusively favors the label. There's reason to why most musicians were not upset to see the death blow administered to the music business.

Touring was one of those great rock and roll jerk offs that sounded so glamorous to anyone who hasn't done one. It is an integral ingredient in the great rock and roll lie. It is also a critical piece if you want people to actually hear your music the way it is intended to be heard—live and in your face. Touring is also the great equalizer. It pits you against yourself. Being trapped in a van for a six-hour drive every day leaves you at the mercy of your past. The longer the ride, the rougher the path.

Sitting there, squeezed between luggage, gear, and sweaty clothes with five other guys is probably not the glorious rock and roll dream you fantasized about when you were a teenager. The sights, the sounds, and the smells—as fascinating as they may very well be—are not enough of a distraction to stop your past from haunting your present situation.

I admit that I always envied the one guy in the band that could sleep through the whole goddamned thing. No matter how safe the trip, and no matter how reliable the driver, trying to sleep in a moving vehicle is impossible for some people, as is the case for me. My naps are generally brief, nightmarish visions of rolling cars and Jayne Mansfield decapitations; a haze of Weegee and Highway Patrol black and white ooze. Hardly something to sleep through. They are always disrupted, intense affairs—deep, sporadic spurts of density littered with winding corridors, sirens, and flashing lights.

Always the sirens and flashing lights. The long arm of Johnny Law is a very real engagement that any band on the road can count on. Being pulled over in a van is really not such a big deal. The premise is almost always drugs, but the excuse is always a busted light or a bunk lane change. In Europe it is almost always because they are looking for smuggling and that means they are usually looking for cigarettes. Of course, the real reason is generally curiosity than out of any real threat to international security. Let's face it, how many times do criminals travel in packs of six crammed in a van to distribute paraphernalia?

I can't even count the number of times I've watched as a groggy band member is dragged out of the sleeping loft because of sirens, but paired with the sounds of thunder, and the flashes of lightening in a storm, and by the sheer volume of such experiences, I can assure you that a comfortable sleep is still not to be had. Multiply that by the number of days on tour, factor in hangovers as necessary, and multiply that by a half a dozen folks and you are starting to get the picture.

Then there is the indignity of it all. Locked in a stinky van full of stinky boys, it is then necessary to take sheer exhaustion and pepper it with sprigs of paranoia, and a dash of the always faux superiority that comes blaring through by someone's idealism. You know, the inevitable knowledge that one dummy always has to blurt out: "I haven't broken any laws!" Of course, somebody in the van probably has, or is certainly in the process of doing exactly that at the very moment the statement is made—and is drowned out by the rushed movement of scurried baggie burials and manic yet graceful sounds of dry pill swallowing and gagging by the other five people in the van.

The curiosity of being pulled over can be a brief or a long and drawn out affair. It really depends on who is doing the dragging, and where you are located on the union mandated break schedule. I have been in a van that was put through an X-ray machine, had my hands swabbed for explosives, and had my luggage scoured for drugs more times than I can count. "In my country, I am a school teacher," I tell them. "What do you do in yours?"

Among my favorite explanations for the volumes of pills I always carry took place while I was in Bavaria: "This one is for my blood pressure, this one for my cholesterol, these are for asthma, this is for my heart, and this one... this one is for anxiety. Do you mind if I take that one right now?"

There is also the beauty of foreign product exchange. Gold Bond is familiar to anyone who travels like this. It is generally used to reduce discomfort associated with, uh, sitting for long periods of time and perspiring. It is a tour necessity. The enthusiastic gendarme as he pours it onto his palm with the familiar "Ah-ha!" associated with finding a container of white powder in every person's luggage—and which, of course, must be cocaine—is most amusing. It is the hardest gaff to intervene on, but the thought of someone taking a whiff of Gold Bond or getting it in their eyes is too much to allow.

Essentially, though, touring in a van is the same no matter where in the world you go. From a sleep standpoint, however, it's all the same. There are long stretches of desolate farmlands, frequent rest stops selling crap you don't need and food you shouldn't ingest, hot desert patches, maybe, and large inhabited cities with cool shit you aren't going to see because you are definitely going to the suburbs or the slum to sit in the club for hours waiting. That's pretty much the scene everywhere. Well, except for Brazil, where there are patches of jungles and rainforests and cops that carry machine guns.

Just as unnerving as the obligatory storm and drag is the rushed scramble that occurs compliments of the distributor of olfactory damage: "Jesus Christ, what the fuck is that?" Amid the howling laughter, writhing pain, gasping for air, and the lunge for the now open window, sits the lone, smiling yet apologetic sadist who promises never to eat "whatever that slop was" ever, ever again. The gagging, retching, and choking alone are more than enough to stop any reasonable person from falling asleep in the van. Sticking one's face into the shirt is hardly solace when the last shower you had was three days ago. Enjoy your patina.

You can look forward to repeating it all tomorrow, but for tonight you can look forward to laying your head on a pillow in some band apartment, sprinkled with the stale smell of old piss, vomit, cigarettes, and fuck. Bon appetite. Your lucky day has arrived, indeed. Everywhere you go, you can rest assured that someone has drawn a penis on the wall. That will, no doubt, be the first thing you see when you wake. For the life of me I will never understand what makes an undersexed and horny band of traveling marauders pull into every backstage and band apartment worldwide and draw a phalluses.

Yet, that is the glory and majesty of rock. It drips in beads of sweat on stage from five dudes (or ladies) and there it sits on those clothes and that body until next time. Or it sits in a stinking sopping wet pile in the van, with those ten stinky ass shoes, socks, and guitar straps. There is where the comparison between rockers and those other nomadic gypsies—the truckers—begins, and ends. Truckers are significantly cleaner.

ACKNOWLEDGMENTS

This book would not exist if it weren't for the covert efforts of my wife, Else Duff, aka Evil E of L.A. Derby Dolls fame. It's because of her that it made its way to Rare Bird when I wasn't looking. Obviously, thanks must be extended to Tyson and Julia at Rare Bird. They are true mavericks in an ever-changing world.

I would also be remiss if I didn't wave a soggy handkerchief at the individuals who didn't hang on long enough to see this mess published. Some participants in the story itself, including guitarist extraordinaire Amy Wichmann and Spanish legend Kike Turmix, have left to disrupt other dimensions. My love interest often referenced in this book, Gina, is also no longer with us, having departed suddenly. Her last name has been omitted from the book out of respect for her family. The two people who would have both loved and hated this the most, my mom and dad, are also not with us. If they've been reading over my shoulders, well, I hope there weren't too many surprises.